Assessing Outcomes in
Child and Family Services

MODERN APPLICATIONS OF SOCIAL WORK
An Aldine de Gruyter Series of Texts and Monographs

SERIES EDITOR
James K. Whittaker, *University of Washington*

Paul Adams and Kristine E. Nelson (eds.), **Reinventing Human Services: Community-and Family-Centered Practice**

Ralph E. Anderson and Irl Carter, with Gary Lowe, **Human Behavior in the Social Environment: A Social Systems Approach** (Fifth Edition)

Richard P. Barth, Mark Courtney, Jill Duerr Berrick, and Vicky Albert, **From Child Abuse to Permanency Planning: Child Welfare Services Pathways and Placements**

Gale Burford and Joe Hudson, **Family Group Conferencing: New Directions in Community-Centered Child and Family Practice**

Robert J. Chaskin, Prudence Brown, Sudhir Venkatesh, and Avis Vidal, **Building Community Capacity**

Dana Christensen, Jeffrey Todahl, and William C. Barrett, **Solution-Based Casework: An Introduction to Clinical and Case Management Skills in Casework Practice**

Marie Connolly with Margaret McKenzie, **Effective Participatory Practice: Family Group Conferencing in Child Protection**

Mark W. Fraser, Peter J. Pecora, and David A. Haapala, **Families in Crisis: The Impact of Intensive Family Preservation Services**

James Garbarino, **Children and Families in the Social Environment** (Second Edition)

Roberta R. Greene, **Human Behavior Theory: A Diversity Framework**

Roberta R. Greene, **Human Behavior Theory and Social Work Practice** (Second Edition)

Roberta R. Greene, **Social Work with the Aged and Their Families** (Second Edition)

André Ivanoff, Betty J. Blythe, and Tony Tripodi, **Involuntary Clients in Social Work Practice: A Research-Based Approach**

Susan P. Kemp, James K. Whittaker, and Elizabeth M. Tracy, **Person-Environment Practice: The Social Ecology of Interpersonal Helping**

Gary R. Lowe and P. Nelson Reid, **The Professionalization of Poverty: Social Work and the Poor in the Twentieth Century**

Anthony N. Maluccio, Cinzia Canali, and Tiziano Vecchiato (eds.), **Assessing Outcomes in Child and Family Services: Comparative Design and Policy Issues**

Robert M. Moroney and Judy Krysik, **Social Policy and Social Work: Critical Essays on the Welfare State** (Second Edition)

Peter J. Pecora, Mark W. Fraser, Kristine Nelson, Jacqueline McCroskey, and William Meezan, **Evaluating Family-Based Services**

Peter J. Pecora, James K. Whittaker, Anthony N. Maluccio and Richard P. Barth, with Robert D. Plotnick, **The Child Welfare Challenge: Policy, Practice, and Research** (Second Edition)

John R. Schuerman, Tina L. Rzepnicki, and Julia H. Littell, **Putting Families First: An Experience in Family Preservation**

Madeleine R. Stoner, **The Civil Rights of Homeless People: Law, Social Policy, and Social Work Practice**

Tiziano Vecchiato, Anthony N. Maluccio, and Cinzia Canali (eds.), **Evaluation in Child and Family Services: Comparative Client and Program Perspectives**

Albert E. Trieschman, James K. Whittaker, and Larry K. Brendtro, **The Other 23 Hours: Child-Care Work with Emotionally Disturbed Children in a Therapeutic Milieu**

Harry H. Vorrath and Larry K. Brendtro, **Positive Peer Culture** (Second Edition)

Betsy S. Vourlekis and Roberta R. Greene (eds.), **Social Work Case Management**

James K. Whittaker and Associates, **Reaching High-Risk Families: Intensive Family Preservation in Human Services**

Assessing Outcomes in Child and Family Services

Comparative Design and Policy Issues

editors

ANTHONY N. MALUCCIO
CINZIA CANALI
TIZIANO VECCHIATO

Aldine de Gruyter

New York

About the Editors

Anthony N. Maluccio is Professor of Social Work at Boston College, Graduate School of Social Work, Chestnut Hill, Massachusetts.
Cinzia Canali is Research Associate at the Fondazione Emanuela Zancan, Padua, Italy.
Tiziano Vecchiato is Scientific Director of the Fondazione Emanuela Zancan, Padua, Italy.

ALDINE DE GRUYTER
A division of Walter de Gruyter, Inc.
200 Saw Mill River Road
Hawthorne, New York 10532

This publication is printed on acid free paper ∞

Library of Congress Cataloging-in-Publication Data

Assessing outcomes in child and family services : comparative design and policy issues / edited by Anthony N. Maluccio, Cinzia Canali, and Tiziano Vecchiato.
        p. cm. — (Modern applications of social work)
Includes bibliographical references and index.
    ISBN 0-202-30704-2 (alk. paper) — ISBN 0-202-30705-0 (pbk. : alk. paper)
    1. Child welfare—Evaluation—Congresses. 2. Family services—Evaluation—Congresses. 3. Evaluation research (Social action programs)—Congresses.   I. Maluccio, Anthony N.   II. Canali, Cinzia,   III. Vecchiato, Tiziano.   IV. Series.
    HV707 .A87 2002
    362.7—dc21   2002002703

Manufactured in the United States of America

10 9 8 7 6 5 4 3 2 1

Contents

Contributors   vii

Preface   ix

Acknowledgments   xi

Introduction: Outcome-Based Evaluation:
   Cross-National Perspectives   1
Anthony N. Maluccio, Cinzia Canali, and Tiziano Vecchiato

1   **Current Initiatives in the Development of Outcome-Based**
     Evaluation of Children's Services   6
     Harriet Ward

2   **The Black Box: Accounting for Program Inputs When**
     Assessing Outcomes   19
     Edith Fein

3   **The Evaluation of "Community Building": Measuring the**
     Social Effects of Community-Based Practice   28
     Robert J. Chaskin

4   **Outcome-Based Evaluation of National Health and**
     Social Programs   48
     Tiziano Vecchiato

5   **Nonexperimental Methods of Evaluating Social Programs:**
     Applications for Child and Family Services   61
     Robert Goerge

6   **An Intervention to Reduce Smoking Habits through**
     Counseling from the General Practitioner   70
     Giovanni Pilati, Elizabeth Tamang, and Luca Gino Sbrogiò

7   **Improving Mental Health Care for Children and Adolescents:**
     Strategies and Lessons   84
     John Landsverk and Inger Davis

8   **Evaluating Social and Health Services with Children,**
     Adults, and Elderly Persons   99
     Alessandro Pompei

9   Outcomes Are Dependent on Inputs: Does Risk Assessment
     Inform Service Delivery?   107
     Marianne Berry and Scottye J. Cash

10   A Learning-Organization Approach to Evaluation   127
     Lois Wright and Kathy Paget

11   Outcome Studies in the Context of Organizational Inertia
     and Political Ideology   141
     Frank Ainsworth

12   Family Service Centers: Lessons From National and
     Local Evaluations   153
     Anita Lightburn

Author Index   174

Subject Index   177

Contributors

Frank Ainsworth, Edith Cowan University, School of International, Cultural and Community Studies, Joondalup Campus, Perth (Western Australia)

Marianne Berry, Office of Child Welfare Research and Development, School of Social Welfare, University of Kansas, Lawrence, Kansas

Cinzia Canali, Fondazione Emanuela Zancan, Padua (Italy)

Scottye J. Cash, School of Social Work, Florida State University, Tallahassee, Florida

Robert J. Chaskin, The Chapin Hall Center for Children, University of Chicago, Chicago, Illinois

Inger Davis, School of Social Work, San Diego State University, San Diego, California

Edith Fein, Dunne, Kimmel and Fein, LLC, West Hartford, Connecticut

Robert Goerge, The Chapin Hall Center for Children, University of Chicago, Chicago, Illinois

John Landsverk, Child and Adolescent Services Research Center, Children's Hospital of San Diego, San Diego, California

Anita Lightburn, School for Social Work, Smith College, Northampton, Massachusetts

Anthony N. Maluccio, Graduate School of Social Work, Boston College, Chestnut Hill, Massachusetts

Kathy Paget, Center for Child and Family Studies, University of South Carolina, College of Social Work, Columbia, South Carolina

Giovanni Pilati, Azienda per i Servizi Sanitari No. 2, Gorizia (Italy)

Alessandro Pompei, Fondazione Emanuela Zancan, Modena (Italy)

Luca Gino Sbrogiò, Azienda ULSS 15 Alta Padovana, Cittadella-Camposampiero, Padua (Italy)

Elizabeth Tamang, Azienda ULSS 15 Alta Padovana, Cittadella-Camposampiero, Padua (Italy)

Tiziano Vecchiato, Fondazione Emanuela Zancan, Padua (Italy)

Harriet Ward, Department of Social Sciences, Loughborough University, Loughborough, Leicestershire (United Kingdom)

Lois Wright, Center for Child and Family Studies, College of Social Work, University of South Carolina, Columbia, South Carolina

Preface

In recent years growing attention has been given by researchers to outcome evaluation in the field of human services, largely in response to demands by funders and others for accountability, assessment of performance, and cost effectiveness. Limited attention has been paid, however, to the findings of evaluation studies conducted in different countries. For this reason, in a recent survey of child welfare outcome research in the United States, the United Kingdom, and Australia, Maluccio, Ainsworth, and Thoburn (*Child Welfare Outcome Research in the United States, the United Kingdom, and Australia*. 2000. Washington, D.C.: CWLA Press) call for greater attention to cross-national studies and challenge us to take up the task of learning from outcome research across the world, to improve the life chances of vulnerable children and youths wherever they may be.

In line with the above challenge, we organized a seminar entitled: "Outcome-based Evaluation: A Cross-national Comparison" in Volterra (Italy) on March 26–29, 2001. The seminar featured the presentation and discussion of a series of invited papers by researchers and administrators from Italy, the United States, Australia, Canada, Israel, Sweden, and the United Kingdom. The seminar was cosponsored by the Fondazione Emanuela Zancan and Boston College Graduate School of Social Work. The Fondazione Zancan, constituted in 1964 and located in Padua, Italy, is a leading center for study, research, and training in the social and health services. Its statutory objective is to foster studies and training for practitioners, educators, and researchers in the social and health sectors.

In this volume, we present a range of papers from the seminar. These focus primarily on outcome evaluation pertaining to design and policy issues in the field of child and family services. In a companion volume edited by T. Vecchiato, A. N. Maluccio, and C. Canali (*Evaluation in Child and Family Services: Comparative Client and Program Perspectives*) we offer papers also presented at the seminar, which focused on client perspectives and programmatic issues in outcome evaluation in child and family services.

As reflected in these papers, there is much more to be done—in carrying out research that can help enhance service delivery, in learning from each other across the globe, and in furthering positive outcomes for young people and their families. Ultimately we hope that these efforts will promote a new culture of human rights and social solidarity. Toward this end, we trust that the volume will be useful for researchers, administrators, practitioners, students, and educators in family and child welfare settings, schools of social work, and related educational programs.

Acknowledgments

We wish to express our deepest appreciation to the many persons and organizations who helped us in implementing the seminar in Volterra as well as in preparing this volume. These include the following cosponsoring organizations:

- Scuola Superiore Sant'Anna di Studi Universitari e di Perfezionamento, Pisa (Italy)
- Cattedra di Gerontologia e Geriatria, Dipartimento di Medicina Interna, Università degli Studi di Milano (Italy)
- The Open University, School of Health and Social Welfare, Milton Keynes (United Kingdom)
- University of Connecticut, School of Social Work, West Hartford, Connecticut (USA)

They also include the following persons:

- Mons. Giuseppe Pasini, President, Fondazione Emanuela Zancan
- Mons. Giovanni Nervo, Honorary President, Fondazione Emanuela Zancan
- Ivo Gabellieri, Mayor of Volterra
- Pierluigi Giovannini, President, Fondazione Cassa di Risparmio, Volterra
- Alberto Godenzi, Dean, Boston College, Graduate School of Social Work, Chestnut Hill, Massachusetts
- Richard Mackey, formerly Interim Dean, Boston College, Graduate School of Social Work, Chestnut Hill, Massachusetts

We also express our appreciation to the secretarial and administrative staff members who provided invaluable service both in connection with the seminar and in preparation of this volume. In particular, Pamela Harrison worked hard and efficiently in typing the entire manuscript, as she has done with our other publications over the years. Edith Fein graciously helped us in editing a number of chapters for content as well as style. Our special thanks also go to James K. Whittaker, who reviewed the manuscript and gave us invaluable suggestions for organizing and editing the papers.

Finally—and most important—we are of course grateful to the contributors, whose papers reflect provocative thinking and careful expression of ideas. Moreover, their thoughtful and prompt responses to our requests facilitated our tasks as editors, and their participation in the seminar contributed to lively discussions and exciting new directions.

Introduction

Outcome-Based Evaluation: Cross-National Perspectives

Anthony N. Maluccio, Cinzia Canali, and Tiziano Vecchiato

In recent years we have witnessed growing commitment in various countries to improving of the quality of health and social services on behalf of families and children. At the same time, interest in *outcome evaluation* has increased, especially in regard to the effectiveness of such services, as reflected in the seminar described in the preface, which took place in Volterra (Italy) in March 2001. In this introduction we delineate selected issues that emerged in regard to conducting cross-cultural research in the above area; describe the major themes covered by participants; and conclude with a brief look at future opportunities for cross-national collaboration. We should add that, while the volume grew out of an international seminar, the participants constituted a "convenience sample." This of course qualifies the generalizability of the themes and conclusions presented by the contributors.

ISSUES IN CROSS-CULTURAL EVALUATION

In this volume we do not attempt to draw systematic, country-by-country comparisons, which would be inappropriate due to the selective nature of the perspectives presented. It may be helpful, however, to identify what the participants repeatedly noted in regard to issues and difficulties inherent in conducting outcome evaluation. These include:

- varying definitions of *outcome;*
- complexities in measuring outcomes of particular interventions with different groups of consumers and documenting the effectiveness of the intervention;
- the tendency to focus on evaluation of *process* more than *outcome;*
- the challenge of involving practitioners in the evaluation task, in part because its value is unclear to them or perceived as distant or untrustworthy;
- the typical inadequacy of resources available for systematic evaluation; and
- the need to inject rigor in the design and execution of evaluation projects.

These and other issues of course become more complex in a cross-cultural context. Outcome evaluation in different countries is at different stages of conceptualization and development; reflects different priorities and methods; and attracts diverse funding and varying professional interests. But it is clear that it is beginning to be regarded as part and parcel of administrative functions and responsibilities in a wide variety of agency settings.

In future collaborative efforts, it is important to deal with the above issues—and others that emerge in the process of conducting comparative evaluation studies—through attention to such themes and guidelines as the following:

- critically examining and comparing the underlying theoretical models used by researchers;
- planning and conducting evaluative studies through collaboration among researchers in different countries;
- collaborating with researchers from a variety of disciplines in addition to social work;
- involving in the evaluation process—and from the beginning—those who are closest to the delivery of services, including administrators, practitioners, and consumers;
- specifying desired outcomes of particular services or projects and documenting the course of service delivery;
- conducting comparative studies of the outcomes of different welfare systems;
- devoting attention to the roles and outcomes of prevention services;
- documenting the process of service delivery to assure that comparisons are made among similar programs; and
- considering whether programs that deliver mandated services should be compared with those where the client or consumer "volunteers" for the services.

MAJOR THEMES

As noted in the preface, the contributors to this volume focus primarily on outcome evaluation pertaining to *design and policy issues* in the field of child and family services. Harriet Ward begins by exploring various questions raised in outcome evaluation of children's services in the United Kingdom, specifically the "Looking After Children" initiative. This is a national system designed to help practitioners and administrators assess outcomes for children and youths placed in out-of-home care. Ward examines the application to this project of performance indicators required by the national government for all "personal" social services, describing a variety of problems with management information systems and their potential solutions. She thus offers suggestions for conducting similar projects in other countries.

In the next chapter, Edith Fein argues that evaluations would benefit from measuring program inputs as well as program outcomes; she illustrates her points through her research on family reunification services in the United States. In particular, she stresses the importance of examining what is inside the "black box" of service delivery before making program comparisons—that is, *describing who actually does what* to assure that like programs are being compared—as well as examining how outcomes must be analyzed in relation to their specific goals and inputs.

Robert Chaskin then focuses on evaluation of the broad effects of community-based efforts to improve the lives of children and families "in need." He delineates comprehensive community initiatives aimed at community building in the United States. On the basis of these experiences, he offers guidelines for applying theories of change to "community building"; taking into account the complexities of communities as well as interventions; and making the case or providing the evidence for the effectiveness of community-based practice.

In Chapter 4, Tiziano Vecchiato begins with a comprehensive discussion of two issues in evaluation of national health and social programs in Italy: confronting the difficulties in selecting indicators of effectiveness and dealing with the complications involved in determining national goals in light of geographic differences. He proposes potential solutions regarding these issues as well as suggestions for improving methods and theories of evaluation.

Robert Goerge, on the other hand, in Chapter 5 focuses on nonexperimental methods of evaluating social programs in the area of child and family services. In particular, he indicates that statistical approaches using longitudinal data offer a good alternative when random assignment evaluations are not feasible due to ethical or operational difficulties. He illustrates his argument through application to evaluation of the effect of welfare reform in an urban area of the United States.

In Chapters 6 through 8, the contributors apply strategies of outcome evaluation to a range of social problems. Giovanni Pilati and his coauthors focus on an example of intervention into a public health problem in Italy—that of smoking—through the use of counseling by general practitioners. John Landsverk and Inger Davis discuss multiple strategies used in a demonstration project in the United States aimed at improving mental health care for children and adolescents. They discuss in detail the strategies and challenges involved in improving the process of care provision. Of special interest is their analysis of outcome assessment in community mental health settings. Alessandro Pompei evaluates the effectiveness of a carefully designed helping process with children, adults, and elderly persons in residential settings in Italy. He illustrates through a specific project the major phases of the helping process: documentation, assignment of responsibilities to various caregivers, analysis of the presenting problems, provision of service, and criteria for evaluation of outcome.

In Chapter 9, Marianne Berry and Scottye J. Cash describe an evaluation of the role of risk assessment methods in child protective agencies in the United States. They examine the interplay of *family risk factors* and *service provisions* at the point of intake, during services, and at case closure. They conclude that the inclusion of risk measures at intake and of service provision measures throughout the course of the case helps researchers and practitioners to understand what works best, for whom, and under what circumstances.

Drawing on the experiences of the Center for Child and Family Studies in a southern state in the United States, in Chapter 10 Lois Wright and Kathy Paget address the use of a "learning organization" approach to evaluation of outcomes in public child welfare agencies; they define this term as partnership between individuals who implement programs and those who engage in evaluation. They then show how such an approach can lead to refinement of the role and activities of the evaluation process and the skills and challenges involved in communicating results meaningfully.

In Chapter 11 Frank Ainsworth explores the impact of organizational inertia and political ideology on outcome research, using examples of studies that he has conducted in diverse agency settings in Australia and South Africa. He describes lessons learned through conducting these studies in bureaucratic organizations, in such areas as organizational inertia, ideological impediments, and use of administrative data sets.

Finally, in Chapter 12 Anita Lightburn presents a case study of national and local evaluations of a Head Start Family Service Center program demonstration in the United States. She discusses insights derived from these evaluations, arguing that the choice of experimental designs in the study was premature and that in future research formative evaluation approaches need to be carried out first, as a foundation for experimental studies.

LOOKING TO THE FUTURE

This volume represents a beginning in the efforts to facilitate and implement cross-national collaboration on outcome evaluation in the areas of health and social services, notably services addressed to the needs of vulnerable children and families. In addition to describing particular programs and initiatives in their respective countries, the contributors suggest possibilities for cross-national collaboration.

Much more work is required, however, to pursue these possibilities and promote such an objective. In particular, there is a need to develop common templates for conducting evaluative research, in such areas as consensus on definitions of terms; agreement on procedures, like specifying objectives before selecting outcome measures; creating a forum for discussing ethical issues such as use of data sets, publication of results, and the importance of informed consent; and assessment of outcomes in diverse practice settings (such as home-based versus residential services) and with different professional approaches (such as single versus multidisciplinary services).

Additional collaborative strategies include replication of successful programs across countries; sharing knowledge of methodology and approaches as well as implementation problems that we encounter in conducting outcome-based research; circulating information about program innovations and their effectiveness; and conducting parallel studies regarding the outcome of diverse approaches to similar problems in different countries.

The contributors to this volume demonstrate strong conviction about sharing research expertise across national boundaries; learning through each other how to cope with organizational impediments to cross-national collaboration; and strengthening the interaction between practice and research. Their positive response to the Volterra seminar suggests that there is wide interest in pursuing cross-national collaboration. Further useful opportunities to conduct such research should be nurtured in the future, building on the initial efforts reflected in the contributions to this volume.

1

Current Initiatives in the Development of Outcome-Based Evaluation of Children's Services

Harriet Ward

Over the last century, England, along with most other developed countries, has introduced a wide range of services designed to promote the satisfactory development of its children. Services such as physical and mental health care, dental care, and education are universally available and, despite a flourishing private sector, are still largely delivered, without charge, by public agencies. Nevertheless, of the eleven million children and young people under eighteen years of age in England today, about four million are thought to be vulnerable in that they "would benefit from extra help from public agencies in order to make the best of their life chances" (Department of Health, Department for Education and Employment and Home Office, 2000:2). Of these, 381,500 are defined as *children in need,* that is, children whose vulnerability is such that they are unlikely to reach or maintain a satisfactory level of health or development, or those whose health and development will be significantly impaired without the provision of additional services (Children Act 1989, Section 17.10). Children Act 1989, which introduces the concept of *children in need,* also lays on local councils an obligation to provide these additional services, generally through their social services departments, although working closely with other agencies.

While it is possible to trace the development of child welfare services in Britain over the last century, it is only over the past twenty years or so that serious attempts have been made to evaluate their outcomes or effectiveness. The introduction of outcome-based evaluation of children's services is, as this book shows, a developing initiative throughout the Western world; in Britain it has been particularly engendered by a loss of confidence in the welfare state, a perceived lack of accountability of public services accompanied by rising costs, and a thriving consumerist movement that demands that services meet the requirements of users (Parker, Ward, Jackson, Aldgate & Wedge, 1991). The systematic evaluation of children's services is part of a much wider movement to introduce outcome-based accountability into all public sector services: health, education, transport, social security and now social services are all increasingly required to provide demonstrable evidence of satisfactory delivery and proof that public money is being well-spent.

Within the above context, this chapter explores the introduction of outcome-based evaluation in services for children in need at both micro and macro levels and considers the issues raised by initiatives such as the Looking After Children project, a methodology designed to help practitioners and their managers assess outcomes for children placed in out-of-home care (Ward, 1995), and the "Performance Assessment Framework" (Department of Health, 1999b)—a series of performance indicators for all the "personal" social services required annually by government and published in the national press.[1] Poor implementation and problems with management information systems have meant that the link between aggregate and individual data has sometimes been lost, a situation that a new Integrated Children's System aims to redress.

THE LOOKING AFTER CHILDREN PROJECT: OUTCOME-BASED EVALUATION AT THE MICRO LEVEL

On almost any criterion, children who have been placed in the care of public agencies tend to be among those most obviously in need, and for many years concerns have been raised about the poor outcomes that they appear to achieve. Recent figures suggest that 70 percent of care leavers have no educational qualifications; 50–80 percent are unemployed a year after discharge; 30 percent of single homeless people have been in care; and one in seven young women leaving care is pregnant or already a mother (Acheson, 1998). These women also receive the most expensive level of service provision: on average, each child looked after away from home currently costs her or his social services department £435 per week, about five times more than each child supported in his or her own family or living independently (Department of Health, 2001:para. 20b). It is therefore unsurprising that the first initiatives to introduce outcome-based evaluation measures have concentrated on the assessment of the effectiveness of services for children placed in care or accommodation. However, although there is some evidence that children's experiences in public care do little to compensate for previous adversities and may indeed compound them, we do not yet know how far this is the case, or whether this extremely disadvantaged group would have displayed even less successful outcomes without the provision of services.

The Department of Health (England) initiative on assessing outcomes for children looked after away from home is known as the Looking After Children project (Parker et al., 1991; Ward, 1995). This long-standing research and development program has been running since 1987, and is now in its fourth stage. In the first stage (1987–1991), a working party of academics and practitioners devised a theoretical framework for assessing outcomes in child care. They argued that appropriate outcome measures should adopt the child's perspective, and therefore assess services by asking how far they promote children's long-term chances of achieving satisfactory well-being in adulthood. Although the working party's remit was to produce measures designed to assess outcomes for children in care or accommodation, they argued that the program should, at least in theory, be applicable to all children rather than focusing solely on issues specific to those in receipt of a particular service.

The working party therefore identified seven developmental dimensions along which all children need to progress if they are to achieve long-term well-being in adulthood: health, education, identity, family and social relationships, social presentation, emotional and behavioral development, and self-care skills. They argued that, at a very basic level, all parents have broadly similar objectives for their children in each of the above dimensions; for instance, they want them to be healthy, literate, confident, popular, attractive, and competent, and are concerned if they show signs of emotional or behavioral disturbance. The objectives should be no different for those children for whom the state has acquired parental responsibility. However, children will only make satisfactory progress if their needs in each of these dimensions are adequately met, primarily by parents but with assistance from social workers, foster carers, and other child welfare professionals where necessary. Both parents and child welfare agencies can be held accountable for the extent to which they attempt to meet children's needs, and the outcome of their efforts can be measured with reference both to children's experience of parenting and to their progress, although it is important to recognize that there is not always a causal relationship between the two (Parker et al., 1991).

The practical application of the theoretical perspectives noted above produced the Assessment and Action Records, a series of six practice tools that ask age-related questions about significant aspects of children's experience and progress, drawn from research knowledge about normative development (Department of Health, 1991). In the second stage of the project, the Assessment and Action Records were extensively piloted: social workers and children and young people in five local authorities tested their viability as practice tools; in addition, data from Assessment and Action Records completed by a representative sample of parents and children not looked after away from home were used to evaluate the relevance of their content to normative parental practice within the community. The records were extensively revised in the light of these findings, and additional materials were produced in order to allow them to be set within existing procedures for information-gathering, planning, and review (Department of Health, 1995; Ward, 1995).[2]

During the third stage of the project (1995–1998) widespread use of the materials was facilitated by a structured program for implementation, which was supported and funded by central government and informed by both theoretical and empirical work undertaken in the second, developmental stage. Although implementation was only made mandatory in Wales, virtually all local authorities in England and Wales made it their policy to use the materials as case management tools for all children who were looked after for substantial periods. Versions adapted to local circumstances and requirements are now also being implemented in Scotland and Northern Ireland. In addition, extensive pilot and implementation projects have been undertaken in Canada, Australia, Germany, Sweden, Hungary, and Russia (Ward, 1998).

Social workers are expected to ensure that an Assessment and Action Record is completed annually for each child looked after away from home for whom they hold responsibility. In theory, therefore, a system is in place in English and Welsh local authorities that should allow for outcome data on all looked after children to be routinely collected and recorded as part of the everyday interaction between social workers, carers, and the children for whom they hold responsibility. It should be possible to aggregate the data held on individual children to assess the outcomes of the service as a whole.

However, perhaps we should not be surprised to find that reality falls considerably short of the theoretical picture. The evidence from an extensive audit program undertaken between 1996 and 1999 demonstrates that, even with substantial support from central government, the use of these materials, though improving over time, is often inconsistent and patchy. While those parts of the system that replicate existing procedures for information-gathering, planning, and review are generally found in 70–80 percent of case files, the innovative Assessment and Action Records, designed to gather data on outcomes, are only used in about 36 percent of relevant cases, and are rarely used repeatedly to gather longitudinal information (Moyers, 1996; Peel, 1997; Scott, 1999).

There is considerable difference of opinion as to whether such findings are indicative of major difficulties inherent in the system as a whole, or whether they demonstrate teething problems in the introduction of a program that requires a radical change in social work culture, compounded by the well-documented difficulties of translating social policy into social work practice (Baldwin, 2000). It seems likely that all of these factors have impeded comprehensive implementation.

Undoubtedly the current version of the Assessment and Action Records is too long, and the format, which repeatedly invites respondents to give tick-box answers to a range of primary and secondary questions, is too mechanistic and off-putting for users. Moreover, the design currently bears an unfortunate resemblance to a public examination paper and could also be improved. A major weakness has been caused by the delay in producing an electronic version of the records, so that at present data can only be aggregated and analyzed by keying them separately into a database. We also know that, in their current version, the records are not always appropriate for use with children and young people with certain disabilities: in particular, the educational progress of children with learning disabilities cannot be adequately measured against normative standards, while the development of self-care skills raises very different issues when children's functioning is substantially impaired by physical conditions affecting, for instance, mobility, sight, hearing, or cognition. However, as noted below, while plans to make radical changes to the materials may make them more user-friendly, even if it were possible to construct a computerized system that could be presented in a manner thoroughly acceptable to all the participants, it would not be adequately implemented unless a number of other issues are addressed.

Systematic outcome-based evaluation of this nature requires participants to gather accurate data on a routine basis in order to demonstrate changes to the service and/or developmental progress in the child or young person concerned. However, the evidence from the audits, and also more particularly from Stage Four of the project (1996–2002), where researchers are demonstrating how the data from case files of 242 children can be transformed into management information, is that the need to gather and record accurate information is not always understood by practitioners.[3] Even where all the materials are completed, case files demonstrate substantial gaps and inaccuracies in key information. It is often impossible to find the answer to simple questions such as the date on which a child was admitted to care or accommodation, or the number of placements he or she has experienced since then; other information such as academic progress or the child's health needs may be out of date or no longer relevant.

Discussions with social workers reveal that many of them have the information in their heads, but they do not regard writing it down as necessary. Indeed, this is at the heart of one of the main criticisms raised by practitioners: that by requiring them to monitor children's progress by answering questions on forms, the system bureaucratizes the social work task (Ward, 1995). This debate is taken further forward by Garrett (1999), who argues that by suggesting that there are a number of recognized indicators of progress that can be monitored in order to evaluate outcomes, the system requires social workers to act as controlling agents who require children in need to conform to societal norms rather than giving free rein to their individuality. It is difficult to see how such criticisms can be addressed by any system designed to produce routine evaluations of outcome.

Up to a point, these criticisms reflect conflicting perceptions of social work accountability. In England, central government produces legislation that local councils are required to implement, but the manner of implementation is largely left to their discretion; procedures followed by social work staff often mirror this relationship, in that the council for which they work translates the legislative requirement into local policy, but as professionals who work in bureaucracies, they are given considerable discretion as to how this is operationalized. An acknowledgment of professional freedom to act is sometimes interpreted as meaning that social workers are relieved of the responsibility of implementing policy, as Garrett (1999) appears to argue. The audits of Looking After Children showed that the success or failure of implementation was often related to middle managers' perception of the amount of discretion they could exert in deciding whether or not to encourage fieldworkers to follow local policy directives. Even in Wales, where the system has been made mandatory, middle managers vary in the extent to which they urge compliance, and implementation frequently follows the letter rather than the spirit of policy: the documentation is more frequently found on files, but questions are more often left unanswered (Nicholson and Ward, 1999).

Implementation of the system, however, while imperfect, has by no means failed. Not only has no council withdrawn from the program, but there is substantial evidence to suggest that, even if the practical completion of the documents is inadequate, the conceptual framework upon which the materials are based is gradually becoming part of accepted social work theory. A comprehensive study of social workers' understanding of children's needs found that those working in local authorities which had implemented the Looking After Children materials were able to describe them in the structured, developmental terms provided by the seven dimensions used in the project (Department of Health, 2000a). A number of councils, having introduced Looking After Children for young people looked after away from home, have begun to use the theoretical framework as a basis for developing procedures for identifying and assessing other children in need; these initiatives were reinforced when the new government guidance for the assessment of need was released in 2000 (Department of Health et al., 2000). This program now requires social workers to build on the developmental basis of the Looking after Children model in assessing all children in need, by identifying how far factors related to parenting capacity, the wider family, and the environment are impeding or promoting children's progress in the seven developmental dimensions.

Not all social workers in England have yet grasped the message that, in their interactions with individual children, they need to gather accurate, structured information that allows them to assess how far services are affecting developmental progress. Nevertheless, this argument is constantly being reinforced and will continue to be so through new procedures and training. In England and Wales, the new Post Qualifying Award in Child Care, introduced in 2000, places an added emphasis on the importance of social workers acquiring a greater understanding of children's developmental needs; there are plans in progress for this also to become a more central part of the curriculum for the basic diploma.[4] New information requirements imposed by government on social services will also make it likely that, in the future, social workers will be expected to devote more attention to the need for comprehensive and accurate recording (Ward, 2000). Moreover, such initiatives are also now being matched at the macro level by a similar emphasis on the need for outcome based evaluation.

PERFORMANCE ASSESSMENT FRAMEWORK: OUTCOME-BASED EVALUATION AT THE MACRO LEVEL

As part of the government program for modernizing and improving social care services (launched in 1998), a performance management system has been introduced, providing a comprehensive framework for measuring the effectiveness of services against identified objectives and setting targets for improvements (Department of Health, 1998, 1999a, 1999b). English councils are now required to work toward eighteen objectives for services for children and adults; their progress will eventually be monitored through fifty performance indicators. Councils are also required to submit data on most of these indicators annually to central government, although the full range will not be available until late 2002. A series of National Priorities Guidance targets has also been set and is designed to ensure that health authorities, education departments, and social services work jointly toward those objectives that require cooperation from several agencies. The annual statistical returns identify individual councils and are published both on the internet and in the press. Additional powers have also been given to the government to take action where local councils consistently fail to meet acceptable standards.

In many ways the performance management program being introduced into children's services at a macro level adopts an approach that complements that of the Looking After Children program at the micro level. Key government objectives for looked after children are framed in developmental terms, and specify, for instance, that services should "ensure that children are securely attached to carers capable of providing safe and effective care for the duration of childhood"; that they should ensure that these children "gain maximum life chance benefits from educational opportunities, health care and social care"; and that care leavers, "as they enter adulthood, should not be isolated and should participate socially and economically as citizens." The indicators that demonstrate how far these objectives are being achieved cover issues such as the proportion of looked after children permanently excluded from school, the proportion with up-to-date immunizations, annual dental checks, and annual health assessments, and the proportion convicted of offenses (Department of Health, 1999b). These indicators are described in the Assessment and Action Records and other Looking After Children materials.

Moreover, in both systems, the developmental approach has led to the identification of objectives and indicators that are applicable to all children rather than those who receive a particular service and has meant that children who are looked after away from home or who receive extensive family support services are not assumed to have lower aspirations or to require a lower standard of services than their peers. This marks an important conceptual advance in Britain, where, decades after the repeal of the Poor Law, it has still been difficult to dispel a widespread assumption that it is inappropriate for the state to provide a higher standard of care than the poorest parents can offer.

USE OF PERFORMANCE INDICATORS

Implementation of the performance assessment framework has raised many issues similar to those highlighted at an individual level by the implementation of Looking After Children. There are the same problems with the absence or inaccuracy of data. For instance, the first attempt to gather national data on indicators of educational outcome revealed that one in three councils were unable to say how many of their looked after children had passed their GCSE examinations (equivalent to high school graduation) (Robbins, 1999). There are also major difficulties with information systems, which frequently are unable to deliver the reports that would allow managers to make use of the data at a local level (Department of Health, 2000b).

While the above may prove to be teething problems endemic to the introduction of new and unfamiliar procedures, more significant difficulties could arise in the way in which the system is used. The introduction of performance management in other public services has sometimes created unintended consequences, where the need to meet targets becomes divorced from the primary objective—to improve services. For example, outcomes of the education system in England and Wales are now evaluated by monitoring the percentage of children who pass particular examinations; it is thought, however, that the need to meet these targets has given head teachers a perverse incentive to exclude disruptive pupils, particularly if they are unlikely to succeed academically (Social Exclusion Unit, 1998). The introduction of penalties and disciplinary measures for departments that fail to meet targets is likely to have exacerbated difficulties such as these.

It is possible that the introduction of performance targets for children's social care services may create similar perverse incentives. A major issue in Britain has been the frequency with which looked after children move from one placement to another. This has led to the introduction of a performance target linked to the objective to ensure stability of care, such as "to reduce to no more than 16 percent in all authorities, by 2001, the number of children looked after who have three or more placements in one year" (Department of Health, 1999b:8). There are concerns that the need to meet this target may become an end in itself, and that children could be left in unsatisfactory placements or that vulnerable teenagers refused admission in order to ensure its achievement (Ward & Skuse, in press).

Despite concerns such as these, in many ways the introduction of outcome-based performance indicators to children's social care services marks a significant advance. Statistical information concerning the numbers of children looked after or the length of time they spend in care or accommodation has been compiled for many years, but this simply gives an indication of activity or *output,* and is a poor proxy for measuring outcome. The developmental approach has ensured that the emphasis has shifted from measuring output to evaluating impact or *outcome.* Of course there are many intervening factors that make it difficult, if not impossible, to identify a clear causal relationship between service and outcome in such complex cases as those coming to the attention of social workers. Nevertheless, the program currently being developed provides the first systematic attempt to monitor the effectiveness of social services for children in need in England and Wales.

DIVORCING THE AGGREGATE FROM THE INDIVIDUAL

The indicators of outcome that are currently being monitored are designed to help local councils assess whether children in receipt of services are making satisfactory progress. Because identical indicators and objectives have been set for all children, including those supported in their own families or looked after away from home, it should eventually be possible to identify whether some councils are providing more effective services than others, or whether there are improvements from one year to the next.

However, outcome indicators such as those currently being monitored will only demonstrate *whether* children are progressing and targets are being met. This may be sufficient at a national level, but at a local level agencies will also need to be able to identify *why* certain children are progressing and not others, and *who* needs additional support if services are genuinely to be improved. At present there are a number of obstacles that prevent outcome data from being used in this way, as delineated below.

First, most agencies are not gathering the contextual information that will allow them to interpret their outcome data. Information about children's needs and the extent to which these are met by appropriate services is necessary in order to understand their progress: for instance, the data on the academic achievements of children in care need to be interpreted in the light of evidence concerning the incidence of learning disability in this vulnerable population and the availability of places in appropriate schools. Moreover, at present, baseline data on children's developmental status are not gathered at the point at which a service is provided, and so it is impossible to assess whether apparently slow progress marks a genuine deterioration or whether it is in fact an improvement on what had gone before.

Second, at present outcome-based evaluation at an aggregate level seems strangely divorced from the evaluation of the progress of individual children. Outcome data from the performance indicators are used to inform management and government whether targets are being met, but they are rarely disaggregated and used to help field social workers or social work teams identify how the progress of individual children might be improved. A number of agencies, for instance, are gathering information to complete statistical returns on the educational outcomes of looked after children not from the children themselves nor from their carers, their schools, or their teachers, but directly from the education departments that run the schools; such information comes in aggregate form, and cannot be related to the individual children concerned. This occurs even in very small councils where only a handful of children are involved (Gatehouse, 2000).

TOWARD AN INTEGRATED CHILDREN'S SYSTEM

The Looking After Children system was designed to provide a link between the micro and the macro assessment of outcome in cases where children were looked after away from home. It was originally envisaged that data on key variables would be collected in the course of social work interactions with individual children, and then harvested from files at routine intervals and aggregated to provide the requisite information for managers. However, poor implementation of the Assessment and Action Records, together with difficulties in their design and the lack of an electronic version, have prevented this from being feasible. Furthermore, the introduction of both the Framework for Assessment of Need and a performance management system that requires outcome-based evaluation of all children's services and not solely those for children placed in out of home care, has produced a much wider remit. Work is now being undertaken to fuse the Framework for Assessment of Need with Looking After Children to form an integrated children's service system; its purpose will be to provide "an assessment, planning, intervention and reviewing model for all children in need" designed to promote satisfactory outcomes (Department of Health, 2000c).

The Integrated Children's System will incorporate three interrelated strands of work. First, a theoretical framework is being developed that will map how the impact of parenting capacity and family and environmental factors on a child's developmental progress can be monitored throughout a child's contact with social services. The aim is to produce a conceptual map that will form a unified basis for evaluating the relationship among need, services, and progress whatever the child's circumstances. The same theoretical framework will therefore underpin all social work interventions, whether children are living at home and receiving family support services or cared for by public agencies and placed in residential units or with foster carers and so on.

Second, formats will be developed to reflect the above-noted conceptual framework in the social work processes of assessing need, making and reviewing plans, and monitoring interventions and outcomes. The aim is to build on the responses both to the implementation of the Looking After Children materials and new documentation designed to operationalize the Assessment Framework currently being piloted (Department of Health and Cleaver, 2000). A major objective will be to produce more user-friendly materials that gather essential information, but aim to reduce the bureaucracy of earlier models.

Third, attempts have been already been made to help social services departments improve the information technology they use by issuing a data model that identifies core information requirements for children's services, together with a process activity model for mapping the various activities through which information will be collected (Department of Health, 2000b, 2000d). Both of these have been introduced by central government and will form a template for the development of management information systems for children's services. The Integrated Children's System will be closely aligned with these models, providing in electronic format the screens through which social workers gather the information required in their work with individual children, and the point at which outcome-based data can be harvested and aggregated for strategic planning purposes. The aim is to restore the link between individual and aggregate data, so that information about outcome can be used to help both field social workers and managers identify how services can be made more effective.

CONCLUSION

The vision, therefore, is to provide an electronic recording system that streamlines the processes of assessment, planning, intervention, and review for social services work with all children in need and at the same time captures data that can be used to assess the outcomes of services at both an individual and an aggregate level. The system will operate both horizontally as it models the different processes that social workers and their managers need to undertake in order to identify need, provide services, and monitor progress, and vertically as it links with wider management information systems through the process activity model and the data specification for children's services.

The Integrated Children's System is likely to form the foundation upon which all social work interventions with children and families in England and Wales are based and, if implemented, will have substantial implications for practice. It assumes that social workers will input data directly onto laptop computers in the course of their everyday interactions with service users. Such a methodology will obviate the need for administrative staff to transfer written information from files onto management information systems, and should thus improve the accuracy of data. It should also make it easier to establish feedback loops, whereby information concerning individual children is aggregated and used both to inform the development of the service as a whole and to identify how far the experience of each child concerned can be improved to enhance his or her chances of achieving long-term well-being. The system will also have major implications for training as it anticipates that social workers will have a thorough understanding not only of children's development and those factors in their parents' capacity, their family, neighborhood, and the wider environment that enhance or inhibit it, but also that they will be computer literate and have a better understanding of the importance of accurate, systematic recording.

There are also major implications for research into the outcomes of children's services. The system is designed to gather data on key issues relating to the developmental progress of children in receipt of social work interventions. If the system is successfully implemented, it should be able to provide accurate and comprehensive data that will allow for outcome-based evaluation at both national and local levels. The benchmarking group of senior managers engaged in the fourth stage of Looking After Children have demonstrated how research messages from the data on children in out-of-home care can be explored and the findings used to improve the quality of their service (Ward, MacDonald, Skuse & Pinnock, in press). The Integrated Children's System should allow for the exploration of more comprehensive data on a wider group of children receiving a multiplicity of services. It also increases the likelihood of our being able to make meaningful comparisons in regard to the outcomes of services between different councils, or indeed between different countries.

Finally, perhaps we should note that the Integrated Children's System is not an unexpected or completely innovative development. Rather, it is the next logical step in a long-term initiative, consisting of many different strands at both macro and micro levels that have, for several years, been moving toward the introduction of outcome measures in children's services in England and Wales.

NOTES

1. Also see Rose (2002) and Thoburn (2002) for further consideration of the Looking After Children project.

2. The complete Looking After Children package consists of Essential Information Record; Care Plan; Placement Plan; Review form; Consultation papers for children, parents, and carers; Assessment and Action Records (for ages under 1, 1–2, 3–4, 5–9, 10–14 and 15+) (Department of Health, 1995).

3. For further details regarding audit results, see Skuse, MacDonald, and Ward (2001) and Ward and Skuse (1999).

4. The basic social work qualification in England and Wales is the Diploma in Social Work; advanced awards, including the new Post Qualifying Award in Child Care, are closely related to an ongoing Program of professional development.

REFERENCES

Acheson D. (1998). *Independent Inquiry into Inequalities in Health*. London: Stationery Office.

Baldwin, M. (2000). *Care Management and Community Care: Social Work Discretion and the Construction of Policy*. Ashgate, England: Aldershot.

Department of Health (1991). *Looking After Children: Assessment and Action Records (1st ed.)*. London: HMSO.

Department of Health (1995). *Looking After Children: Assessment and Action Records (2nd ed.)*. London: HMSO.

Department of Health (1998). *Modernising Social Services: Promoting Independence, Improving Protection, Raising Standards*. White Paper Cm. 4169. London: Stationery Office.

Department of Health (1999a). *Social Services Performance in 1998–99: The Personal Social Services Performance Assessment Framework*. London: Author.

Department of Health (1999b). *The Government's Objectives for Children's Social Services*. London: Author.

Department of Health (2000a). *Studies Which Inform the Development of the Framework for the Assessment of Children in Need*. London: Stationery Office.

Department of Health (2000b). *Integrated Children's System,* Briefing Paper No 1. London: Author.

Department of Health (2000c). *Data Specification for Children's Services*. London, Author.

Department of Health (2000d). *Process Activity Model for Children's Service*. London, Author.

Department of Health (2001). *Children in Need in England*. London: Author.

Department of Health & Cleaver, H. (2000). *Initial and Core Assessment Record*. London: Stationery Office.

Department of Health, Department for Education and Employment, & Home Office (2000). *Framework for the Assessment of Children in Need and Their Families*. London, Department of Health.

Garrett, P. M. (1999). Producing the moral citizen: The looking after children system and the regulation of children and young people in public care. *Critical Social Policy* 19:291–312.

Gatehouse, M. (2000). *Looking After Children: Data Analysis Network for Children's Services: Annual Report*. Loughborough, England: Loughborough University.

Moyers, S. (1996). *Looking After Children: Audit of Implementation in Year One (1995–96)*. Totnes, England: Dartington Social Research Unit.

Nicholson, D. & Ward, H. (1999). *Looking After Children: Good Parenting, Good Outcomes: Report of an Audit of Implementation in Eleven Local Authorities in Wales.* Loughborough, England: Loughborough University.

Parker, R., Ward, H., Jackson, S., Aldgate, J., & Wedge, P. (1991). *Looking After Children: Assessing Outcomes in Child Care.* London, HMSO.

Peel, M. (1997). *Looking After Children; Audit of Implementation in Year Two (1996–97).* Leicester, England: University of Leicester.

Robbins, D. (1999). *Mapping Quality in Children's Services: An Evaluation of Local Responses to the Quality Protects Program.* London: Department of Health.

Rose, W. (2002). Achieving better outcomes for children and families by improving assessment of need. In T. Vecchiato, A. N. Maluccio, & C. Canali (Eds.). *Evaluation in Child and Family Services: Comparative Client and Program Perspectives.* Hawthorne, NY: Aldine de Gruyter.

Scott, J. (1999). *Looking After Children: Audit of Implementation in Year Three (1997–98).* Leicester, England: University of Leicester.

Skuse, T., MacDonald, I., & Ward, H. (2001). *Looking After Children. Transforming Data into Management Information: Report on the Longitudinal Study at the Third Data Collection Point.* Loughborough, England: Loughborough University.

Social Exclusion Unit (1998). *Truancy and School Exclusion,* Cm. 3957. London: Stationery Office.

Thoburn, J. (2002). Outcomes of permanent substitute family placement for children in care. In T. Vecchiato, A. N. Maluccio, & C. Canali (Eds.). *Evaluation in Child and Family Services: Comparative Client and Program Perspectives.* Hawthorne, NY: Aldine de Gruyter.

Ward, H. (Ed.) (1995). *Looking After Children: Research into Practice.* London, HMSO.

Ward, H. (Ed.) (1998). Assessing outcome in child care: an international perspective, *Children and Society,* 12(3):151–248.

Ward, H. (2000). Translating messages from research on child development into social work training and practice, *Social Work Education* 19:543–51.

Ward, H., MacDonald, I., Pinnock, M., & Skuse, T. (in press). Monitoring and improving outcomes for children in out of home care. In K. Kufeldt & B. McKenzie (Eds.). *Child Welfare: Connecting Research, Policy and Practice.* Waterloo, Ontario: Wilfrid Laurier.

Ward, H. & Skuse, T. (1999). *Looking After Children: Transforming Data into Management Information: Report on First Year of Data Collection.* Totnes, England: Dartington Social Research Unit.

Ward, H. & Skuse, T. (in press). Performance targets and stability of placements for children long looked after away from home, *Children and Society.*

2

The Black Box
Accounting for Program Inputs When Assessing Outcomes

Edith Fein

Program outcomes are a vital evaluation tool, but to be used fairly they must be related to actual program processes and inputs because programs vary in the services they deliver even if they are described as being identical or similar. This chapter uses the evaluation of a family reunification program in the United States to illustrate this thesis. Implications for practice, planning, and evaluation are discussed.

BACKGROUND

Family reunification services are intensive, home-based services, time-limited in applications, using paraprofessionals for at least part of the service delivery (Warsh, Pine, & Maluccio, 1996). (For discussion of process and outcome measurements in family reunification services, see Pine, Healy, & Maluccio, 2002.) The small number of studies of reunification services (Fein & Staff, 1993; Fraser, 1991; Lerner, 1990) show lower "success" rates than family preservation services with which they are often compared (Maluccio, 2000; Nelson & Landsman, 1992). Moreover, recent examination of the validity of the outcome measures, appropriateness of control groups, and other methodological issues has raised questions concerning outcomes studies in the areas of family preservation and clinical practice, along with doubts about the power of reported findings (Drisko, 2000; Landsverk & Davis, Chapter 7 in this volume; McCroskey & Meezan, 1997; Rossi, 1992). In this chapter we do not join in the specifics of that debate; rather we suggest that, given the early stage of most of these programs and their evaluations, the primary focus for these studies should be the process of the service delivery, or what is "inside the black box."

What is the best window into the black box? Cheetham (1992:276) offers some suggestions in this regard:

> A first but often ignored priority is some focus on the content and manner of the service being delivered. In research that is intended to have an impact on policy and practice, there is little point in knowing about the effects of an intervention on clients unless we know how that intervention may be repeated, modified, or avoided. All bets

about the relationship between outcome and intervention are pointless unless you know what the social workers did.

As suggested above, basic for program replication is the determination of what the workers in the program did with and for their clients. One approach, not often taken, is an examination of the mix of activities that defined the program, in particular how much time was spent in the various aspects of service delivery. This information admittedly affords only a limited peek into the complexity that constitutes the black box, but it is a valuable starting point because the data have potential use for resource allocation, practice modifications, and policy changes. Various studies of family preservation programs have attempted to obtain detailed information of program activities, but methodological problems limited the studies' usefulness (Berry, 1997). These problems reflect the difficulties in capturing what, with whom, when, how often, and for how long services were provided. The information collected was not useful in capturing the intricacies of the service delivery process even though practitioners, who are best able to portray their own activities, were involved as data collectors (Berry, 1997; University Associates, 1992). As Aldgate (2002) indicates, it is essential that we continue to gather the perspectives of clients as well as social workers on the process and outcome of services.

PROGRAM DESCRIPTION

The reunification program under study was offered by a private child welfare agency that has offices in a number of states. The program works with abused and neglected children and their families, referred by each state's child protection agency as candidates for reunification but in need of more services than the states can offer. The program teams a social worker and a family support worker to prepare the child and family for reunification and to provide in-home services for up to eighteen months after the child returns home. The duration of service is thirty days for assessment, six months for the reunification decision, and twenty-four months for case closing. The service delivery is structured by a formal case plan developed by the team of workers and the family, setting forth explicit goals about how the family situation must change to effect reunification and outlining action plans of the steps necessary to achieve the goals (Fein & Staff, 1991a).

A formative evaluation, in place since the beginning of the program, examined case progress and outcomes and some of the process of service delivery, in particular the use of explicit goal-oriented case plans. Through the third year of the program, 34 (30 percent) of the 112 children were reunified with their families; 23 (21 percent) were still with their families by the end of the third program year. Two of the three sites accounted for most of the reunifications (14 and 15 children, respectively) and for 10 and 11 of those children still at home after reunification.

During the third year of the program, one of its components held particular interest for management: the roles of the social worker and family support worker on the team and the intensity of services they provided. A three-month study therefore focused on program activities at the two sites with the larger caseloads.

METHODOLOGY

Describing how time is allocated to the complexity of activities taking place in intensive home-based services is a major methodological problem. For example, when a worker drives a mother and child to the local welfare office to apply for benefits, the hour-long round trip provides transportation for the family but also includes modeling parent skills, counseling the client on her problems with domestic violence, and connecting her with community resources. How can the time used be described to give an accurate picture of the mix of services? If one activity is given precedence, for example, *providing transportation,* information about the other three is lost. If the hour in the car is divided among the four activities, some activity will be undercounted, probably providing transportation, which truly does take the full hour. If combinations of activities are listed along with single activities (for example, travel, travel and counseling, travel and modeling child care), the activity list would expand to unmanageable lengths.

Because earlier studies in family preservation and family reunification services did not provide useful models, as noted above, the coding methodology selected for this study was based on research previously conducted in the agency using a unique system of describing elements of time with two categories of descriptors (Fein and Staff, 1991b). *Activity* categories were used to name what was done, and *purpose* categories to describe the function or reason for the activity. Staff members were asked to complete daily time sheets on which they noted each task by selecting an appropriate combination of activity and purpose categories and indicating how much time each task took. They also noted which case the work was related to and whether they were alone or with the other member of the team when they contacted clients and other professionals.

The two-part coding handled the rich variety of workers' tasks without the need for tediously long coding lists, and dealt with the problem of multipurpose activities, as described in the example above, by separating the actual task (driving with client) from the purposes served (using community services, counseling, teaching parent skills, etc.); thus the hour of transportation can be marked as having three purposes. By this device, relatively short, useful lists describe a broad array of professional actions with clients. In addition, the time-study data were cross-referenced with information about case status to explore service delivery during three stages of the case: assessment, work toward reunification, and work after reunification.

FINDINGS

Nature of Services Provided

Social workers and family support workers spent 24 percent of their time in contact with client families and 12 percent in contact with other professionals in the child welfare system. Concrete services (22 percent) and visiting time and preparation (16 percent) received greater emphasis than direct counseling (8 percent). Traveling was an important component, taking almost one-fifth of all worker time (18 percent). The parent and child educational and support groups established at one of the sites during the last month of the study took 14 percent of the time at that site for the month for presentation and preparation. The teams that were assigned to each family acted in unison for 23 percent of the time spent with clients and collateral professionals. A substantial amount of time (20 percent) was spent in meetings among staff members for planning and discussion.

Workers' Role Differences

The program was staffed both with master's level social workers and with family support workers who did not have formal clinical training and certification but were experienced in delivering services to families. Differences were anticipated in the amount of time used and thus the extent of responsibility each type of worker had for both the clinically oriented efforts and the concrete services provided to the families. The anticipated differences were found. As compared to social workers, family support workers spent more of their time in direct contact with families (29 vs. 19 percent), traveling (23 vs. 13 percent), providing concrete services (31 vs. 10 percent), arranging and attending family visits (22 vs. 10 percent), and providing direct child care (11 vs. 3 percent). They spent a smaller portion of their time counseling clients (5 vs. 10 percent), meeting with and calling collateral professionals (8 vs. 16 percent), and doing narrative recording (5 vs. 11 percent). Both types of workers spent fairly equal amounts of time in staff meetings (21 and 22 percent).

Site Differences

The service model was the same for both sites, which began the program at the same time, but considerable variation developed in the way the service was delivered. Workers at Site A spent more time in and preparing for groups (14 vs. 0 percent; Site B did not have groups during the third year), and in narrative recording (12 vs. 5 percent). Those at Site B spent larger percentages of their time in direct contact with individual families (28 vs. 20 percent), counseling clients (10 vs. 6 percent), offering concrete services (25 vs. 15 percent), attending or arranging family visits (18 vs. 14 percent), and meeting with each other (25 vs. 19 percent). The amount of traveling time (17 and 19 percent) was similar despite differences in the density of population and size of the geographic areas served by each site, as was the time spent with collateral professionals (11 and 13 percent).

Worker Role Differentiation at the Two Sites

Social workers and family support workers had different patterns of responsibility at the two locations. The proportion of direct and collateral contact time spent together as a team was 17 percent at Site A and 28 percent at Site B. This was one aspect of a pattern of greater similarity of function at Site B and more differentiation at Site A. At each location social workers spent less time than family support workers providing concrete services and visiting, but more time in contacts with collateral professionals. What were small or moderate differences at Site B were large differences at Site A, where the proportion of time one type of worker spent was three to five times greater than was spent by the other.

Intensity of Service Delivery

The program was originally developed to offer a more intensive level of services than the state could provide. However, the percentage of worker time devoted to direct service categories such as direct client contact and contact with collateral professionals was not greater than that found for another of the agency's programs, long-term foster care, previously studied (Fein & Staff, 1991b). Each program used approximately 35 to 40 percent of its time in direct contact with clients and collaterals. This similarity between reunification's intensive services and those of a "regular program," however, represents only the perspective of worker time. From the perspective of the reunifying families, they were the recipients of an intense amount of contact; they received an average of twelve hours of service each week, with a range of three to thirty-five hours.

Intensity at Different Stages of Intervention

During the time study, active cases were at various stages of the service delivery process: assessment, working toward reunification, and postreunification. The largest subgroup of families was working toward reunification; they experienced an average of sixteen hours of service per week within a range of nine to thirty-five hours. The intensity was lower for families being assessed and those already reunified, averaging ten and six hours, respectively. The intense amount of contact was possible because workers had low caseloads (social workers averaged four to five families, family support workers two to three) and used the team approach (families interacted with two workers throughout service delivery).

Site Differences in Intensity of Service

The two sites showed differences in the intensity of the service as well as the nature of the service provided. Families at Site A averaged nine hours of service per week, those at Site B nineteen hours. Families working toward reunification, beyond the initial assessment period, had a similar pattern. At Site A they received an average of thirteen hours per week compared to twenty-one hours at Site B.

Services Provided

The data above indicate that families being assessed for the program and those whose children were already reunified received less intensive services than those who were beyond the assessment period and working to achieve reunification. The nature of the services also differed. During the approximately month-long assessment phase, compared with the period spent with families already accepted into the program, workers spent a smaller percentage of their time in direct contact with families (24 vs. 37 percent), traveling with or for the family (19 vs. 23 percent), providing counseling (4 vs. 12 percent) and concrete services (13 vs. 29 percent), and attending and arranging visits (14 vs. 24 percent). Also, social workers and family support workers spent more of the client and collateral contact time during assessment acting together (51 vs. 21 percent). The pattern of different service delivery during assessment was most evident at Site A, where the provision of counseling (1 percent), concrete services (1 percent), and visiting coordination (3 percent) was almost nil during assessment. The team work difference was particularly dramatic (55 percent during assessment vs. 14 percent during the work toward reunification).

Summary

What does this look inside the black box reveal about the services provided by the reunification program? It is an intensive service program with an emphasis on the provision of concrete services rather than reliance on counseling alone. The intensity measured by the number of hours of service experienced by the families is high, made possible by low caseloads and team assignments.

The intensity and nature of the services changed during the course of service delivery: intensity was somewhat lower during the initial assessment phase and a shift occurred after reunification toward more counseling time and less time for provision of concrete services. The team concept was working; families were interacting with both a social worker and family support worker who worked closely together while the families' eligibility for the program was assessed and then worked somewhat more independently, providing different services as efforts toward reunification occurred.

The implementation of the program was not uniform at different locations; on the contrary, two different approaches to service delivery were illustrated by the time study data. At one site, workers spent less time with individual families but met with them in group sessions for parents and children. Less intensive services were provided (fewer hours per case), with a smaller proportion of workers' time spent on counseling, concrete services, and visiting. Social workers and family support workers had more clearly delineated roles and worked more independently of each other with families accepted into the program. At the other site, more intense services were offered, with more of the workers' time devoted to client contact and concrete services, for example. Teams worked together more frequently.

These differences were consistent with other differences noted by the ongoing evaluation during the three years of the program. Compared to the second location, the first site had higher caseloads; assessed and accepted more families into the program; more closely followed the time guidelines for assessment, reunification, and closing; made more use of referrals to other agencies for counseling and other services; and created more action plans calling for independent activities by family and workers. The time study data clarified differences that management felt were occurring at the two sites, without knowing the nature or importance of the differences.

UTILIZATION OF FINDINGS AND IMPLICATIONS

The study described in this chapter examined one aspect of the service delivery of a single family reunification program and in the process helped the management of the agency to understand the program better. As a consequence of the study, workers as well as managers became interested in, sometimes challenged by, and sometime comforted by learning how colleagues were providing services.

Practice Implications

Despite some predictable grumbling about extra paperwork, workers showed considerable interest in contributing to the time study. Many found the exercise revealing, making them more aware of how they used their time. In fact, the program supervisor at one of the sites felt that workers were more focused in their work and took a more planful approach to case interventions as the study progressed, affected only by the process of systematic self-reflection and before any formal data presentation.

During the reunification service's early program planning and worker recruitment, the proposed emphasis on intensity of services led several of the program planners to believe that the workers' responsibilities would be focused heavily on field work and direct contact with clients. They recruited staff members with that understanding. The time study's demonstration that responsibilities for planning, meetings, and case documentation remained strong even when direct services were intense has clear implications for worker recruitment, training, and expectations.

Program Planning

Shortly after the completion of the study, Site B began increasing referrals and caseloads, a change in policy motivated by a management decision to serve more clients. The time study did not instigate the change but it revealed to management and workers at Site B that they had been offering a more intensive version of service delivery than their coworkers at the other site and demonstrated to them that providing fewer hours of service to more families could be done responsibly and with similar results, at least as measured by reunification counts. This information eased the transition to larger caseloads, making more acceptable what could have been a difficult situation for staff morale.

Implications of this study for program planning stem from the site differences in implementation that are often found in multisite programs. Many new programs, though initiated by a single agency or funding source, are established by contract at different agencies with different staffing and management structures. The two sites involved in this time study were two offices of the same agency, reporting to the same agency management, which began the program simultaneously with staff members hired specifically for the program. A program model that was to be followed and a series of early program meetings constituted a forum to promote consensus about the model and the implementation process. An ongoing in-house evaluation of the program included case monitoring and promulgated a structured goal and plan orientation that influenced and presumably systematized case practice and management.

The extent of the differences found at the two implementation sites in this study, however, was great given the planning and practice procedures that might have been expected to promote greater consistency. If, despite all these procedures, the style and orientation differences of workers were strong enough to affect the mode of service delivery as much as they did, how variable must multiagency programs be? Are programs based on one model but run completely independently by different agencies and states at all comparable? This has important implications for program managers and evaluators of these programs. Are the conclusions being made about program training, costs, and outcomes valid when they are based on assumptions of program consistency? Should attempts be made to use uniform models in disparate situations or, as Schorr suggests, should the "emphasis [be] on the attributes of effective programs, rather than on effective program models, because while you can learn a lot from these programs, I don't think you can clone them" (1992:11).

SIGNIFICANCE FOR RESEARCH AND EVALUATION

A significant interest of all evaluations is in the ultimate outcomes produced by the programs. Thus, even during the early stages of program implementation and before results can be fairly measured, the pressure is strong, as noted by Schuerman, Rzepnicki, and Littell (1994) as well as Piening and Warsh (2002), to determine the outcomes: *how the program is doing*. In such a rush to obtain information, programs based on similar models are perhaps inappropriately aggregated and compared or contrasted.

One problem with considering only program outcomes is that they often are not carefully defined by those struggling to evaluate child welfare and other human service projects. For example, in the reunification program described in this chapter, if a government agency is paying for services, then Site A, which processed more families, would earn more money for its agency. If *reunified families* are paid for, then both sites achieved similar numbers of reunifications, though Site A's percentages were lower. If *costs* are important, then Site B's style, where lower cost family support workers had many of the same functions as more expensive social workers, would be cheaper. Care must be taken to note the similarities and differences in program measures.

A second problem is that, whatever the outcomes, typically there is a dearth of information about program process: the actions and interventions included in the program whose outcomes are being examined. Yet information about how programs produce their outcomes is vital in order to replicate or improve services. Outcome evaluations must be sensitive to these hidden variables, which can be as influential as the identified outcome variables being studied.

All evaluations would benefit, therefore, from defining and measuring program inputs as well as the all-important outcomes. Indeed, the use of outcome data as a program planning guide should always be tempered by examining what is inside the black box of service delivery. Only then can confidence exist that program labels are not hiding service delivery differences.

REFERENCES

Berry, M. (1997). *The Family at Risk: Issues and Trends in Family Preservation.* Columbia: University of South Carolina Press.

Cheetham, J. (1992). Evaluating social work effectiveness. *Research on Social Work Practice* 2:265–87.

Drisko, J. W. (Ed.) (2000). Clinical practice evaluation: Conceptual issues, empirical studies, and practice implications. *Smith College Studies in Social Work* 70(2; special issue).

Fein, E. & Staff, I. (1991a). Implementing reunification services. *Families in Society* 72: 35–43.

Fein, E. & Staff, I. (1991b). Measuring the use of time. *Administration in Social Work* 15: 81–93.

Fein, E. & Staff, I. (1993). Last best chance: Findings from a reunification services program. *Child Welfare* 72:25–40.

Fraser, M. (1991). In-home family-based reunification services: Preliminary evaluation findings positive. *Research Exchange* 1:1–2.

Lerner, S. (1990). *The Geography of Foster Care. Keeping the Children in the Neighborhood.* New York: Foundation for Child Development.

Maluccio, A. N. (2000). Foster care and family reunification. In P. A. Curtis, G. Dale, & J. C. Kendall (Eds.). *The Foster Care Crisis: Translating Research into Policy and Practice* (pp. 211–24). Lincoln: University of Nebraska Press, in association with the Child Welfare League of America.

McCroskey, J. & Meezan, W. (1997). *Family Preservation and Family Functioning.* Washington, DC: Child Welfare League of America.

Nelson, K. E., & Landsman, M. J. (1992). *Alternative Models of Family Preservation: Family-Based Services in Context.* Springfield, IL: Charles C. Thomas.

Piening, S. & Warsh, R. (2002). Collaboration between evaluators and agency staff in outcome-based evaluation. In T. Vecchiato, A. N. Maluccio, & C. Canali (Eds.). *Evaluation in Child and Family Services: Comparative Client and Program Perspectives.* Hawthorne, NY: Aldine de Gruyter.

Pine, B. A., Healy, L. M., & Maluccio, A. N. (2002). Developing measurable program objectives: A key to evaluation of family reunification programs. In T. Vecchiato, A. N. Maluccio, & C. Canali (Eds.). *Evaluation in Child and Family Services: Comparative Client and Program Perspectives.* Hawthorne, NY: Aldine de Gruyter.

Rossi, P. H. (1992). Assessing family preservation programs. *Children and Youth Services Review* 14:77–98.

Schorr, L. (1992). Making a difference. *Focus* 2:10–12. Baltimore, MD: Annie E. Casey Foundation.

Schuerman, J. R., Rzepnicki, T. L., & Littell, J. (1994). *Putting Families First: An Experiment in Family Preservation.* Hawthorne, NY: Aldine de Gruyter.

University Associates (1992). Evaluation of Michigan's Family First Program. *Research Exchange* 2:15–16.

Warsh, R., Pine, B. A., & Maluccio, A. N. (1996). *Reconnecting Families: A Guide to Strengthening Family Reunification Services.* Washington, DC: Child Welfare League of America.

3

The Evaluation of "Community Building"

Measuring the Social Effects of Community-Based Practice

Robert J. Chaskin

There has been an increased focus in recent years in the United States on community-based efforts to improve the lives of children and families in need. These include various kinds of community-based service reform efforts (focusing on issues ranging from child abuse and neglect to health to juvenile justice and crime); efforts to promote community-based developmental opportunities for youth (such as recreational and after-school programs); and broad-based community development or "community building" initiatives to make disadvantaged neighborhoods more supportive environments for children, youth, and their families.

Community-based efforts across this spectrum treat the local community as both the context for and the principle around which practice should be organized. As *context,* community is "taken account of" in order to make policies and programs more relevant, responsive, and effective. As *organizing principle,* community is seen as the unit of planning and action toward which policy is directed, for which programs are developed, around which strategic goals are established, or through which activities and services are provided.

A common assumption of many of these efforts is the importance of a community's "social fabric" as both an outcome goal and as a mediating variable that influences how—and to what extent—community change can occur. These community-based interventions thus seek both to work through the social infrastructure of communities in order to achieve particular outcome objectives (e.g., reductions in child abuse, improvements in school achievement, or higher levels of employment) and to strengthen the social infrastructure itself; they seek to "build community" by strengthening community resources, enhancing social interaction among members, and promoting "social capital" as a collective good available to community members.

The evaluations of these efforts, however, are largely silent on the extent to which changes in a community's social fabric are effected. In general, they have focused on a combination of program-level outputs (such as houses built or jobs created), community-level outcomes as indicated by available data (such as median family income or high school dropout rates), and understanding implementation issues through a focus on decision-making processes, organizational arrangements, and the dynamics of participation, funding, and technical support.

This chapter explores the problem of measuring the social effects of community-based interventions. It outlines the theoretical assumptions about community social structure and functioning that drive these interventions, focusing on one (broadly defined) set of such efforts—comprehensive community initiatives (CCIs).[1] It briefly describes the nature of these interventions, the dilemmas of evaluation that face them, and the state of evaluation technology within them. It then reviews several ways of understanding community strength and "social fabric," outlines some of the constructs that are used to define it, and considers some of the methods and approaches used to measure these constructs. Finally, it draws some conclusions about the value and relative benefits of different approaches to measuring these constructs as a component of the evaluation of community-based efforts.

COMPREHENSIVE COMMUNITY INITIATIVES AND
THE EVALUATION OF "COMMUNITY BUILDING"

Among the many community-based efforts spawned over the last fifteen years in the United States that seek to improve the lives of children and families, Comprehensive Community Initiatives (CCIs) are perhaps the most explicit about their reliance on and intent to rebuild the social fabric of particular communities. These are explicitly community-building endeavors that view local communities (often urban neighborhoods) as definable social and functional units in which residents share both physical proximity and some set of shared circumstances. Such circumstances include access to key institutions (such as schools and churches), services and facilities provided by community organizations, informal social organizations and sets of relationships among community members, and a local environmental context—the quality and availability of public space, a level of safety, the state of the built environment, access to transportation—that can promote or inhibit sound institutional functioning and positive social interaction. Indeed, it is the convergence of these shared conditions that provides the fundamental rationale for organizing CCIs in neighborhoods: neighborhoods are seen by the designers of such programs as the place where many of the needs and circumstances of people come together and where they can best be addressed (Chaskin, 1998).

In part, CCIs were developed as a reaction against immediate past practice and, in part, as a reformulation of earlier (and ongoing) approaches (Kubisch et al., 1997). CCIs seek to replace piecemeal, categorical approaches with "comprehensive" efforts that attempt to build on the interconnections among economic, social, and physical needs, opportunities, and circumstances. They also build on the conceptual foundations and practice of earlier private-sector efforts in the United States (e.g., the Gray Areas Projects and the Community Development Corporation movement) and public policies (e.g., the Community Action and Model Cities programs).[2] However, they translate these concepts—characterized primarily by a focus on comprehensive, coordinated strategies through the creation of local mechanisms to foster collaboration and community participation—using different organizational approaches and some different programmatic strategies.

While the individual efforts that comprise this field differ along several dimensions, they hold in common a set of fundamental goals and are guided by adherence to a shared set of general principles. The goals are both broad and ambitious: to fundamentally change the circumstances of poor neighborhoods and the people who live in them. The principles are equally broad: community-building practice requires (1) a comprehensive or holistic approach and set of strategies and (2) the participation of community "stakeholders"—residents, community organizations, businesses, local institutions, government—in the development and implementation of such strategies. CCIs thus seek to support and develop sustainable processes, organizations, and relationships that can address the physical, social, and economic circumstances of poor neighborhoods and their residents and to build on and strengthen more informal community strengths—leadership, resident engagement, informal networks—that could provide the foundation for an ongoing capacity in the neighborhood to address its needs and support the well-being of its members.

THE EVALUATION OF COMPREHENSIVE COMMUNITY INITIATIVES

Challenging as they are to implement, CCIs are equally challenging (some would say impossible) to evaluate. This is true for several reasons. First, they are highly complex, seeking to work across sectors (social, economic, physical) and levels (individual, organizational, community) simultaneously. Second, they are highly evolutionary. Rather than beginning with a clear set of outcome objectives and a clearly defined intervention, both tend to be developed over time by local participants, with objectives multiplying and shifting over time. Third, they are highly contextual, seeking to be responsive to local circumstances and to have an effect on entire communities—which are themselves "open" systems subject to myriad influences beyond that of any given initiative—making the establishment of counterfactuals extremely difficult. Fourth, issues of process and organization are often deemed as crucial to the understanding of the possibilities and limitations of these efforts as any measure of neighborhood change. (These include, for example, how "comprehensiveness" gets defined and its impact on programmatic action; how collaborative governance is structured and operates; and how resident engagement and participation is incorporated and what are its effects). Finally, some of the kinds of outcomes they seek—"strengthened community capacity, enhanced social capital, an empowered neighborhood" (Kubisch, Fulbright-Anderson, & Connell, 1998)— are imprecisely defined and present particular measurement problems for which there are few widely accepted solutions (Chaskin, 2000; Chaskin, Brown, Venkatesh, & Vidal, 2001; Kubisch et al., 1998; Rossi, 1999).

Given these complexities, most evaluations of CCIs (where they have been evaluated) have tended to focus little on the question of outcomes, and still less on those that are most elusive—those concerning the social and interactional aspects of community building. Instead, they have focused largely on implementation processes, following out the conduct and activities of the initiatives as they develop. These implementation studies have provided documentation of the planning process, accountings of programmatic developments, descriptions of the dynamics of participation and decision-making, analyses of the role and influence of funding and technical support, and assessments of initiative successes and shortcomings and the factors that contributed to them (e.g., Brown, Butler, & Hamilton, 2000; Brown & Stetzer, 1998; Chaskin, Chipenda-Dansokho, & Toler, 2000). Often, they have served a diagnostic function, informing the initiatives as they evolve through interim analysis and formative feedback. This is a vitally important aspect of this work and should not be undervalued; interim analysis allows for midcourse strategic review and correction by initiative actors, helps build local capacity for using evaluation as a strategic tool, and provides a basis for accountability throughout the planning and implementation process (Brown, 1998; Fetterman, Kaftarian, & Wandersman, 1996; Rossi, 1999).

Documented outcomes, however, have often been limited to various "benchmarks" of progress (e.g., the development of the administrative framework for a new program; the purchase of property for redevelopment) and the concrete outputs of programmatic activity (e.g., new housing units; individuals placed in jobs; youth participating in an after-school program). More distal outcomes—measurable impacts on individuals, organizations, and the target community as a whole—have been more rarely captured, through surveys of participants (e.g., for individual assessments of impact) or through monitoring changes in indicators available using existing data (e.g., to track changes in school achievement, rates of employment, or levels of criminal activity). When they *have* been measured, CCI evaluations have often relied on pre-post measures of change without the benefit of a randomized control or comparison-group design to provide a counterfactual that could support assigning attribution of changes to initiative action, and have tended in any case not to attempt to measure changes in community social organization.[3]

In recent years, there have been important developments relevant for the evaluation of these initiatives that can help address the limitations on evaluation posed by the complexity, uncertainty, and evolutionary nature of CCIs. These include the development of a "theory of change" approach to evaluation and advances in mining and mapping administrative data for small-area analysis.

Theory of Change Approach to Evaluation
The theory of change approach seeks to address the problems of evaluating CCIs by engaging in a grounded, participatory process to articulate the assumptions about community circumstances, key activities, and likely outcomes that lie behind a particular CCI, and tailoring evaluation activities to follow out these presumed pathways of change (Connell & Kubisch, 1998; Weiss, 1995).[4] Such a process is generally facilitated by the evaluator to incorporate the input of various "stakeholders" in the initiative, often including some combination of staff, resi-

dents of the target neighborhood, members of the governance body that has over-sight responsibility for planning, and funders. It then has these stakeholders work "backwards" from their anticipated long-term outcomes, through early and inter-mediate outcomes (or "benchmarks"), the initial activities that are posited to lead to them, and the resources available and needed to implement these activities in the context in which the initiative is taking place.

Finally, this approach to evaluation seeks to reconcile diverging theories of change in such a way that a "good" theory[5] on which stakeholders can all agree is adopted, and to identify appropriate outcome measures and data collection strate-gies for tracking progress and providing useful, credible analyses of initiative ac-tion and effects over time (Connell & Kubisch, 1998; Milligan, Coulton, York, & Register, 1998). Evaluation design thus becomes a tool for the planning and man-agement of the initiative at the same time that it seeks to tame the initiative's com-plexity, reduce its uncertainty, and harness its evolutionary nature in order to make it more evaluable. (For more on strengthening the relationship between evaluation and program implementation, see Piening & Warsh [2002], and Wright & Paget, Chapter 10 in this volume.)[6] In these respects, the theory of change approach to evaluation shows real promise for CCIs and similar efforts.

Major challenges, of course, remain. Not all participants will hold the same theory of change, and reconciling competing theories is not always easy. The process as a whole requires significant up-front investment in establishing rela-tionships and an agreed-upon process that will guide the work, sufficient re-sources to do the research, and a belief in and commitment to supporting the research as both a planning and evaluation tool. There are also significant chal-lenges of measurement, which require attention both to initiative activities and initiative outcomes, as well as a diachronic perspective that provides an under-standing of process and the temporal staging of trajectories of work, since "activ-ities . . . occur over time in inter-related clusters at different levels of observation, with later activities being shaped by the outcomes of earlier activities" (Connell & Kubisch, 1998:32).

In addition, although the approach clarifies intent and provides the foundation to construct strategies for measuring relevant outcomes in particular cases, it does not by itself solve any of the *particular* measurement problems that plague CCIs. It may tell us, for example, that given the theory of change of a particular initiative, a rise in "community identity and optimism" and "more responsive institutions" are some of the social outcomes looked for (e.g., Milligan et al., 1998), but how such outcomes are best measured must still be worked out. Still, the theory of change approach at least sets the stage upon which these issues can be resolved reasonably and usefully within the context of a community initiative:

> Plausible theories of change will no doubt be complex and pluralistic, but if they are to be implemented (doable) they cannot be contradictory and if they are to be evalu-ated (testable) they cannot be unarticulated. (Connell & Kubisch, 1998:31)

USING ADMINISTRATIVE DATA

In addition to this approach (and in some cases as a component of it), there has been increasing focus on the manipulation and use of administrative and other existing data to allow for outcome analysis at the community level. The intent here is to be able to tap into existing data resources both to inform the planning of CCIs and other local efforts and to provide indicators of community change relevant to their evaluation. Administrative data, where they exist, can be beneficial in this regard for several reasons: Since data already exist, they can be used both to construct a retrospective baseline and to follow out change longitudinally without the expense of new data collection, and since in many cases data sources "cover the entire city, district, or county within which the CCI target community is located," using geographic information system (GIS) technology allows for the aggregation of data into community units within the larger area that can be compared with one another (Coulton & Hollister, 1998:166).

Beyond generally available data like those provided by the U.S. Census, sources of administrative data available in the United States will differ from locality to locality, but include data on housing and land use (e.g., land ownership and property tax records); the local economy (e.g., income tax and public community development expenditure records); safety (e.g., police records); education (e.g., public school records); health (e.g., immunization records); social services (e.g., public assistance and child welfare records); community resources (e.g., community directories and organizational membership records); and social behavior (e.g., teen childbirth and delinquency records) (Coulton & Hollister, 1998; Coulton 1995; Sawicki & Flynn, 1996). In some cases, data from various administrative sources can be linked to understand the dynamics of service utilization by individuals across systems (Goerge, Voorhis, & Lee, 1994).

Again, there are limitations and complications. First, communities are variously defined, and existing data on community circumstances and dynamics are collected based on different units of analysis (e.g., census tracts, zip codes, police precincts, service catchment areas). Where addresses or other locator information is included in these data sets, however, it is possible to use GIS technology to map them to conform to the community unit(s) of relevance for a particular initiative. Second, data are collected over different periods of time, and in some cases too infrequently to allow for monitoring of community change useful to initiatives or community organizations. Third, the data collected are of uneven quality, and may not speak effectively to critical questions a community initiative may have in order to identify priorities or measure the kinds of changes relevant to evaluate the effectiveness of its work. Fourth, much of the data that exist are held by actors outside the community, such as government agencies, universities, and private organizations. Gaining access to this information often requires time-consuming, sometimes difficult, and not always successful negotiation with agency personnel; bureaucratic hurdles and concerns about confidentiality may effectively bar community actors from access, or make their use of the data too complicated to be of ready help. Fifth, in many cases data that might be helpful are not routinely collected by community organizations and other institutions, which differ in their capacity and the resources necessary to ask productive questions, gain access to and work with information, and engage in data collection strategies where information does not exist. This is particularly difficult given the inherent constraints under which many community organizations work, including limited staff capacity, financial resources, and time. Finally, some information relevant to understanding community circumstances and change is not available at all through existing data sources. For example, information on qualitative aspects of community life, resident and stakeholder perceptions of community strengths and needs, and information on networks and relational dynamics are not routinely collected or available.

Unfortunately, it is these kinds of data that speak most directly to the questions of "social fabric." Administrative and other available data can be used effectively to understand other kinds of community outcomes that are targeted by community initiatives (e.g., reductions in child abuse and crime; increases in high school graduation and household income; improvements in the community's physical infrastructure). They may also provide useful proxy measures for certain "community building" kinds of change with which they are associated (e.g., residential stability as a proxy for community cohesion).[7] However, to measure such changes directly, new data collection will be necessary in most cases.

CONSTRUCTS, RESEARCH APPROACHES, AND MEASURES

What, then, needs to be measured to understand the effect of community initiatives on a community's strengths and "social fabric," and what approaches to measurement are most likely to be useful—both sufficient and feasible—within the context of the evaluation of such efforts?

To answer these questions, we must of course return to the theory-of-change problem: what a particular initiative should measure depends on what it is trying to change. Several constructs may be applicable, falling perhaps into three broad areas: measures of community "assets," measures of community attitudes and perception, and measures of community social structure and behavior. These groupings are somewhat ideal-typical; there is some overlap in both the key constructs that fall within them and in the methods used to measure them, and several of the constructs most often invoked in community initiatives—social capital, community capacity—require explicitly combining measures from more than one of these areas.

Community Assets

One goal of community initiatives is often to increase and strengthen the range of indigenous resources—a kind of "web" of supports and capacities—within a community available to its members. Measuring these "assets" is often a critical part of the planning process, since doing so provides a baseline for understanding both need and opportunities upon which initiative action might build, as well as a baseline for understanding any change in such resources over time.

Approaches to this task generally incorporate some combination of mining existing data, community inventory or "mapping" exercises, and survey research. Mining existing data for indicators of organizational presence and provision is generally a first-order task. For example, telephone directories, government agency listings, and some reference books (like the *Encyclopedia of Associations*) can be used to enumerate organizations that provide particular services, and large funders of community-based nonprofits (such as the United Way) may keep data on the organizations they fund, which can then be geocoded to determine their distribution and concentration.

A second, more direct, and broad-based approach in particular communities is through inventories and surveys of existing assets, including but not limited to organizations. Because "asset mapping" (Kretzmann & McKnight, 1993) is often associated with action-oriented research that has at its core a principled commitment to community building, the research is often participatory, using community actors in the conceptualization, implementation, and analysis of data collected. For example, "community youth mapping" is a process that has been used in a number of cities in the United States in which local youths are recruited to locate and document resources—facilities, organizations, services, contact people—that they consider important in their local community. Youths go block by block to map such resources, guided in their reporting by an observational protocol and a set of questions to ask organizational leaders and program staff about programs offered, facilities available, eligibility requirements, and so forth (Academy for Educational Development, 2000). In addition to the data produced, proponents of youth mapping suggest that youths, through their engagement in the process, become greater community resources themselves, both more knowledgeable and potentially influential in community activities and service provision, and more likely to participate and become connected to new relationships and opportunities.

Similarly, many community organizations and initiatives have used a combination of inventory approaches and survey instruments to determine the availability of local resources as well as to recruit community members to participate in initiative activities, from organizing campaigns to planning events to more ongoing roles or membership. These instruments provide a framework for enumerating both organizational assets—from major institutions (schools, libraries) to small local associations (block clubs, churches)—and individual skills that community members possess that can be harnessed for action. Again, mapping organizational and institutional assets begins with information available through various lists and directories, which are often followed up with brief key-informant interviews or mail-in questionnaires to organizational leadership. Knowledge of individual skills can be gathered through the use of survey instruments such as the "capacity inventory." Here, community residents are asked to enumerate their particular skills and interests, organized by kind of work (e.g., health, construction, child care), by providing yes/no responses for particular skills within them (e.g., caring for the elderly, painting, taking children on field trips). They are also asked about their experience with community activities, such as participating in block clubs or church groups, and to rank their skills and provide an assessment of their marketability (Kretzmann & McKnight, 1993).

In some cases, specific community assets have been evaluated in the context of particular programs or through resident assessments of the work of certain organizations or efforts. Sometimes, these are self-assessment measures provided through surveys of participants; in other cases, a random sample of community residents is surveyed. For example, residents have been surveyed regarding their perceptions of block club efficacy and community organization legitimacy (e.g., Perkins, Florin, Rich, Wandersman, & Chavis, 1990); church leaders and members have been surveyed to assess the fit between church activities and congregational and community needs (e.g., Guest & Lee, 1987); community planning council members have reported on various aspects of membership and council quality (such as leadership, knowledge, effectiveness, inclusiveness, influence) (e.g., Hughey, Speer, & Peterson, 1999); and community leaders (such as directors of service organizations) have been surveyed to measure levels of their awareness of community needs, action taken by leaders' organizations, and their perceptions of the efficacy of particular programs (e.g., Goodman et al., 1996).

Community Attitudes and Perceptions

A second set of constructs that may be relevant for understanding the social effects of community-based practice concerns the perceptions and feelings of residents about their community as a whole, and how they change over time. Indeed, in many cases community initiatives seek to have an impact not just on objective community circumstances (housing, employment) but on the subjective experience of community residents (satisfaction, sense of hope). Survey methods are the most common approach to measuring residents' satisfaction, concerns, priorities, sense of belonging, and "sense of community," although they are sometimes used in combination with (or supplanted by) qualitative methods such as key-informant interviews, focus groups, and structured observation.

Community satisfaction surveys often include a range of items to measure residents' perceptions of several aspects of community characteristics and functioning, such as crime and safety; cleanliness; quality and availability of housing and social services; sense of belonging; attitudes toward police and other public services; confidence in the future; and satisfaction with services, environment, and the quality and timing of response to community needs by public agencies and community-serving organizations (e.g., Briggs & Mueller, 1997; Hughey & Bardo, 1987). Measures are generally constructed from a combination of responses to items eliciting both perception and behavior, and focus on both general assessments and responses to questions about specific characteristics or dynamics. For example, respondents might be asked to what extent they are satisfied with their neighborhood as a whole, followed by a series of questions ranking their satisfaction with particular facets of neighborhood life (e.g., To what extent do you feel safe in your neighborhood at night? To what extent is building maintenance a problem in your neighborhood?), and combined with items that ask for self-reports of behavior (e.g., Which services in the neighborhood do you use? Do you belong to any local organizations or groups?).

Measures of residents' connection and sense of belonging have also been developed, again largely through survey methods. "Sense of community," for example, has been defined as a combination of perceptions of membership, influence, integration, and emotional connection and argued to have positive influence on residents' perception of the environment, social relations, and sense of control, as well as on their participation in community development activities (Chavis & Wandersman, 1990). Survey measures of sense of community have been constructed from items concerning perceptions and self-reported behaviors regarding residents' feelings of belonging; the extent to which they feel their needs are met by the community; the extent to which they are concerned about and feel they make a difference in the community; and the sense that there are shared respect, values, and commitment among members (Chavis & Wandersman, 1990; Goodman et al., 1998).

Social Structure and Behavior

In addition to building organizational and individual assets and attempting to enhance levels of satisfaction with and the affective connection residents feel toward their community, many community-building efforts focus on community social structure—"concrete social relationships among specific social actors" (Wellman & Berkowitz, 1988). These efforts often address social structure as both an independent and a dependent variable: networks of relations among community members can be harnessed to promote social change, and positive changes in networks of relations are one important outcome that community-building efforts seek to influence.

Social support, network structure, social capital, and collective efficacy are some of the key constructs that focus centrally on social structure and interactive behavior among community members. Measures of social support, for example, focus on the number of providers of support that are available to a respondent and those used (available and utilized support networks, respectively); the nature of support provided (e.g., information, advice, assistance); and respondents' subjective assessment of the quality of support given (Barrera, Sandler, & Ramsay, 1981). In some cases, efforts to measure social structure and interaction will rely on more general reports of network size (e.g., How many people in the neighborhood do you know by name? How many people in the neighborhood would you turn to for assistance?); of participation (e.g., To what extent do you participate in community activities such as organizational membership, meeting attendance, and organizational leadership?); and of perceptions of likely neighboring behavior (e.g., perceived likelihood that neighbors would keep an eye on your house if you were away) (Briggs & Mueller, 1997; Chavis & Wandersman, 1990). In other cases, formal network analysis will attempt to map and model network structure and interaction more specifically.

Network analysis may entail a focus on the existence of interpersonal (or inter-group) linkages along several dimensions, such as the *shape* of networks and the patterning of relationships (including their density, "reachability," and range) and the *nature* of the linkages (such as their content, durability, intensity, and frequency) (Mitchell, 1969). Generally, respondents' relations are mapped based on responses to highly specific survey questions about their networks. They are asked to list the (first) names of people to whom they would go for particular types of favors, talk with about particular types of issues, rely on for particular types of assistance, or spend time with in different circumstances. They may also be asked about the intensity of their ties with different people, the contexts in which they meet, and their ties to local organizations (e.g., Fischer, 1982). Mapping these responses and analyzing the patterns of relationships they describe provides an understanding of an individual's (or group's) placement within a network of relationships, and (aggregating out) the relationship among networks and the possible flow of resources within and across them.

Two aspects of social networks are of particular interest in the context of communities and community-building efforts. One concerns the degree of network closure—the extent to which people know the people who know you. This is particularly important in supporting informal mechanisms of social control and support. Youths, for example, are less likely to engage in antisocial behavior if their actions are likely to be reported to their parents, and watchful neighbors who know their circumstances are more likely to be able and willing to lend informal help (Anderson, 1990; Coleman, 1988). The second has to do with what are often called "weak ties" (Granovetter, 1973). These are casual or instrumental rather than intimate bonds that can connect individuals to networks of association held by others beyond the local community and that provide access to information, resources, and opportunities beyond their networks of close association. Indeed, it is weak ties to external networks that appear to be most critical, for example, for securing employment (Granovetter, 1973), and the management of "bridging" ties to other networks is a crucial component of strategic engagement in social networks (Burt, 1992).[8]

The existence of relations among individuals (including access to networks that work in both these directions) and aspects of social structure that support action—i.e., that actors can use "as resources . . . to achieve their interests" (Coleman, 1988:S101), is often referred to as *social capital*. Social capital is an evocative construct, and has been so much and so variously used recently that is hard to pin down.[9] Treatments of social capital range from a principal focus on collective obligations and expectations, information channels, and norms (three "forms" of social capital) facilitated by relational networks (Coleman, 1988), to an emphasis on trust and civic engagement (Putnam, 1993), to a focus on individual access to social leverage and social support (Briggs, 1998), to a stress on "sociocultural milieu" (identity, interaction, linkages, sentiments, social space) and institutional infrastructure (Temkin & Rohe, 1998), to a focus on embedded and autonomous social relations at both the micro and macro levels (Woolcock, 1998). In this way, social capital has developed a kind of "circus-tent quality: all things positive and social are piled beneath it" (Briggs, 1998:178), although some analysts stress the potential negative aspects of social capital as well (Foley & Edwards, 1997; Woolcock, 1998).

Given this diversity of definition and emphasis, measuring social capital becomes quite problematic. In the context of evaluating community-building efforts, few attempts have been made. One serious recent attempt in the United States is a study of the social effects of community development corporations (CDCs), in which measures of relationships, attitudes, and behaviors were combined (Briggs & Mueller, 1997). These measures were derived largely from survey responses of CDC residents and a sample of residents in comparison neighborhoods to questions about (1) how many people (relatives and friends) respondents knew in and out of the neighborhood; (2) perceptions of likely support from neighbors and overall "sense of community" using the scale developed by Chavis and Wandersman (1990); and (3) respondents' organizational participation and "collective activism"—that is, engagement in civically oriented actions such as signing a petition or getting together with neighbors to solve a problem. Results of surveys of the CDC residents were compared to those of residents in the comparison neighborhoods, and ethnographic data were used to help enrich and interpret survey findings.

A related construct relevant for understanding community strengths and social fabric, but not yet explicitly applied to the evaluation of community-based interventions, is that of *collective efficacy*—the "capacity of collective action shared by neighbors" (Duncan & Raudenbush, 1999:32). Collective efficacy is measured by two sets of five-item scales, one measuring "informal social control" and the other measuring "social cohesion and trust," based on respondents' answers to survey questions about, respectively, the extent to which they could count on neighbors to intervene in specific situations and the extent to which they feel about how well people in the neighborhood get along and share values (Sampson, Raudenbush, & Earls, 1997). High levels of neighborhood collective efficacy were found to be strongly associated with lower levels of neighborhood violence, personal victimization, and homicide, and to partially mediate the effects of neighborhood social composition (e.g., poverty, race and ethnicity, residential stability) on violence (Sampson et al., 1997).

EVALUATING "COMMUNITY BUILDING"

Depending on the nature of the intervention, it may be important to attempt to understand changes in a community's individual and organizational assets, attitudes, and social structure as part of the evaluation of a community initiative, in addition to focusing on initiative process, program outputs, and existing indicators of individual-level outcomes and community change. The constructs, methods, and measures outlined above provide some foundation for doing so, but decisions on specific strategies, measures, and instrumentalities will need to be tailored to the particular goals, contexts, and constraints provided in specific cases. Some key issues are briefly outlined below.

Theories of Change and Reasonable Expectations

The clearer the theory of change that drives community-based practice, the more guidance it can provide to both practice and evaluation. To serve both purposes in efforts like CCIs that are participatory and developmental, the theory requires a rational and well-supported process that explicitly—and from the beginning—ties strategic planning activities to evaluation requirements, identifies objectives and appropriate measures, collects baseline data across sites, and establishes management information systems that can be maintained by local actors who are provided with dedicated resources and support to do so.

It also requires attention to reasonable expectations, and to specifying outcome goals and aligning evaluation activities with the level and focus of the intervention. In many CCIs, for example, the overarching goals of "comprehensive change" and "neighborhood transformation" contrast with a level of investment and targeted programmatic activity that, at least taken piece by piece, is relatively traditional, narrow in its scope, and targeted to particular sets of outcomes (such as more housing or better schools)—which is not to say that these component activities are not vital or difficult in their own right nor that such efforts should not push beyond them toward broader change. On the one hand, bold ambitions for broad change can capture the imagination and resources needed to catalyze serious action; on the other, unreasonable expectations can lead to disillusionment, especially among community residents who have seen such promises fail to come to fruition in the past.

That said, many practitioners and community residents involved in such efforts are committed to and believe they can have an impact on the social fabric of communities. Indeed, many claim fundamentally to be concerned with these broader and more elusive aspects of "social fabric"—they are about not just building housing or providing social programs, but about building community and a community's "capacity" to promote and sustain positive social change.[10] To understand their effects, and to clarify the possibilities and limitations of such efforts in reaching these goals, evaluations of such efforts must begin to take them into account.

Taking Account of Complexity: Combining Methods

Given the complexity of communities as units of action and analysis and both the complexity and uncertainty that characterize most interventions seeking to promote change within them, a mixed-method approach to evaluating community initiatives is likely to be most effective. Such an approach could include a combination of survey research, qualitative research on initiative implementation and community dynamics, analysis of administrative data, and monitoring program conduct and outputs. (For application of such strategies as use of administrative data in the area of family preservation, see Berry and Cash—Chapter 9 in this volume.)

Survey research is best suited for systematically collecting data on attitudes, networks, and residents' perceptions of community resources, neighboring behaviors, assets, and expectations. Instruments can be developed that draw from measures of relevant constructs previously tested and can provide representative assessments of key elements of social structure and dynamics, as well as be analyzed to make statistical inferences. Surveys can also be implemented in some cases using local residents as interviewers and analysts or in partnership with local organizations or community-change efforts (e.g., Littell, Smoot, & Chaskin, 1993). In this way, research can also be used as an outreach, training, and employment tool.

Qualitative research—ethnography, structured observation, key-informant interviews, focus groups—can, if done well and systematically, provide a critical understanding of the complex dynamics of initiative or program implementation and community action. Regarding the former, it can provide the foundational "story line" of initiative conduct to provide a diagnostic analysis over time and against which any outcome measures can be better understood. Regarding the latter, it allows for an inductive understanding of social circumstances and processes, the meanings attributed to them by community actors, and the interaction among individuals, groups, program activities, and the environment. It can be used effectively to provide "thick description" of the social environment and rich illustrations of action within it; to inform the development of survey instruments and sampling strategies; and to extend and inform the interpretation of survey findings, corroborating patterns or suggesting alternative interpretations and providing a "feedback loop" that can refine analyses or suggest new directions for research (Briggs & Mueller, 1997).

The use of existing administrative data and its potential value for the evaluation of community efforts were outlined earlier. A useful extension of this approach could also be to work with initiatives, implementing agencies, and community organizations to develop management information systems that can provide the core documentation of program development, outputs, and use. This is most likely to work well when these actors can collect the data during the normal course of their administration, in relatively straightforward and unobtrusive ways, and where the information collected is of clear and immediate value to their work. Even so, this is not necessarily an easy task. Even when the responsibility to do so is clear (e.g., as a stated condition of financial support) and interest and commitment is present, dedicated resources for these activities will need to be provided to the implementing agencies, systems will need to be devised with them, and consistent and ongoing technical assistance may be necessary for some time. If successful, however, this approach has the advantage of building the capacity of implementing organizations to monitor their work (self-evaluate) and increases the chances that data collected are relevant and useful.

Making the Case: Evidence and Audience

Putting in place a mixed-method evaluation can be limited not only by resource constraints, but by more fundamental methodological dilemmas or political realities. Perhaps the most thorny issue regarding the former in the context of community initiatives concerns establishing causality in the absence of the ability to conduct an experimental research using randomized controls. Some have argued for the value of an interrupted time-series approach using comparison communities or randomized site selection, particularly where the effects are expected to be large (Gueron, 1999), or "blending" such a design with other quantitative and qualitative methods in an integrated way (Granger, 1998). Given sufficient resources, such an approach can be powerful. Sufficient resources are not always available, however, and it is often impossible, given the timing of program implementation, to make an adequate number of preintervention observations to establish a baseline for the time-series analysis. Compromises may need to be made. The issue here is how to make a credible case: "Since evaluations are done to help people make decisions, the credibility of any causal inference should be commensurate with the importance of the judgment it will influence" (Granger, 1998:228).

The ability to make this case is to some degree dependent on the social and political context in which the effort is to unfold. In some cases, tolerance for evaluation may be low: program managers and local participants may believe that formal evaluation is unnecessary to attribute change ("We'll know it when we see it"), may fear evaluation as a threat, or may see funding for evaluation as money that should be spent on program operations (e.g., Ainsworth, Chapter 11 in this volume; Chaskin, 2000). In other cases, funders or policymakers may need to be convinced with compelling evidence of success in order to continue support. In yet others, these two tendencies may converge, engendering disagreement about what kinds of information should be prioritized, at what level of detail and rigor it should be sought, who should decide, and how it should be presented to be most useful (and to whom). At a minimum, it will be necessary to focus on systematic program documentation, following out the various component projects sponsored or supported by an effort to understand their conduct and specific outputs. Comparing these to community-level changes that have been identified as goals of the effort allows a provisional argument for impact to be made, although it does not provide sufficient evidence of attribution.

Whatever the design, another aspect of making the case concerns the relationship among evaluation, implementation, and policy and the presentation of findings to multiple audiences. Such audiences may include policymakers, funders, program managers and staff, members of boards and governance bodies overseeing planning and implementation, program clients, and community residents. Speaking effectively to each requires understanding their needs and interests; tailoring reporting to be responsive to them (e.g., substantive focus, format and presentation, level of detail, and periodicity of reporting); and perhaps engaging them in different ways in the process of developing questions and research approaches, identifying data sources, and interpreting findings.

CONCLUSION

The combination of the above-noted factors suggests that building an understanding of the social effects of community-building efforts requires striking a balance between broader support for rigorous evaluations and demonstrations that attempt to measure these effects directly and with attendance to establishing a strong case for attributing causality, and a pragmatic approach to systematic, diagnostic evaluations of particular efforts underway, perhaps including support for comparative case studies or meta-analyses of a range of such efforts. Although challenging, doing so may help build both a capacity and interest in evaluation as a tool for action as well as a stronger foundation of knowledge that can inform policy and practice more broadly.

NOTES

1.   For overview of the field of CCIs, see Kubisch et al. (1997), Kingsley, McNeely and Gibson (1997), and Jackson and Marris (1996).

2.   On the Ford Foundation's Gray Areas Projects, see, e.g., Marris and Rein (1982). On Community Development Corporations, see, e.g., Berndt (1977), Pierce and Steinbach (1987), and Vidal (1992). On Community Action and Model Cities, see, e.g., Frieden and Kaplan (1975), Haar (1975), and Kramer (1969). On the link between these efforts and contemporary neighborhood initiatives, see Halpern (1995).

3.   For discussion of the problem of the counterfactual in community initiatives, see Rossi (1999). Briggs and Mueller (1997) provide one exception to this tendency, which will be discussed briefly below. Some other evaluations have used comparison-community designs, but have generally used more bounded units of analysis to define the communities, such as public housing developments rather than "neighborhoods" (e.g., Riccio, 1999).

4.   Cf. Fetterman et al. (1996) on "empowerment evaluation" and the use of logic models and Wright and Paget (Chapter 10 in this volume) on applications of the logic model in the field of child and family services.

5.   A good theory of change in this context, according to Connell and Kubisch, is one that is "plausible, doable, and testable" (1998:19).

6.   For more on strengthening the relationship between evaluation and program implementation, see Piening and Warsh (2002) and Wright and Paget (Chapter 10 in this volume).

7.   Communities characterized by greater residential stability are likely to exhibit a greater density of acquaintance among members, and therefore greater social cohesion (e.g., Sampson, 1988).

8.   A central aspect of this, according to Burt (1992), is the optimization of *structural holes*. A structural hole is the "chasm spanned" between clusters of social actors, and optimizing structural holes involves building and maintaining bridges across these chasms. The goal is to create an "efficient-effective network" that balances network size and network diversity, i.e., that (1) promotes the inclusion of a large number of *nonredundant* ties and (2) focuses resources on maintaining those relationships among nodes that embody access to other networks ("primary contacts"), and therefore to the information, resources, and opportunities they represent (ibid.). Of relevance to community efforts that seek to strengthen relational networks, the strategic role of individuals is not limited to making use of the structural position they find themselves in. The structure itself is open to manipulation and navigation: "Where structural holes do not exist, they can be manufactured, or the constraint of their absence can be neutralized" (ibid.:230).

9.   For a thorough review and critique of the construct of *social capital*, see Woolcock (1998).

10.   For a treatment of the definition and approaches to building "community capacity," see Chaskin et al. (2001).

REFERENCES

Academy for Educational Development (2000). *Website*. Available: http://www.aed.org.

Anderson, E. (1990). *Streetwise: Race, Class and Change in an Urban Community*. Chicago: University of Chicago Press.

Barrera, M., Sandler, I., & Ramsay, T. (1981). Preliminary development of a scale of social support: Studies on college students. *American Journal of Community Psychology* 9:435–47.

Berndt, H. E. (1977). *New Rulers in the Ghetto: The Community Development Corporation and Urban Poverty*. Westport, CT: Greenwood.

Briggs, X. (1998). Brown kids in white suburbs: housing mobility and the many faces of social capital. *Housing Policy Debate* 9(1):177–221.

Briggs, X. & Mueller, E., with M. Sullivan. (1997). *From Neighborhood to Community: Evidence on the Social Effects of Community Development*. New York: Community Development Research Center.

Brown, P. (1998). Shaping the evaluator's role in a theory of change evaluation: Practitioner reflections. In K. Fulbright-Anderson, A. C. Kubisch, & J. P. Connell (Eds.), *New Approaches to Evaluating Community Initiatives, Vol. 2: Theory, Measurement, and Analysis* (pp. 101–12). Washington, DC: Aspen Institute.

Brown, P., Butler, B., & Hamilton, R. (2000). *A Review of the Sandtown-Winchester Neighborhood Transformation Initiative. A Report Prepared for the Enterprise Foundation*. Chicago: Chapin Hall Center for Children at the University of Chicago.

Brown, P. & Stetzer, P. S. (1998). *Glades Community Development Corporation: A Chronicle of a Community Development Intermediary*. Chicago: Chapin Hall Center for Children at the University of Chicago.

Burt, R. S. (1992). *Structural Holes: The Social Construction of Competition*. Cambridge, MA: Harvard University Press.

Chaskin, R. J. (1998). Neighborhood as a unit of planning and action: A heuristic approach. *Journal of Planning Literature* 13(1):11–30.

Chaskin, R. J. (2000). Two-tiered evaluation in the neighborhood and family initiative: Dilemmas of implementation. Paper presented at the annual meeting of the Association for Public Policy Analysis and Management, Seattle, WA.

Chaskin, R. J., Brown, P., Venkatesh, S., & Vidal, A. (2001). *Building Community Capacity*. Hawthorne, NY: Aldine de Gruyter.

Chaskin, R. J., Chipenda-Dansokho, S., & Toler, A. K. (2000). *Moving Beyond the Neighborhood and Family Initiative: The Final Phase and Lessons Learned*. Chicago: Chapin Hall Center for Children at the University of Chicago.

Chavis, D. M. & Wandersman, A. (1990). Sense of community in the urban environment: A catalyst for participation and community development. *American Journal of Community Psychology* 18:55–81.

Coleman, J. S. (1988). Social capital in the creation of human capital. *American Journal of Sociology* 94:95–120.

Connell, J. P. & Kubisch, A. C. (1998). Applying a theory of change approach to the evaluation of comprehensive community initiatives: Progress, prospects, and problems. In K. Fulbright-Anderson, A. C. Kubisch & J. P. Connell (Eds.), *New Approaches to Evaluating Community Initiatives, Vol. 2: Theory, Measurement, and Analysis* (pp. 15–44). Washington, DC: Aspen Institute.

Coulton, C. J. (1995). Using community-level indicators of children's well-being in comprehensive community initiatives. In J. P. Connell, A. C. Kubisch, L. B. Schorr, & C. H. Weiss (Eds.), *New Approaches to Evaluating Community Initiatives, Vol. 1: Concepts, Methods, and Contexts* (pp. 173–200). Washington, DC: Aspen Institute.

Coulton, C. & Hollister, R. (1998). Measuring comprehensive community initiative outcomes using data available for small areas. In K. Fulbright-Anderson, A. C. Kubisch, & J. P. Connell (Eds.), *New Approaches to Evaluating Community Initiatives,* Vol. 2: *Theory, Measurement, and Analysis* (pp. 165–220). Washington, DC: Aspen Institute.

Duncan, G. J. & Raudenbush, S. W. (1999). Assessing the effects of context in studies of child and youth development. *Educational Psychologist* 34(1):29–41.

Fetterman, D. M., Kaftarian, S. J., & Wandersman, A. (Eds.) (1996). *Empowerment Evaluation: Knowledge and Tools for Self-Assessment and Accountability.* Thousand Oaks, CA: Sage.

Fischer, C. (1982). *To Dwell among Friends: Personal Networks in Town and City.* Chicago: University of Chicago Press.

Foley, M. W. & Edwards, B. (1997). Escape from politics? Social theory and the social capital debate. *American Behavioral Scientist* 40 (5):550–61.

Frieden, B. J. & Kaplan, M. (1975). *The Politics of Neglect: Urban Aid from Model Cities to Revenue Sharing.* Cambridge, MA: MIT Press.

Goerge, R., Voorhis, J. V., & Lee, B. J. (1994). Illinois's longitudinal and relational child and family research database. *Social Science Computer Review* 12(3):351–65.

Goodman, R., Speers, M. A., McLeroy, K., Fawcett, S., Kegler, M., Parker, E., Smith, S. R., Sterling, T. D., & Wallerstein, N. (1998). Identifying and defining the dimensions of community capacity to provide a basis for measurement. *Health Education & Behavior* 25(3):258–78.

Goodman, R. M., Wandersman, A., Chinman, M., Imm, P., & Morrissey, E. (1996). An ecological assessment of community-based interventions for prevention and health promotion: Approaches to measuring community coalitions. *American Journal of Community Psychology* 24(1):33–61.

Granger, R. C. (1998). Establishing causality in evaluations of comprehensive community initiatives. In K. Fulbright-Anderson, A. C. Kubisch, & J. P. Connell (Eds.), *New Approaches to Evaluating Community Initiatives,* Vol. 2: *Theory, Measurement, and Analysis* (pp. 221–46). Washington, DC: Aspen Institute.

Granovetter, M. (1973). *Getting a Job: A Study of Contacts and Careers.* Cambridge, MA: Harvard University Press.

Gueron, J. M. (1999). Comment on Rossi's chapter entitled Evaluating community development programs: Problems and prospects. In R. F. Ferguson & W. T. Dickens (Eds.), *Urban Problems and Community Development* (pp. 559–65). Washington, DC: Brookings Institution Press.

Guest, A. M. & Lee, B. A. (1987). Metropolitan residential environments and church organizational activities. *Sociological Analysis* 47:335–54.

Haar, C. M. (1975). *Between the Idea and the Reality: A Study in the Origin, Fate and Legacy of the Model Cities Program.* Boston: Little, Brown.

Halpern, R. (1995). *Rebuilding the Inner City: A History of Neighborhood Initiatives to Address Poverty in the United States.* New York: Columbia University Press.

Hughey, J. B. & Bardo, J. W. (1987). Social psychological dimensions of community satisfaction and quality of life: Some obtained relations. *Psychological Reports* 61:239–46.

Hughey, J., Speer, P. W., & Peterson, N. A. (1999). Sense of community in community organizations: Structure and evidence of validity. *Journal of Community Psychology* 27(1):97–113.

Jackson, M. R. & Marris, P. (1996). *Collaborative Comprehensive Community Initiatives: Overview of an Emerging Community Improvement Orientation.* Washington, DC: Urban Institute.

Kingsley, G. T., McNeely, J. B., & Gibson, J. O. (1997). *Community Building: Coming of Age.* Washington, DC: Development Training Institute and Urban Institute.

Kramer, R. (1969). *Participation of the Poor: Comparative Community Case Studies in the War on Poverty*. Englewood Cliffs, NJ: Prentice-Hall.

Kretzmann, J. P. & McKnight, J. L. (1993). *Building Communities from the Inside Out: A Path toward Finding and Mobilizing a Community's Assets*. Evanston, IL: Center for Urban Affairs and Policy Research, Neighborhood Innovations Network, Northwestern University.

Kubisch, A., Brown, P., Chaskin, R., Hirota, J., Joseph, M., Richman, H., & Roberts, M. (Eds.) (1997). *Voices From the Field: Learning from the Early Work of Comprehensive Community Initiatives*. Washington, DC: Aspen Institute.

Kubisch, A. C., Fulbright-Anderson, K., & Connell, J. P. (1998). Evaluating community initiatives: A progress report. In K. Fulbright-Anderson, A. C. Kubisch, & J. P. Connell (Eds.), *New Approaches to Evaluating Community Initiatives, Vol. 2: Theory, Measurement, and Analysis* (pp. 1–14). Washington, DC: Aspen Institute.

Littell, J. H., Smoot, P., & Chaskin, R. J. (1993). *The Neighborhood and Family Initiative: Findings from a Survey of Residents in Two Neighborhoods. A Report to the Ford Foundation*. Chicago: Chapin Hall Center for Children at the University of Chicago.

Marris, P. & Rein M. (1982). *Dilemmas of Social Reform: Poverty and Community Action in the United States* (2nd Ed.). Chicago: University of Chicago Press.

Milligan, S., Coulton, C., York, P., & Register, R. (1998). Implementing a theory of change evaluation in the Cleveland Community-Building Initiative: A case study. In K. Fulbright-Anderson, A. C. Kubisch, & J. P. Connell (Eds.), *New Approaches to Evaluating Community Initiatives, Vol. 2: Theory, Measurement, and Analysis* (pp. 45–86). Washington, DC: Aspen Institute.

Mitchell, J. C. (1969). The concept and use of social networks. In J. C. Mitchell (Ed.), *Social Networks in Urban Situations: Analyses of Personal Relationships in Central African Towns* (pp. 1–50). Manchester: Institute of Social Research at the University of Zambia.

Perkins, D. D., Florin, P., Rich, R. C., Wandersman, A., & Chavis, D. M. (1990). Participation and the social and physical environment of residential blocks: Crime and community context. *American Journal of Community Psychology* 18(1):83–115.

Piening, S. & Warsh, R. (2002). Collaboration between evaluators and agency staff in outcome-based evaluation. In T. Vecchiato, A. N. Maluccio, & C. Canali (Eds.), *Evaluation in Child and Family Services: Comparative Client and Program Perspectives*. Hawthorne, NY: Aldine de Gruyter.

Pierce, N. R. & Steinbach, C. F. (1987). *Corrective Capitalism: The Rise of America's Community Development Corporations*. New York: Ford Foundation.

Putnam, R. D. (1993). *Making Democracy Work: Civic Traditions in Modern Italy*. Cambridge, MA: Harvard University Press.

Riccio, J. A. (1999). *Mobilizing Public Housing Communities for Work: Origins and Early Accomplishments of the Jobs-Plus Demonstration*. New York: Manpower Demonstration Research Corporation.

Rossi, P. H. (1999). Evaluating community development programs: Problems and prospects. In R. F. Ferguson & W. T. Dickens (Eds.), *Urban Problems and Community Development* (pp. 521–67). Washington, DC: Brookings Institution Press.

Sampson, R. J. (1988). Local friendship ties and community attachment in mass society: A multilevel systemic model. *American Sociological Review* 53:766–79.

Sampson, R. J., Raudenbush, S., & Earls, F. (1997). Neighborhoods and violent crime: A multi-level study of collective efficacy. *Science* 277 (15):918–24.

Sawicki, D. S. & Flynn, P. (1996). Neighborhood indicators: A review of the literature and an assessment of conceptual and methodological issues. *Journal of the American Planning Association* 62(2):165–83.

Temkin, K. & Rohe, W. (1998). Social capital and neighborhood stability: An empirical investigation. *Housing Policy Debate* 9(1):61–88.

Vidal, A. C. (1992). *Rebuilding Communities: A National Study of Urban Community Development Corporations*. New York: New School for Social Research.

Weiss, C. H. (1995). Nothing as practical as good theory: Exploring theory-based evaluation for comprehensive community initiatives for children and families. In J. P. Connell, A. C. Kubisch, L. B. Schorr, & C. H. Weiss (Eds.), *New Approaches to Evaluating Community Initiatives,* Vol. 1: *Concepts, Methods, and Contexts* (pp. 65–92). Washington, DC: Aspen Institute.

Wellman, B. & Berkowitz, S. D. (1988). Introduction: Studying social structures. In B. Wellman & S. D. Berkowitz (Eds.), *Social Structures: A Network Approach* (pp. 1–14). New York: Cambridge University Press.

Woolcock, M. (1998). Social capital and economic development: Toward a theoretical synthesis and policy framework. *Theory and Society* 27:151–208.

4

Outcome-Based Evaluation of National Health and Social Programs

Tiziano Vecchiato

In recent years the planning for social and health services in Italy has highlighted two major issues: the difficulties in defining measurable outcomes and the conditions required for evaluating the effectiveness of services. In particular, the first issue, defining measurable outcomes, reflects problems involved in accounting for geographic differences when determining national goals for outcomes, and also in defining realistic standards for expected results. The second issue, evaluating effectiveness, concerns the difficulties in selecting indicators of effectiveness and determining the time needed to obtain reliable data that relate to the results. Building on the Italian experience, in this chapter we address both issues, in order to improve the theory and methods of evaluation, and to discuss some results that are already available for comparisons among diverse methods.

LIMITS OF NATIONAL PLANNING

More studies on how to improve planning for health and social programs are needed for the following reasons (Vecchiato, 1995, 2000a, 2000b):

- to understand why it is ordinarily difficult to assess the achievement of results;
- to learn what obstacles prevent the use of programs at regional and local levels;
- to discover why the planning method is so cumbersome;
- to examine why it is so difficult to turn general goals into specific goals at regional and local levels; and
- to explore why planning absorbs so much energy without devoting at least some attention to the evaluation of results.

Planning is usually associated with political choices. For instance, in universal welfare systems, the protection of frail people and the reduction of inequalities in accessing services are two priorities that coexist in both national and local planning (Vecchiato, 1999a, 1999b, 1999c). Thus, public policies for health protection are often characterized by the search for points of balance between these two priorities. In some cases, policies have a *solidaristic* nature, that is, decisions are made based on fiscal or other "social solidarity" considerations as part of public welfare politics. In other cases, policies have a *utilitarian* nature, relying on private insurance programs that can safeguard the collective interest by offering services to those who cannot meet the welfare criteria. Solidaristic and utilitarian approaches together create an ecological vision of service provision that reconciles the needs of frail people with the desire not to exclude those who do not qualify (Vecchiato, 2001).

In Italy resources in universal welfare systems are concentrated on the planning process, that is, on political and technical choices that regulate the welfare system. These choices are reflected in the 1999 national health reform law, the 1998 National Health Plan, and the 2000 reform of social services.[1] All of these laws share social policies based on the following principles:

1. Universality of access: access to services is not limited by the results of the assessment process or by available assets, but depends on professional evaluation of the person's need for health, social or integrated services.

2. Equal access to a wide range of uniformly distributed services: the removal of geographical barriers to access is guaranteed by local planning of services.

3. Sharing the financial risk: the financing system guarantees that an individual's payment does not depend on the severity of need or on the services provided, but exclusively on the person's capacity to contribute financially.

Welfare systems founded on the principle of social solidarity provide a guarantee of the *essential levels of care*. The idea of essential levels is related to a political and technical judgment on the *necessary conditions* for matching the needs (of promotion, maintenance, and recovery of health conditions) as well as professional assessment of the *appropriateness* of the request for services and the availability of services uniformly throughout the territory.

These considerations present a challenge: how to affirm the right to health or social assistance, recognized as important by everyone, with organizational imperatives, that is, creating resources, defining service strategies, and performing professional responsibilities so that the goals mesh with interventions and measurable results. Indeed, the right to health care and the right to social assistance are, in great part, "conditional rights"; that is, there are certain structural, organizational, and professional requirements for the rights to be workable. For instance, if a system of services for children and families is not able to guarantee performances that are of good quality, distributed throughout the territory and accessible, there will not be concrete and effective results.

In practice, a right works if there exist the necessary conditions (political, organizational, professional, etc.) for implementing it in the form of goods, services, and strategies for matching diverse needs. In *The Cost of Rights,* Holmes and Sunstein (1999) suggest that the protection of social rights depends on the capacity to finance social rights through taxes; the ability to build responsibility around their attainment; and the recognition of the (solidaristic) link that ties individual outcomes for a single person or family to the attainment of effective results for the whole community.

The emphasis on good management of resources for societal well-being is a re-action to a number of failures in planning, which arise because it is often impos-sible to document either results or their lack if there is no measurement and assessment at all. Occasionally, evaluations are avoided to hide such failures, but failures are recognized even in the absence of adequate evaluations. Indeed, when a program is evaluated, poor results can often be related to planning deficiencies, such as formulating vague or broad objectives, not defining specific plans, not as-signing individual responsibilities, or not keeping in mind the available resources. In such cases, the general objectives are not followed by a clear definition of spe-cific objectives or indicators for measuring their attainment.

TOWARD IMPROVED PLANNING

To improve planning in the area of health and social programs, we need to en-rich the theoretical bases of the services, improve their methodologies, provide re-sources that are consistent with expected results, and facilitate their attainment.[2] In addition various levels of evaluation should be considered—process evaluation, outcome evaluation, and assessment of satisfaction—and evaluation should be un-dertaken in a systematic way. This includes monitoring responsibilities; specify-ing the objectives in an operational sense and quantifying them as expected "results"; comparing measures at different times; and examining how the results of measurements can be analyzed. Also, the planning process must not be based on broad statement of aims (e.g., "promote," "improve," "increase," "decrease"), but on realistic decisions that determine the contents of objectives and the mea-surement of their attainment. In this respect, an initial evaluation could be to com-pare the client's situation at one time with the situation as it develops subsequently after the service itself, on the basis of qualitative and quantitative indicators that are defined in advance and can be represented graphically, for example, using *baselines* and follow-up measures (cf. Unrau, Gabor, & Grinnell, 2001).

Evaluations should be based on a preliminary assessment of the client and the problem's dimensions *before* program implementation. Often this is not the usual way of working and, at the end, only some ex-post evaluations are used that do not have not the strength of a pre-post assessment. In addition, the preliminary as-sessment can be used to define the problem's dimensions and delineate the neces-sary conditions for effective service.

Normally, the practitioner's decisions in planning for services can be repre-sented in the following sequence: objectives, actions, subjects, resources, times, and evaluation, as shown in Figure 4.1.

In general, the mindset of practitioners who adopt the above sequence is ori-ented to the *things to do* and *people who should do them,* with little thought given to evaluation questions. To change this thinking and practice planning activities

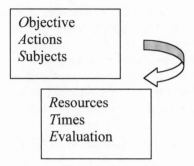

Figure 4.1.   Common indicators of practitioners' decisions.

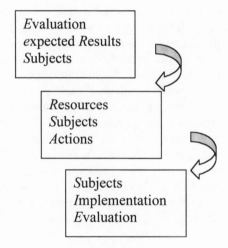

Figure 4.2.   Planning for evaluation in practitioners' decisions.

with a different vision, it is necessary to define the relationship between evaluation and planning differently, as shown in Figure 4.2.

The above sequence demonstrates some of the complex features of the planning process. For instance, defining the responsibilities for obtaining the expected results is present for subjects in each triad (*EeRS*): in the second triad, the subjects must plan actions using appropriate resources (*RSA*); and in the third triad, subjects must guarantee implementation and evaluation (*SIE*). In this representation, assessment appears in a preliminary step (*EeRS*) as well as in the following ones, in order to carry out evaluation of process, output and outcome. For this reason the function *Evaluation* opens and closes the sequence.

The definitions of expected results (*eR*) need to be consistent with their different natures, in terms of improvement, stabilization, or deceleration. With improvement and deceleration, for example, differences must be measured, while "maintenance" implies stability of outcomes. This is exemplified in the field of care for non-self-sufficient elderly people, where a maintenance goal seeks avoid a deterioration of a person's quality of life. In fact the 1998–2000 National Health Plan considers "actively coping with chronicity" as one of its main goals.

The early definition of objectives optimizes the planning process, because it prevents the formulation of overly ambitious objectives, and those that are not realistic or consistent with the mission of the organization.

EVALUATION OF EFFECTIVENESS IN RECENT NATIONAL PLANNING

Recent national planning in the area of human services in Italy is contained in the 1998–2000 National Health Plan; the National Plan for children and adolescents; the 2000–2003 Action Program of the government for handicapped people; the 2001–2003 National Social Plan; and the draft of the 2001–2003 National Health Plan.[3] To determine if these plans set forth indicators that can measure expected results, we will take, as an example, the draft of the 2001–2003 National Health Plan. In developing it, one of the first problems that was faced was the selection of outcome indicators. Usually, the indicators used in different countries for evaluating outcomes in health are divided into two main categories: mortality indicators and general/specific morbidity. From there it is then possible to specify more particular measures, as shown in Table 4.1.

The data sources are usually based on administrative databases, surveys, hospital and medical records, estimates of incidence, and perceived health status. Nevertheless, these criteria are not enough for planning a systematic outcome evaluation. In this connection, the Health World Report (World Health Organization, 2000) includes an explanatory model that correlates the functions a health system performs and the objectives of the system (see Figure 4.3).

Table 4.1.   Health Indicators for Outcome-Oriented Evaluation

Mortality	— Life expectancy
	— Infant mortality
	— Causes of mortality rates
	— Premature mortality: potential years of life lost (PYLL)
Morbidity and Quality of Life	
• *General Morbidity*	— Perceived health status
	— Measures of impairment, disability, and handicap
	— Multidimensional health status measures
	— Prevalence and incidence of disease
• *Disease-Specific Morbidity*	
Composite Health Measures	— Health expectancies [e.g., disability-free life
(Mortality + Morbidity)	expectancy (DFLE), disability-adjusted life expectancy
	(DALE) and health-adjusted life expectancy (HALE)]
	— Disability-adjusted life years (DALYs)

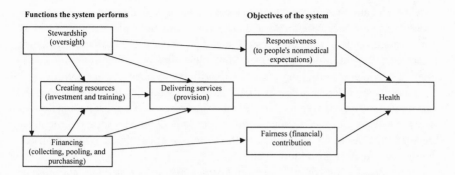

Figure 4.3. Relationships between functions and objectives of a health system.

The evaluations of the WHO are based on five groups of indicators:

- general level of health of the population of each single state;
- existing health inequalities in different groups of the population;
- capacity of the health system to match the demands for health of the population;
- distribution of health services among different social classes; and
- health fund distribution among different components of the population.

To assess overall population health and thus judge how well the objective of good health is being achieved, WHO has chosen to use disability-adjusted life expectancy (DALE), which has the advantage of being directly comparable to life expectancy estimated from mortality alone and is readily compared across populations.

The two principal approaches to verify the health of a population are based on measures of good health compared to a long life free of disability, and some measure of life expectancy, adjusted to take account of time lived with a disability. Disability-adjusted life expectancy is estimated from three kinds of information: the fraction of the population surviving to each age (calculated from birth and death rates); the prevalence of each type of disability at each age; and the weight assigned to each type of disability, which may or may not vary with age.

One important difference between the burden of disease estimation using disability-adjusted life years (DALYs) and that of DALE is that the former do, but the latter does not, distinguish among the contributions of each disease to the overall result. DALE has the advantage of not requiring as many choices of parameters for the calculation; in addition, it is directly comparable to the more familiar notion of life expectancy without adjustment (Murray, Salomon, & Mathers, 1999).

The WHO Report (World Health Organization, 2000) contains a comparative analysis that attributes different positions to the countries; for instance, in a comparison of 191 WHO countries, Italy is in second position with regard to *health outcomes,* in eleventh for *efficiency,* and in twenty-second for *output capacity*. The trend of data and the consequent positioning have provoked much discussion, because some countries with an advanced economy did not achieve a high position. For instance, some of the countries criticized the excessive importance attributed to outcome indicators in comparison to output indicators, even though achievement of health and well-being is what primarily interests people and families.

These questions exist in the international debate and they have also fueled the European debate on shared indicators, which has recently been resolved in the *Design for a Set of European Community Health Indicators* (European Community Health Indicators, 2000). In particular, this proposal is articulated in four main categories, as indicated in Table 4.2.

For the goals of outcome evaluation, *health status* indicators and *determinants of health* are particularly important. These have the characteristics indicated in Table 4.3.

An evaluation strategy related to this set of determinants of health does not necessarily take into account the expected results of the health indicators established at the beginning of the planning process. It represents a map to follow for selecting the indicators that better guarantee a before-after comparison that allows for measurement of outcomes. If this does not take place, there is only one possibility: to consider the situation as it occurs and to compare it with other situations, without systematic outcome evaluation but giving only positive or negative meanings to the trend. For example, critics of the Italian welfare system claim that Italy ranked second after France in the WHO report outcome indicators in the Year 2000 *not* because of the positive effects of national politics (such as the 1998–2000 National Health Plan) but because of the benefits of the Mediterranean diet. It is clear that results cannot be automatically ascribed to the effects of national and local

Table 4.2. Main Categories for the ECHI Health Indicator Set

1. Demographic and socioeconomic factors
    1.1. Population
    1.2. Socio-economic factors
2. Health status
    2.1. Mortality
    2.2. Morbidity, disease-specific
    2.3. Generic health status
    2.4. Composite health status measures
3. Determinants of health
    3.1. Personal and biological factors
    3.2. Health behaviors
    3.3. Living and working conditions
4. Health systems
    4.1. Prevention, health protection, and health promotion
    4.2. Health care resources
    4.3. Health care utilization
    4.4. Health expenditures and financing
    4.5. Health care quality/performance

Table 4.3. Determinants of Health

3.1. Personal and biological factors	3.2 Health behaviors
3.1.1. *Biological (risk) factors*	**3.2.1. *Substance use***
Body mass index	Regular smoking
Low birth weight	Smoking in pregnant women
Blood pressure	Former smoking
Serum cholesterol	Amount smoked
Nutritional status indicators	Alcohol use: nondrinkers
	Alcohol use pattern
3.1.2. *Personal conditions*	Total alcohol consumption
Coping ability	(II) licit drug use
Sense of mastery	Road traffic accidents involving
Optimism	alcohol
Knowledge/attitudes on health issues	
	3.3 Living and Working conditions
3.1.3. *Nutrition*	**3.3.1 *Physical environment***
Energy from food	Outdoor air
% energy from fat	Housing
% energy from protein	Drinking water supply
% energy from sat. fatty acids	Sewage system
Consumption of bread/cereals	Ionizing radiation
Consumption of fruit excl. juice	Noise
Consumption of vegetables excl. potatoes	
Consumption of fish	**3.3.2 *Working conditions***
Consumption of micronutrients	Physical workplace exposures
Breastfeeding	Mental workplace exposures
Contaminants	Accidents related to work
	Occupational diseases
3.1.4. *Other health-related behaviors*	
Physical activity	**3.3.3 *Social & cultural environment***
Sexual behavior	Social support
Induced abortions	Social isolation/networks
Traffic behavior	Life events
Other health promotion behaviors?	Violence

programs; they probably occur from complex determinants of different nature and in this case nutrition habits are certainly a factor.

For this reason, more and more often national plans invest in programs that affect lifestyles and daily habits in general, in order to have a positive impact on the well-being of people and families. It has become evident that the determinants of health do not depend only on the efficiency of health services but also on other factors (such as lifestyles, community solidarity, and prevention). For this reason, the impact of national programs cannot be evaluated *only* as a direct effect of social and health planning, but *also* in relation to broader determinants of well-being. The long-range character of national and regional plans does not lead in itself to evaluating effectiveness, that is, to relating verified outcomes to specific causes.

An important related evaluation question is whether the outcomes resulted from effective measures created prior to undertaking treatment. In dealing with this question, two measures are necessary: (1) comparisons among well-being indicators (such as in the 2000 WHO report) and (2) comparisons among outcome measures in relation to the goals established during the preliminary assessment, as a *relationship between expected and obtained outcomes*. On this basis, we would have two sets of indicators: (a) those expected as a result of preexisting programs (*absolute outcomes*); and (b) those obtained as a result of specific planning programs (*relative outcomes*).

The performances of countries or regions could then be described as: *absolute* and *relative outcomes*. Theoretically, relative measures can be ascribed to the efforts carried out by a country or region to arrive at the expected results. For instance, the economic outcomes for developing countries could be understood by comparing absolute income and growth data over time and among countries. This way of thinking about outcome evaluation is used for some problems considered in the draft proposal of the 2001–2003 Italian National Health Plan. For example, in defining the goals for certain of the main pathologies, specific outcome measures are used, citing minimum and maximum values for each region. Thus, in the

Table 4.4. Preliminary Data from Study of People Suffering from Allergies: Percentages and Estimate in Respect to the Population (thousands) (1999–2000) (Confidence Level 95%)*

	%	Minimum	Maximum
Piemonte	10.3	394	474
Valle d'Aosta	12.7	13	17
Lombardia	11.3	937	1083
Trentino–Alto Adige	10.3	94	95
Veneto	11.1	450	533
Friuli–Venezia Giulia	9.6	102	123
Liguria	12.2	179	214
Emilia-Romagna	12.5	463	524
Toscana	10.7	341	405
Umbria	10.7	80	97
Marche	9.7	126	155
Lazio	11.0	526	621
Abruzzi	10.0	116	139
Molise	8.2	24	30
Campania	5.9	302	372
Puglia	6.4	234	289
Basilicata	9.4	50	63
Calabria	10.0	184	224
Sicilia	7.9	355	444
Sardegna	9.1	149	150
Italia	9.7	5,409	56,755

*Source: Istituto Superiore di Sanitá, Ministero della Salute.

case of allergies, the values for the percentages and the confidence intervals are based on a national survey of those people suffering from this illness (See Table 4.4). This can also be done with children's problems, such as abuse and neglect.

In like manner, a regional planner could specify local outcome goals, using as a reference the measure of national outcomes and organizing resources and strategies to achieve the expected results on the local level. In addition, for other problems it may be possible to use epidemiological data from various surveys such as that of HIV, where an association exists between the number of cases in the population and the incidence of HIV. From Figure 4.4 it can be seen, just from the slope of the graph, that (a) the improvement measure (in this case, incidence reduction) can be obtained without any intervention; and (b) to influence the slope if it is considered unsatisfactory, intervention must occur with specific actions and strategies that modify the invested resources to reach the expected results.

Another example of the importance of epidemiological data is the use of the Body Mass Index (BMI), which is linearly correlated with mortality in both sexes, or the use of the rate of suicides in adolescence, which varies with areas or regions.[4] Further, in the National Health Plan in Italy it is estimated that overweight, obesity, and physical inactivity are involved in the increased incidence of some types of malignant neoplasm (breast cancer and cancer of the endometrious in females; colon cancer in males); diabetes mellitus type 2 in elderly people, male and female; cardiovascular diseases, such as iscaemic coronary cardiopathy; arteriosis and osteoporosis and their consequences, including femur fractures in elderly people; litiasis bilious; and night apnea.

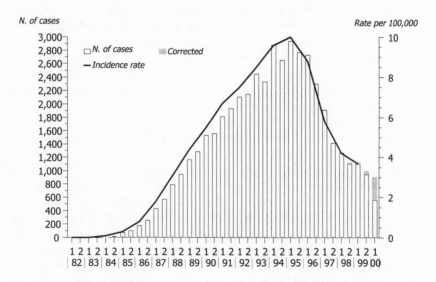

Figure 4.4.   HIV example.

Considering the BMI example, it is logical to assume that diseases connected with the diet involve a large part of the population, not only at-risk groups; therefore, nutrition is one of the main strategies for maintaining or promoting a positive state of health. Nevertheless, in order to create a goal that is more than a theoretical recommendation, actions must be planned based on evidence or at least on research that documents positive results. Plans for intervention can vary, as follows:

- a good level of evidence exists for a particular intervention;
- uncertain or incomplete evidence suggests that intervention should start;
- an unsatisfactory level of evidence suggests that intervention should not be started, even if it could start on the basis of other considerations;
- uncertain or incomplete evidence suggests that intervention should not be started; and
- a good level of evidence suggests that the intervention should not be started.

CONCLUSION

The question of measuring effectiveness in the health and social services is now a focus of scientific debate in Italy. For this reason, it is important to have guidelines based on scientific literature and research studies that can assist planners in their search to obtain effective results.[5]

A major problem in the area of health and social programs is the insufficiency of the scientific literature to support planning recommendations; much of the literature consists of case studies or other evidence that needs further documentation. In particular, when considering clinical and organizational problems, research and experimentation must be undertaken to plan adequately for interventions. These areas of research deal with conditions for effectiveness of integrated care: multidimensional evaluation; documentation management; economic impact of decisions; organization of responsibilities; continuity in utilizing care; collaboration among residential and territorial structures; appropriate paths for different kinds of needs; and outcome evaluation.

An important aspect of effectiveness evaluation relates to the monitoring of equal access to services. This was discussed in considering whether a solidaristic welfare system reaches its own goals of universal access, reduction of inequalities, and protection of frail people. These consumers live in poverty, with little education, in poor neighborhoods, and in old houses; compared to others they frequently experience illness, have a lower life expectancy, and have less opportunity to access the services and interventions to which they are entitled. They more likely have insufficient cures, inadequate care, and inability to ask for their rights, along with at-risk lifestyles, alcohol abuse, inadequate diet, and domestic problems.

Evaluation indicators, therefore, must take into account not only specific outcomes but also general measures of equity in different welfare systems. In the Italian case, this can be found in the strategies and the specific goals of the recent national planning documents noted earlier in this chapter. In Italy the evaluation of effectiveness is embarking on its first steps and there is huge space for improvement. These problems are also present in other countries, so for now it is not easy to make systematic comparisons among countries, using absolute indicators (as in World Health Organization, 2000) or relative indicators, as defined earlier in this chapter. This could be the challenge for us for the next few years.

NOTES

1. These laws refer, respectively, to Legislative Decree June 29, 1999, No. 229 (published in the official Italian government bulletin *Gazzetta Ufficiale*, No. 132/L (July 16, 1999); Presidential Decree July 23, 1998 (published in the *Gazzetta Ufficiale*, No. 201 (December 10, 1998); and Law of November 8, 2000, No. 328 (published in *Gazzetta Ufficiale*, No. 186/L (November 13, 2000).

2. For discussion of outcome-based evaluation of national programs in the United States, see Chapter 3 by Chaskin and Chapter 12 by Lightburn (in this volume).

3. These are plans that have been approved by the Italian government.

4. The BMI study is described in the *Osservatorio Epidemologico Cardiovascolare* (1998).

5. In Italy, as in other countries, there are programs producing clinical guidelines for professional choices as well as processes and organizational solutions (Agenzia per i Servizi Sanitari Regionali, 1999).

REFERENCES

Agenzia per i Servizi Sanitari Regionali (1999). *Programma Nazionale Linee Guida*. Rome: Ministero della Sanitá.

European Community Health Indicators (2000). *Design for a Set of European Community Health Indicators: Final Report by the ECHI Project*. Bilthoven, The Netherlands: National Institute of Public Health and the Environment.

Holmes, S. & Sunstein, C. R. (1999). *The Cost of Rights*. New York: W. W. Norton.

Murray, C. L., Salomon, J. A., & Mathers, C. (1999). A critical examination of summary measures of population health. GPE Discussion Paper No. 12. Geneva: World Health Organization.

Osservatorio Epidemologico Cardiovascolare (Ed.) (1998). *The Body Mass Index Study*. Rome: Istituto Superiore di Sanitá.

Unrau, Y. A., Gabor, P. A., & Grinnell, R. M. (2001). *Evaluation in the Human Services*. Itasca, IL: F. E. Peacock.

Vecchiato, T. (Ed.) (1995). *La Valutazione dei Servizi Sociali e Sanitari*. Padova, Italy: Fondazione "E. Zancan."

Vecchiato, T. (1999a). La verifica e valutazione dei piani di zona. *Servizi Sociali* 4:76–96.

Vecchiato, T. (1999b). Nuovi contenuti e metodi della programmazione sanitaria. *Annali della Sanit Pubblica* 4:53–58. Rome: Ministero della Sanitá.

Vecchiato, T. (1999c). I soggetti deboli nel piano sanitario 1998–2000. In C. Bedetti, S. Geraci, & R. Guerra. *Le Nuove Povertá: Un Problema Complesso di Sanitá Pubblica* (Serie 3, pp. 4–15)). Rome: Istituto superiore di sanitá.

Vecchiato, T. (Ed.) (2000a). *La Valutazione della Qualitá nei Servizi*. Padova, Italy: Fondazione Zancan.

Vecchiato, T. (2000b). Italian experiences of evaluation. *Journal of Social Work Research and Evaluation* 1(2):153–63.

Vecchiato, T. (2001). Principi e criteri per confrontare modelli di welfare. *Studi Zancan* 2(1):40–59.

World Health Organization (2000). *The World Health Report 2000. Health Systems: Improving Performance*. Geneva: Author.

5

Nonexperimental Methods of Evaluating Social Programs

Applications for Child And Family Services

Robert M. Goerge

When faced with doing an evaluation of an intervention, a researcher's first instinct is to employ a randomized experimental design where members of the study population are randomly assigned to treatment and control groups. With this design, one has the strongest chance of addressing the other possible causes of any change in the outcome of interest, although there is always a question of how generalizable the results would be beyond the study population.

However, doing a randomized experiment is not always possible. In actuality, they are rarely done because of the problem of providing no treatment or an alternative treatment that is believed to be less effective than the treatment that is being tested to the control group. Policymakers, administrators, social workers, advocates, and researchers often cannot justify not providing service even if a randomized experiment would provide reliable knowledge on the effectiveness of an intervention. One of the times that an experiment can be done is when the intervention is in short supply and there is expected to be a waiting list or simply some individuals who will be eligible, but who will not participate. The question then is whether the lack of participation has anything to do with any of the characteristics of the individual or if there is a reason apart from the individual, such as a lottery, that caused the person not to participate.

Since it is difficult to implement a randomized experiment, we are left with nonexperimental methods of evaluation in most situations. Some call these *natural* experiments. We seek a comparison group that is not receiving the intervention, but that is similar enough to the study population to suggest that their outcomes would constitute the outcomes of a counterfactual. These are the outcomes that would have occurred if the intervention had not taken place.

In this chapter we describe a method that compares a participant population with a population that was eligible for the intervention, but did not choose, for whatever reason, to participate in the program. This latter group constitutes the counterfactual. We believe that the outcomes that they experienced are the outcomes that the treatment group would have experienced had they not chosen to participate in the program. Therefore, the difference in outcome between the treatment group and the counterfactual group is the effect of the program.

One threat to this design is that the group that chose not to participate may be different from the group that did in important ways that affect experiencing the outcome of interest. Therefore, we must also account for reasons why the participants did participate and the nonparticipants did not. If we do not, our comparison of the two groups could be biased.

STUDY EXAMPLE

The example we will describe is evaluating the effect of reform of antipoverty programs on completion of high school. Welfare reform in the United States during the 1990s attempted to make participants in that program more self-sufficient so that their long-term outcomes would improve (Burtless, 1999; Lewis, George, & Puntenney, 1999). The major reform was that parents would no longer receive an open-ended entitlement to cash assistance. The time limit to their receipt of cash would be twenty-four consecutive months and five years over their lifetime. Also, if they did not seek employment or become employed, their cash assistance might also end. While many believed that this would have positive long-term effects, there was a concern that there would be negative effects on parenting of children. Some predicted that children would be more unsupervised and neglected, as single mothers leave the home to work or seek work without appropriate child care. One possible outcome of this would be that adolescent children would be less likely to engage in school and perhaps drop out. However, there is also theory to suggest that if a parent becomes employed, if his or her self-esteem increases, and if his or her financial status improves—that is, his or her human capital improves—then his or her children's desire to succeed and continue in school would also increase.

The period of the study is from 1990 through 2001. The study population is the families of children who were in the Chicago Public Schools (CPS) in the state of Illinois at any point from 1990 through 2000. This population accounts for 85 percent of all children living in Chicago at a point in time.

Our primary research questions are:

1. How have changes in the cash assistance programs affected the possibility of school dropout of youths?

2. As parents are required to work or seek work, how has this affected the possibility that a child would leave school before graduation?

APPROACH

The major challenge is to develop an analysis model that can be used to isolate the effect of welfare reform apart from that of other changes in the environment. We want to compare those families who have experienced welfare reform with those who might have experienced it and did not.

Literature on non–experimentally based statistical methods using longitudinal data suggests that, when a rigorous statistical approach is used with required longitudinal data, a nonexperimental design can be a very effective method for evaluating the impact of ongoing programs (e.g., Heckman & Hotz, 1989).

We employ two major strategies to separate the families who did experience welfare reform from those who did not. The first is a before-and-after design, where we compare families who were on welfare prior to reform to those on welfare after reform. The primary concern here is that the families before and after are in some important ways different. The second strategy is comparing those families who were eligible and participated in welfare programs with those who were eligible and did not participate. Since we believe that those who are eligible and participate in the program are different from those who are eligible and do not participate, we statistically adjust for the likelihood that the outcomes that children experience are likely related to the family's choice to participate or not.

We first compare the outcomes for children before and after both state- and federal-level welfare reform. We do this with a time-varying covariate that varies with the periods of reform.

The fact that there is a group of eligible recipients who are not participating in the welfare program allows us to compare eligible recipients with noneligible recipients for the entire period of the study. We will have a time-varying covariate that says when families are eligible for the income maintenance program and whether they are receiving the grant. We also measure the cumulative time on welfare. Therefore, we will know both the effect of being on an income maintenance grant and the effect of having been on income maintenance at some point and for varying durations.

What introduces bias into this design is the possibility that something unobservable to us is causing those who are eligible to not participate and that what is unobservable is also affecting the child outcomes. We hypothesize that a family's nonparticipation has either to do with their being too proud to receive welfare and wanting to avoid stigma or actually having informal or unreported income.

Therefore, in order to account for this bias, we must statistically model it. If we can account for the differences in participation, our estimate of the effect of welfare reform on child outcomes will be less affected by the selection bias. For this type of design, it is important to have considerable information about all of our households and the neighborhoods in which they live; it is likely that we are going to be able to account for much of the difference in participation rates among subpopulations. The school information system allows us to track information about parents through multiple information sources including, but not limited to, wages, welfare, nutrition, and health programs. The CPS data also provide household income, household size, and other information that can be used to determine eligibility for means-tested programs.

Selection of the Comparison Group

What would the outcome for the children who are affected by welfare reform have been if welfare reform had not happened? It is likely that many parents would not have become employed. However, the fact that the strong state economy led to lower unemployment means many of these women might have become employed regardless of welfare reform.

We can also compare older siblings to younger siblings. Older siblings have been affected more by the prereform regime than their younger siblings. The older siblings have been more exposed to parents under Aid to Families with Dependent Children (AFDC) and perhaps less exposed to their parents under Temporary Assistance for Needy Families (TANF). For example, a child who was six years old in 1992 in Illinois had never experienced changes in income maintenance policy or welfare reform (WR), either through federal welfare reform—the Personal Responsibility and Work Reconciliation Act of 1996 (PRWORA), implemented in 1997—or "Work Pays," implemented in 1993, during her or his developmental years. However, a child who was six years old in 1997 experienced "Work Pays" and the pre–welfare reform anticipatory effects that seem to have caused more parents to enter the workforce. Exposure by siblings (except for twins) to welfare reform and to periods in which the parents were employed varies within families.

A key concern of a nonexperimental study such as ours in determining the effect of welfare reform is selection bias. The unobservable factors affecting child outcomes are likely to be correlated with unobservable factors that affect the choice of participating in the welfare program. For example, families who believe that they do not need the assistance may also have more resources to achieve better outcomes for their children. They might be more motivated to earn more income eventually or simply have more unreported income. To address the issues of endogeneity owing to possible selection bias, we propose to use Heckman's sample selection equations (Heckman & Hotz, 1989). Using the simultaneous equation approach, we first use probit regressions as auxiliary equations to explain whether or not a family will participate. We illustrate our approach in more detail in the statistical analysis section below.

Statistical Methodology

Here we use the child outcome of high school dropout as the example for applying the statistical methodology. We employ a hierarchical model that allows us to look at the effects of neighborhood characteristics (level 1) and family characteristics (level 2) on child outcomes. In this way, we control for the time-invariant characteristics of a parent and their differential effect on children (level 3) in the same family, but account for the changes in employment of the parents and the exposure to welfare reform.

We will estimate a hazard model of school dropout. We expect to find evidence that continued being on welfare and not becoming employed increases the child's risk of dropping out. We will also likely find that unobserved mother-specific characteristics affect children's dropping out. It is quite likely that the mothers themselves are aware of at least some of those characteristics. What if they respond to this private knowledge such that those women who are at above-average risk of their child dropping out decide to reduce the risks by staying on welfare and not becoming employed? The result will be that the welfare rolls will see more children with high school diplomas. If ignored, this adverse selection will underestimate the beneficial effect of being on TANF. We therefore address the potential endogeneity and estimate a joint model of school dropout and welfare receipt.

More generally speaking, correlation between explanatory covariates and residuals leads to biased estimates. If the only source of correlation is at the mother level, then incorporating the correlated residuals in the model will eliminate the bias. (Additional correlation at the child level would require the introduction of instruments, i.e., child-specific covariates affecting use of TANF, but not directly affecting child dropout.)

The joint model consists of two sets of equations:

1. Hazard of child dropout: $ln\ h_j(t) = \gamma T(t) + \alpha X_j + \delta,$

where subscript j indicates child number and t indicates spell duration. This is a two-level model with mothers as the unit of observation and children as repeated outcomes within observations. We suppressed the observation subscript for mothers. The baseline log-hazard is assumed to be piecewise linear in the child's age (explained below); represents regressors, including hospital delivery; and captures unobserved heterogeneity at the mother level.

2. Probit of income maintenance participation: $H^*j = \beta X + \varepsilon + \upsilon_j,$

where j indicates the child number, X are explanatory variables (see data section below); ε represents unobserved heterogeneity at the mother level; and υ captures transitory variation.

If the unobservables δ and ε in each of these equations are allowed to be correlated, we can eliminate the bias by making the source of the bias (the correlation) part of the model. In the example, the effect of remaining unemployed and being on welfare may be biased because of nonrandom welfare receipt/remaining unemployed decisions. We therefore estimate a joint ("multiprocess") model of child dropout and remaining on welfare and unemployed.

DATA

We utilize the Integrated Database on Children and Family Services in Illinois (IDB) as the primary data source of this analysis (Goerge, Van Voorhis, & Lee, 1994). While the IDB has been in existence for nearly a decade now, it has continued to grow not only in terms of the areas and programs, but also the period that it covers. The database contains individual case and person data on nearly all social welfare programs in Illinois from at least 1990 to the present. For this project, we are likely to have tracked individuals who have been in the AFDC or TANF programs at some point through December 2000 and track their income maintenance, employment experiences through March 2001, and also their children's experiences through March 2001. At last count, the database contained nearly five million individuals who have participated in income maintenance, food stamp, Medicaid, child welfare, substance abuse, mental health, developmental disability, WIC, aging, special education and regular education, juvenile justice, public health, and rehabilitation programs. Recently, wage records have been linked to the same database. Records for persons and cases have been linked across programs and over time so that one can get an accurate history of program participation for individuals regardless of their status at a particular point in time. Matching techniques going beyond the usual linking with Social Security numbers have been employed to insure high-quality linkage over time and program.

The inclusion of CPS, juvenile justice, and unemployment insurance data takes the IDB beyond the social service program domain. These three sets of data are collected when individuals do not participate in particular programs and thereby provide us with information regardless of whether a family or individual is participating in a particular program.

Many of the data for these analyses come from the IDB. The IDB is a state-level, longitudinal database constructed from administrative data gathered by public agencies that serve children and families in Illinois (Goerge, Van Voorhis, & Lee, 1994). The IDB combines individual- and family-level social service receipt and socioeconomic and demographic data across time to produce a longitudinal database of service use. Specifically for this research, we use individual-level longitudinal service records constructed from administrative data for all CPS School Lunch programs, Food Stamp program and cash assistance (AFDC/TANF), Unemployment Insurance wage reporting data, and Medicaid data covering the period September 1992 through December 2000.

Because the original data used for this study come from different agency information systems that do not share a common identification number (ID), linking data records reliably and accurately across different data sources is an important issue. The databases of each agency have been linked into the IDB on the basis of common information on each of the individuals in each of the databases (including such variables as name, birth date, race and ethnicity, county of residency, and Social Security number) using a technique called probabilistic record linkage (Goerge, Van Voorhis, & Lee, 1994). The method was first developed by researchers in the fields of demography and epidemiology (Newcombe, 1988; Jaro, 1989). The method is known as the most reliable means of matching records across multiple data files under conditions of uncertainty

Below we describe briefly the data sets we propose to use in this research.

Illinois Client Database, Illinois Department of Human Services. The client database records receipt of AFDC/TANF and food stamps and documents all those who are registered as eligible for Medicaid from 1989 to the present. The client database records service receipt information by both case and individual (case members) levels. Socioeconomic and demographic information is available for all those who receive services.

Chicago Public Schools Data. The data available on pupils span 1992 to 2000 and contain considerable demographic information, including residence, year of entry to the United States, language spoken at home, and race/ethnicity. This dataset also includes participation in the School Lunch Program (SLP) and information on the verification of that participation.

Data on Local Area Practices. The Automated Intake System (AIS) assists local office staff in processing applications and determining eligibility for most state and federal public assistance programs, including TANF and food stamps. It contains most information related to eligibility, including identifiers, demographic information, household composition, employment information, and educational level.

Unemployment Insurance Wage Report Data. Unemployment Insurance (UI) wage records consist of total quarterly earnings reported by employers to state UI agencies for each employee. The database contains information on quarterly earnings, employee Social Security number (SSN), employer SSN, and employer address. The Chapin Hall Center for Children receives the Illinois Department of Employment Security quarterly UI wage report data from the Illinois Department of Human Services through an interagency data-sharing agreement. The quarterly data are linked over time at the individual level. The data cover the period from 1995 to the present.

Relevant Variables. Table 5.1 lists the major variables and their data sources. IDB in parentheses indicates that the source data has been linked with all other administrative data in the Integrated Database on Child and Family Services, maintained by the investigators.

CONCLUSION

This approach is currently being implemented and the analysis should be completed during 2002. Since all the data are in hand, we do not expect any obstacles in completing the project.

The approach described in this chapter is one that is applicable to research on many social services. Given the difficulty, both ethically and operationally, of implementing random assignment evaluations, statistical approaches to evaluation offer a good alternative when rich longitudinal data are available from either administrative sources or surveys.

While in this chapter we stress the use of administrative data, in this case because of their availability, high-quality survey data could also allow one to do the same analysis. However, unless the survey sample provides sufficient observations of the population of interest and allows the compilation of neighborhood level characteristics, it may not be a feasible source of data for such analysis.

Table 5.1. Major Variables and Datasets

Neigborhood-level variables (at the census tract level)	Data Source
Race/ethnicity composition of households with children	CPS data (IDB)
Proportion of single-parent households Proportion of households below poverty line Median household income Proportion age 25 and over without a high school diploma Proportion of individuals who are immigrants	U.S. Census data (investigators have developed estimating techniques to update 1990 Census data to latter years of the decade)
Proportion of births with low birth weight Proportion of births to teen mothers Proportion of births without adequate prenatal care	Vital statistics data
Proportion of eligible households receiving FSP	SLP and FSP (IDB)
Program (Local Area Office) variables	
FSP error rate Denied FSP applications Percentage of TANF recipients who are employed Percentage of TANF exiters who receive transitional Medicaid	IL Department of Human Services performance data and Client Database (IDB)
Family (Household) variables	
Household income	UI data (IDB)
Residential mobility Race/ethnicity Household structure Date entered USA Language spoken at home	CPS data (IDB)
Food stamp receipt history Medicaid receipt history WIC (Women, Infant, Children) receipt history Child care receipt history	IL DHS data in the IDB
Policy variables	
Before and after Work Pays Before and after PRWORA passage Before and after Illinois PRWORA implementation	Calculated by Investigators

REFERENCES

Burtless, G. (1999). The transition from welfare to work: Policies to reduce public dependency. In L. Joseph (Ed.), *Families, Poverty, and Welfare Reform: Confronting a New Policy Era* (pp. 175–206). Chicago: Center for Urban Research and Policy Studies, University of Chicago.

Goerge, R. M., Van Voorhis, J., & Lee, B. J. (1994). Illinois's longitudinal and relational child and family research database. *Social Science Computer Review* 12(3):351–65.

Heckman, J., & Hotz, J. (1989). Choosing among Alternative Nonexperimental Methods for Estimating the Impact of Social Programs: The Case of Manpower Training (in Applications and Case Studies). *Journal of the American Statistical Association* 84(408):862–74.

Jaro, M. A. (1989). Advances in record-linkage methodology as applied to matching the 1985 census of Tampa, Florida. *Journal of the American Statistical Association* 84(406):414–20.

Lewis, D. A., George, C. C., & Puntenney, D. (1999). Welfare reform efforts in Illinois. In Joseph, L. (Ed.), *Families, Poverty, and Welfare Reform: Confronting a New Policy Era* (pp. 185–95). Chicago: Center for Urban Research and Policy Studies, University of Chicago.

Newcombe, H. B. (1988). Handbook of Record Linkage: Methods for Health and Statistical Studies, Administration, and Business. New York: Oxford University Press.

6

An Intervention to Reduce Smoking Habits through Counseling from the General Practitioner

Giovanni Pilati, Elizabeth Tamang, and Luca Gino Sbrogió

Tobacco smoking represents a serious public health problem for Italy as it does for many other countries. It is a problem that directly or indirectly affects many families. Since numerous studies have shown that counseling by the general practitioner (GP) is an effective method for helping patients to stop smoking and that this effectiveness increases with the addition of standard aids,[1] in the last few years various Italian local health authorities have tried to put into effect counseling programs. Following a review of research on the effectiveness of counseling, in this chapter we present the experience of a smoking reduction program in Padova (in northern Italy) guided by the Centre for Health Education.

EFFECTIVENESS OF COUNSELING

The general practitioner can be of fundamental importance in helping the population to change unhealthy behavior that can lead to negative health effects, since he or she is the principal reference point for their health. Each year a GP sees around 75 percent of her or his patients at least once and in five years time sees 90 percent (Focarile, 1990; Russell, Merriman, Stapleton, & Taylor, 1983). Besides the activities of diagnosis and treatment, it is usual for a GP to offer counsel on protecting or promoting one's health. People tend to hold the doctor's advice in high esteem and put it into practice, although advice is most convincing when patients suffer from problems with clear correlation to hazardous health behavior. In any case, it has been demonstrated that counseling by GPs is more effective if done in a systematic way, following a well-defined protocol preceded by appropriate experimentation and accurate evaluation. As far as smoking is concerned, numerous studies have shown that doctors can influence their patients' habits significantly.

Schwartz (1991) has summarized the results of twenty-eight studies conducted between 1965 and 1984 that focused on stopping smoking based on a doctor's intervention. These experiences were divided into two groups: those involving only giving advice and those including additional elements. The fifteen interventions based on delivering simple counsel had a "quit rate" of 3 to 13 percent, with an average of 5 percent. The thirteen interventions that included other elements besides simple counseling had a quit rate of 13 to 40 percent, with an average rate of 29 percent (at six months following) and 22.5 percent (at follow-up of one year). In these experiences the counseling was reinforced by procedures like very strong messages, warnings, written prescriptions, various types of follow-ups, a participating contract, or a breathing test demonstration. Kottke, Brekke, Solberg, and Hughes (1988) examined smoking cessation interventions carried out by physicians and found that the percentages of quit rate following intervention were higher than those in the control groups. In particular, the percentage of the quit rate was positively related to the numbers and intensity of contacts with the patients, especially during follow-up visits.

Schwartz (1991) has also reviewed findings of studies regarding (1) compliance with doctor's recommendations to stop smoking among patients with heart and lung problems and (2) compliance with similar instructions for pregnant women. The cessation rate by the latter group varies from 1 to 35 percent. It has also been seen that the presence of heart or lung problems adds credibility to the physician's message and results in a higher percentage of smoking cessation rates: the quit rates of patients with lung problems vary from 10 to 70 percent, with an average of 31.5 percent after one year; for those with heart problems, the quit rate was from 11 to 73 percent, with an average of 43 percent after one year.

Other studies (e.g., Rosso, Senore, Ponti, & Segnan, 1991) conclude that the effectiveness of interventions carried out by GPs is proportional to the time dedicated by them to their patients and the number of successive contacts, whereas the same cannot be said about nicotine replacement therapy and the measuring of carbon monoxide in the patient's breath.

The effectiveness of counseling by GPs against smoking has been demonstrated in a study by Rose and Colwel (1992), who verified the effects on health (in terms of mortality and morbidity) after twenty years. In addition, a longitudinal study of 16,016 government workers was carried out in 1968–1970 in which 1,445 smokers with high risk for cardiorespiratory diseases were identified. Two groups homogeneous in number and characteristics were formed: a control group of 731 persons and an intervention group of 714 persons who were subjected to individual counseling and reinforcement within one year on four occasions, when their medical situation was explained and they were asked to stop smoking.

After one year 84 percent of the intervention group members were interviewed. Of these, 63 percent declared that they had stopped cigarette smoking (but one-third had switched to smoking pipes or cigars). After ten years, there were 30 percent more ex-smokers in the intervention group than in the control group. Also, mortality in the intervention group was significantly reduced as compared to mortality in the control group: 13 percent for ischemic heart attacks; 11 percent for lung cancer; 7 percent for general mortality rate. In short, this meant that for every hundred persons who had stopped smoking after medical counseling, from six to ten more persons were still alive after twenty years, presumably because they had stopped smoking (Rose & Colwel, 1992).

The recent systematic review done by Silagy (2000) further confirms the effectiveness of brief antitobacco counseling. The aims of this review were to assess the effectiveness of advice from physicians in promoting smoking cessation; to compare minimal interventions by physicians with more intensive interventions; to assess the effectiveness of various aids to advice in promoting smoking cessation; and to determine the effect of antismoking advice on specific diseases and all causes of mortality.

Thirty-one trials were identified in the above study, conducted between 1972 and 1997, and included over 26,000 smokers. In some trials, subjects were at risk of specified diseases (chest disease, diabetes, ischemic heart disease), but most were from unselected (general) populations. The most common setting for delivery of advice was primary care; other settings included hospital wards, outpatient clinics, and industrial clinics. Pooled data from sixteen trials of brief advice versus no advice (or usual care) revealed a small but statistically significant increase in the odds of quitting (odds ratio 1.69; 95 percent confidence, interval 1.45 to 1.98). This equates to an absolute difference in the cessation rate of about 2.5 percent.

There was insufficient evidence, from indirect comparisons, for establishing a significant difference in the effectiveness of physician advice according to the intensity of the intervention, the amount of follow-up provided, and whether or not various aids were used at the time of the consultation in addition to providing advice. However, direct comparison of intensive versus minimal advice showed a small advantage for intensive advice (odds ratio 1.44; 95 percent confidence, interval 1.23 to 1.68). In one study that focused on the effect of smoking advice on mortality at twenty years, there were no statistically significant differences in death rates in the group receiving advice. Reviewers' conclusions were that simple advice has a small effect on cessation rates on a long-term basis. Additional strategies appear to have only a small effect, though more intensive interventions are marginally more effective than minimal interventions.

AN INTERVENTION BY GENERAL PRACTITIONERS
TO REDUCE SMOKING: THE EXPERIENCE OF PADOVA

Objectives

The aim of the program conducted by the Centre for Health Education in Padova was to reduce smoking habits through contacts between smokers and their GPs and to reduce the number of cigarettes smoked among those who did not stop smoking. The specific objectives formulated to achieve this aim were as follows:

- increase the number of GPs carrying out a systematic screening of their patients' smoking habits;

- increase the effectiveness of GPs counseling against smoking, utilizing protocols of demonstrated effectiveness; and
- increase the number of GPs utilizing a protocol of systematic screening.

Data pertaining to these objectives were obtained every six months for a period of three years. An initial period of three years was considered adequate to observe variations in smoking habits and related health parameters. Once the intervention got under way, the observations were carried out periodically to register the degree of achievement of the specific targets in relation to morbidity and smoking behavior.

As far as behavior was concerned, the targets were to:

- increase the number of smokers who stop and do not have relapses for at least one year;
- increase the number of smokers who have periods of abstinence between relapses;
- increase the number smokers who reduce the number of cigarettes smoked (without switching to the use of other products like pipes, cigars, or chewing or sniffing tobacco);
- reduce the number of smokers by at least one-third after three years among the intervention population (in fact, it is difficult to obtain further changes in smoking habits among the general population after successfully stopping those who already wanted to; the expected result, that is, the reduction of smokers by one-third after three years, depends mostly on the motivation of the GPs and on the special relationship they have with their patients); and
- reduce by at least 8–10 percent the incidence of smoke-correlated diseases at the end of three years among those who quit completely.

The project further established the following targets regarding the actions carried out by the GPs:

- increase up to 90 percent (within the first six months after the start of the intervention) the number of participating GPs who ask their patients about their smoking habits, thus identifying all the smokers;
- increase up to 80 percent the number of patients who, by the end of the first year, receive counseling from the GP on the opportunity of quitting smoking;
- among the patients who continue to smoke (for whatever reason) increase to 65 percent the number of those who receive further counseling reinforcement on the opportunity of quitting during their successive visits to the GP;
- by giving publicity to the success of the first group of GPs in applying the intervention protocol against smoking, increase by at least one-third the number of the other GPs (those who are not part of the first group) who manifest a strong interest and desire to apply the protocol to their patients.

Finally, another expected result was an increase of smoking GPs who desire to stop and to participate in a health education intervention to help them to stop.

Study Design

The main study phases can be outlined as follows:

1. Determination of baseline situation:

- development of a survey questionnaire for the physicians;
- questionnaire distribution among the GPs;
- telephone interviews with nonrespondents; and
- elaboration of the questionnaire.

2. Preparation of materials:

- counseling manual;
- register for screening patients and registering follow-ups; and
- booklet with advice on how to stop smoking and other supporting materials (handouts, posters, etc.)

3. Training of physicians:

- meetings to present the materials and methods before starting the counseling intervention;
- visits to the GPs, two to six weeks after the start of the intervention; and
- periodic supporting visits.

4. Intervention evaluation:

- systematic data recording by the GPs;
- mailing of summary of collected data to the GPs every six months;
- annual monitoring on counseling effectiveness; and
- final evaluation after three years.

5. Reports:

- basic situation report;
- annual reports; and
- final report.

Materials and Methods

A guide on methodology, which had been specially created along guidelines set by the World Health Organization (WHO) regional office for Europe (WHO, 1987; Zannoni, Mamon, and Pilati, 1992), was used: a register was created to help the doctors screen the patients, record counseling activities, and annotate the evaluation; leaflets, posters, and other materials were produced to reinforce the educational aspect of the intervention; and the GPs taking part were given training.

A survey was carried out among the GPs of the local health unit in Padua in October 1991 to identify which of them were smokers and to find out how interested they were in applying a smoking cessation protocol to their patients (Pilati & Tamang, 1994; Pilati, Mamon, & Tamang, 1992). On the basis of the information received, the most suitable doctors were selected to take part in the educational program trial. Three training evenings were held in April 1992 to provide information about the initiative.

At the beginning of November 1993 approximately twenty doctors started the intervention, of whom eighteen completed it (April 1994). The phases of GPs intervention were as follows:

- create a smoke-free surgical office;
- identify the smokers;
- inform the smokers of the harmful effects of smoking and the benefits gained by quitting;
- develop personalized strategies; and
- follow up at each successive visit.

In January and July 1993 trained personnel carried out follow-up activities at the offices of the doctors involved in the program in order to check how counseling was being done, how a smoke-free office was being created, and how the records were being filled in.

The evaluation phase of the intervention finally got under way on 1 November 1993 and continued until 31 March 1994. Without resorting to letters or phone calls to solicit patients for replies about their current smoking habits, only those who came to their GP during this phase, for reasons that did not concern the non-smoking intervention, were considered for the study. During the summer of 1994 all records were collected and the input and processing of the data started in September. After data elaboration, results were available in 1995.

RESULTS

Of the 295 GPs present in the Local Health Unit 21 (ULSS 21) in 1992, 217 (73.5 percent) answered the study questionnaire.[2] Eighteen of them then took part in the counseling project. In terms of the percentage of population to be treated, 6.5 percent (25,515 of the 390,000 patients in the particular health unit) were involved in the study.

Over the period 1 November 1992–1 November 1993, 16,094 patients, or 63 percent of the general population examined (46.16 percent male and 53.84 percent female), were recorded in the participating GPs' registers. Of the population over ten years of age, 17.2 percent were identified as smokers (22.2 percent male and 12.9 percent female). (See Table 6.1 for comparison with the population in Italy and in the Veneto region.)

Over the period 1 November 1993–31 March 1994 (the evaluation period), 1,348 of the 2,705 identified smokers were seen again, equal to 49.83 percent of the originally identified smokers. Of these 2,705 smokers, 59.21 percent were male and

Table 6.1. Percentage of Italian Smokers above
10 Years of Age*

	Males	Females	Total
Italy	37.9	16.3	26.7
Veneto	31.7	16.1	23.6
Italy	34.5	16.4	25.2
Veneto	26.7	15.6	21.0
ULSS 21 (Padova)	22.2	12.9	17.2

*ISTAT (1991, 1994).

Table 6.2. Initial Number of Cigarettes Smoked According to Gender;
Smoking Population Identified by the GPs Of ULSS 21 of Padova
(Cases Missing, 35)

	Frequency (%)		
Number of cigarettes	Males	Females	Total
1–5	221 (8.28)	274 (10.26)	495 (18.54)
6–10	434 (16.25)	383 (14.34)	817 (30.60)
11–20	731 (27.38)	379 (14.19)	1110 (41.57)
>20	195 (7.30)	53 (1.99)	248 (9.29)
Total	1581 (59.21)	1089 (40.79)	2670 (100.00)

40.79 percent female and the mean age was forty-two years (s.d. 14.8) (see Table 6.2). The majority of the smokers smoked more than ten cigarettes per day. Heavy smokers were mostly males and around forty-five years old (see Table 6.3).

Of the 1,348 smokers who were assessed (49.83 percent of all the identified smokers), 648 (48 percent) reported that they had not altered their behavior, 254 (18.8 percent) that they had stopped smoking, 356 (26.4 percent) that they had reduced their cigarette consumption, and 90 (6.7 percent) that they had increased their consumption.

On assessing the variation in smoking habits according to gender, age, cigarette consumption, contact frequency with the GP, and the duration of intervention, the following associations were observed:

- no statistically significant association exists in relation to gender;
- there is a significant association regarding age, number of cigarettes smoked, number of contacts with GP, time between the first contact (screening) with the patient and the execution of the evaluation.

We now provide further details regarding the findings. Evaluating the variables of smoking habits according to gender, age, cigarette consumption, number of

Table 6.3. Number of Initial Cigarettes According to Age; Smoking Population Identified by the GPs of ULSS 21 of Padova (Cases Missing, 35)

Cigarettes	Frequency (%) (by age)						
	<15	15–24	25–44	45–64	65–74	>74	Total
1–5	2 (0.07)	108 (4.04)	210 (7.87)	138 (5.17)	24 (0.90)	13 (0.49)	495 (18.54)
6–10	7 (0.26)	119 (4.46)	371 (13.90)	253 (9.48)	49 (1.84)	18 (0.67)	817 (30.60)
11–20	9 (0.34)	89 (3.33)	527 (19.74)	407 (15.24)	64 (2.40)	14 (0.52)	1110 (41.57)
>20	1 (0.04)	10 (0.37)	97 (3.63)	124 (4.64)	15 (0.56)	1 (0.04)	248 (9.29)
Total	19 (0.71)	326 (12.21)	1205 (45.13)	922 (34.53)	152 (5.69)	46 (1.72)	2670 (100.0)

contacts with the GPs, and intervention duration, the following associations were seen, using the chi-square test:

- there is no statistically significant association with *gender* ($P < 0.5$)(Table 6.4);
- there is a statistically significant association with *age* (in the age groups of 45–64, 65–74, and 74 there is a higher tendency to reduce cigarette consumption or to stop smoking; $P < 0.001$)(Table 6.5);
- there is a statistically significant association with the *number of cigarettes smoked* (the light smokers have a higher tendency to increase or not to modify their smoking habits, whereas the average and heavy smokers have a higher tendency to reduce or stop smoking; $P < 0.0001$)(Table 6.6);
- there is a statistically significant association with the *number of contacts* (among the smokers belonging to the category who had 3, 4, 5, or more contacts with the GPs, a higher number of persons who stopped or reduced consumption was seen; $P < 0.005$) Table 6.7); and
- there is a significant difference (based on ANOVA test) between the average duration of time elapsed from the first contact (screening) of the patient and completion of the evaluation ($P < 0.001$).

EVALUATION

As we compare the collected data with the expected data, it appears that:

- the number of patients recorded in the register during the examined period is 63 percent (a value expected from data deduced from other related studies is 75 percent in one year) (Focarile, 1990; Russell et al., 1983);
- the prevalence of smokers among the population aged over ten years is 17.2 percent (the expected value was 25 percent, in accordance with anonymous questionnaire surveys;

Table 6.4. Smoking Habits Variations According to Gender; Smoking Population Identified by the GPs of ULSS 21 of Padova*

	Frequency (%)		
Consumption	Males	Females	Total
Reduction	205 (15.21)	151 (11.20)	356 (26.41)
Increase	49 (3.64)	41 (3.04)	90 (6.68)
No change	377 (27.97)	271 (20.10)	648 (48.07)
Cessation	156 (11.57)	98 (7.27)	254 (18.84)
Total	561 (41.62)	787 (58.38)	1348 (100.00)

*Chi-square, 1.64; $P = 0.650$.

Table 6.5. Smoking Habit Variations According to Age; Smoking Population Identified by the GPs of ULSS 21 of Padova*

Consumption	Frequency (%)						
	<15	15–24	25–44	45–64	65–74	>74	Total
Reduction	49 (3.64)	36 (2.67)	72 (5.34)	93 (6.90)	65 (4.82)	41 (3.04)	356 (26.41)
Increase	28 (2.08)	13 (0.96)	18 (1.34)	11 (0.82)	12 (0.89)	8 (0.59)	90 (6.68)
No Change	145 (10.76)	98 (7.27)	132 (9.79)	129 (9.57)	89 (6.60)	55 (4.08)	648 (48.07)
Cessation	43 (3.19)	33 (2.45)	48 (3.56)	53 (3.93)	46 (3.41)	31 (2.30)	254 (18.84)
Total	265 (19.66)	180 (13.35)	270 (20.03)	286 (21.22)	212 (15.73)	135 (10.01)	1348 (100.00)

*Chi-square, 36.310; $P = 0.0002$.

Table 6.6. Smoking Habit Variations According to Categories; Smoking
Population Identified by the GPs of ULSS 21 of Padova (Cases Missing, 7)*

Consumption	Frequency (%)				
	1–5	6–10	11–20	>20	Total
Reduction	12 (0.89)	71 (5.29)	190 (14.17)	83 (6.19)	356 (26.55)
Increase	32 (2.39)	34 (2.54)	21 (1.57)	3 (0.22)	90 (6.71)
No Change	107 (7.98)	191 (14.24)	302 (22.52)	48 (3.58)	648 (48.32)
Cessation	48 (3.58)	84 (6.26)	94 (7.01)	21 (1.57)	247 (18.42)
Total	199 (14.84)	380 (28.34)	607 (45.26)	155 (11.56)	1341 (100.00)

*Chi-square, 154.412; $P = 0.000$.

Table 6.7. Average Difference in Number of
Cigarettes Smoked by Patients Who Have
Reduced Consumption in Relation to the
Number of Contacts*

Contacts	N	median	s.d.
1	49	6.6	4.7
2	36	5.4	3.3
3	72	7.2	7.9
4	93	7.7	4.9
5	65	8.4	5.1
6 or more	41	11.2	7.1

*ANOVA: F value, 4.68; $P = 0.0004$.

• in terms of percentage, the 1,348 smokers on whom the evaluation was carried out is 49.83 percent, as compared with 73–100 percent of responses in
another follow-up study (Rosso et al., 1991).

An evaluation of the program's effectiveness requires a comparison between the
data collected in the registers by the GPs who have applied the guide and the data
on smoking prevalence and cessation deduced from ad hoc surveys in the literature.

The number of smokers who quit in one year is equal to 18.8 percent (a value
expected according to analogous studies (see Schwartz, 1991): annual range
13–38 percent, mean 22.5 percent; value expected based on the study protocol: 30
percent in three years).

As for the "natural quitting rate," obtained by calculating the percentage variation in the number of smokers on samples representative of the same population
(that is, those studied in the ISTAT surveys, 1986/87 and 1990/91), the value is 11
percent over four years in the Veneto region (2.75 percent per year) and 5.6 percent (1.4 percent per year) for Italy (ISTAT, 1991, 1994).

Since the population that was the object of the intervention is the same as the ISTAT sample, although counseling activities differed, the wide diversity between the data suggests that the process was effective. The evaluation of effectiveness was calculated in terms of percentage change in the patients' smoking habit (reduction of cigarette consumption, smoking cessation) obtained in the total number of patients who received counseling. In the case of smoking cessation, the evaluation was obtained by comparing the quitting rate achieved after counseling with respect to the natural quitting rate in the Veneto region according to data provided by ISTAT. Considering the results of this study, 26.4 percent of the patients reduced the number of cigarettes smoked, whereas 18.8 percent quit smoking in the course of a year. Since the natural quitting rate for Veneto is 2.75 percent a year, about 16 percent of the change (18.8–2.75) in smoking habit among the patients who had received counseling can be attributed exclusively to counseling.

CONCLUSION

In evaluating the impact that a standard antitobacco counseling campaign carried out by selected GPs has on the population, this study has also supplied results that are consistent with other studies described in the international literature and previously noted in this chapter. Now the question is whether and how these procedures can be extended to the daily routine of a medical office (taking into account the time to be dedicated to the intervention, continued follow-up counseling, and organization of the practice so that checkups can be carried out).

A great deal of course depends on the doctor's own initiative, but he or she is often confused in the face of the not always clear indications that flood the prevention sector aimed at individuals. Other problems, such as university training that is more inclined toward the therapeutic aspects rather than the preventive ones and the time allocated to the necessary routine, create further limitations.

In this context, the Centre for Health Education in Padova has played an important role in helping doctors set up a network of GPs to do counseling, a network that encourages the exchange of experience between them, produces educational material, and supervises the interventions. This collaboration, offered by trained operators within an organized structure, has greatly contributed to making the intervention effective and practicable, emphasizing the function of the GP as the indisputable, main health promoter.

In the years 1995–2000 the activities described in this chapter became standard intervention for several local health units in the Veneto and Friuli–Venezia Giulia regions and subsequently in other municipalities. The pooling of the data emerging from the different areas will provide further information about effectiveness and expansion of the program.

It should be remembered that this intervention is carried out together with other tobacco prevention activities, thereby increasing the overall effectiveness. In fact, besides counseling by GPs, in Padova as in other areas (especially in Veneto and

Friuli) the tobacco control strategy involves different settings like *schools* (with projects such as Health Promotion in Schools, Smoke-Free Class Competition, and use of didactic guides on smoking prevention by teachers in secondary schools); *hospitals* (Health Promoting Hospitals, Smoke-Free Hospitals); and *workplaces* and leisure time facilities (smoke-free companies, restaurants, cities, etc.). Smoking cessation courses are provided as well through such programs as "Quit and Win Competition" to help smokers quit. All of these activities lead to a comprehensive strategy favoring interaction between young people and grown-ups, teachers and health professionals, media, and business workers. Building on the conviction that tobacco consumption is a primary, challenging, and complex public health program, the focus is on smoking prevention rather than cessation, so as to create a favorable context for resisting pressures in favor of tobacco and for adoption of healthy habits and lifestyles.

NOTES

1.   For studies on helping people to stop smoking, see Lancaster and Stead (2001), Rose and Colwel (1992), Russell et al. (1983), Silagy (2000), and Schwartz (1991).
2.   ULSS refers to the local health unit: Unitá Locale Sociosanitaria.

REFERENCES

Focarile, F. (1990). Efficacia e costi di interventi educativi contro l'abitudine al fumo. *Educazione Sanitaria e promozione della Salute* 13(4):251–58.

Istituto Centrale di Statistica (ISTAT) (1991). *Indagine statistica sulle condizioni di salute della popolazione e sul ricorso ai servizi sanitari* (November 1986–April 1987). Rome: Author.

Istituto Centrale di Statistica (ISTAT) (1994). *Indagine statistica sulle condizioni di salute della popolazione e sul ricorso ai servizi sanitari* (November 1991–April 1992). Rome: Author.

Kottke, T. E., Brekke, M. L., Solberg, L. I., & Hughes, J. R. (1989). A randomized trial to increase smoking intervention by physicians. Doctors Helping Smokers, Round I. *Journal of the American Medical Association* 261:2101–6.

Lancaster, T. and Stead, L. F. (2001). Individual behavioural counselling for smoking cessation. *Cochrane Review* (Issue 3). Oxford, UK: Update Software.

Pilati, G., Mamon, J., & Tamang, E. (1992). Come aiutare i pazienti a smettere di fumare. *Proceedings of the Fifth National Congress of the Italian Society of Quality Assurance* (October; pp. 21–24), Padova, Italy.

Pilati, G., & Tamang, E. (1994). Health professionals against tobacco smoking. *Proceedings of the Second International Conference on Health Promoting Hospitals* (April; pp. 15–16), Padova, Italy.

Rose, G. & Colwel, L. (1992). Randomised controlled trial of anti-smoking advice: Final (20 years) results. *Journal of Epidemiology and Community Health* 46:75–77.

Rosso, S., Senore, C., Ponti, A., & Segnan, N. (1991). Medici di base e interventi contro il fumo: Una rassegna critica degli interventi. *Epidemiologia e Prevenzione* 46:37–44.

Russell, M. A. H., Merriman, R., Stapleton, J., & Taylor W. (1983). Effects of nicotine chewing gum as an adjunct to general practitioner's advice against smoking. *British Medical Journal* 287:1782–85.

Schwartz, J. (1991). Methods for smoking cessation. *Clinics in Chest Medicine* 12 (4): 737–53.

Silagy, C. (2000). Physician advice for smoking cessation. *Cochrane Review* (Issue 4). Oxford, UK: Update Software.

World Health Organization (1987). *Smoke-Free Europe: The Physician's Role.* Geneva: WHO Regional Office for Europe.

Zannoni, F., Mamon, J., & Pilati, G. (1992). *Come Aiutare i Pazienti a Smettere di Fumare: Una Guida per Medici di Medicina Generale.* Padova, Italy: Centro di Educazione alla Salute.

7

Improving Mental Health Care for Children and Adolescents
Strategies and Lessons

John Landsverk and Inger Davis

The past decade has witnessed an increasing professional, administrative, and political interest in the United States in measuring and improving the quality of health and social services. This chapter focuses on these efforts in a specific public health sector, namely, mental health care for children and adolescents. The chapter reviews the history and current status of these efforts, dividing them into two periods: (1) an early period that emphasized changes at the system or macro level, and (2) a later period that developed multiple strategies for trying to improve the actual processes of care and their outcomes at more micro levels within service systems. These strategies will be illustrated by reference to specific projects currently under way at the Child and Adolescent Services Research Center (CASRC) and linked research groups.[1] The projects to be discussed focus on children and adolescents served by the public mental health care sector and do not usually include children and families served by the private or commercial insurance sector. Finally, we will discuss the numerous challenges that have developed during this decade of attempting to improve the quality of care delivered to children and adolescents at risk for the development of mental disorders and severely maladaptive life trajectories.

EARLY HISTORY OF MENTAL HEALTH CARE AT THE MACRO LEVEL

Based on the best available epidemiological studies, it is estimated that between 5 and 11 percent of children have a mental health or substance use disorder and significant functional impairment (Costello et al., 1996). Due to the increased risk for mental health problems among individuals in poverty and to patterns of insurance coverage, many youths with mental health problems are treated in public mental health service systems. Over the last two decades, these public service systems have come under reform efforts broadly labeled as "system of care" initiatives.

In 1982, Jane Knitzer published a stinging critique of the public service systems that serve mentally ill youth under the provocative title *Unclaimed Children: The*

Failure of Public Responsibility to Children and Adolescents in Need of Mental Health Services (Knitzer, 1982). Her observations focused on the lack of integration in mental health services for children and adolescents in the United States and led to system of care initiative (Stroul & Friedman, 1986). This initiative recognized that children and adolescents with significant need for mental health treatment are found and cared for in multiple sectors of care beyond the specialty mental health sector, including child welfare, juvenile justice, education, general health/primary care, and alcohol and drug services. Through this initiative, substantial attention has been given to the organization of public sector systems serving children and adolescents, and to recommendations for improving care by making adjustments to service systems, such as expanding the continuum of mental health services available, creating stronger linkages between public agencies serving children, and eliminating redundancies in care mechanisms (Stroul & Friedman, 1986). Policy efforts to better integrate child and youth services across service sectors are reflected in the national Child and Adolescent Service System Program (CASSP) (Day & Roberts, 1991). Under this policy initiative, sixty-seven communities have been funded since 1993 by the federal program Comprehensive Community Mental Health Services for Children and Their Families. Current funding for this innovative program exceeds eight million dollars per year.

Three major evaluation studies have been conducted to date that address the impact of "system of care" changes on the processes of care and the benefits for children and families. Two of these have employed rigorous quasi-experimental designs and have been completed, while the third has used a less rigorous design and is still in process. Results from the two completed studies, one at Fort Bragg (Bickman, 1997) and the other in Stark County, Ohio (Bickman, Noser, & Summerfelt, 1999), have consistently shown better outcomes at the service system level such as less use of restrictive care (residential treatment, or in-patient hospitalization), decreased waiting time for initiating care, and increased levels of satisfaction at the family level. However, these studies have found no change in individual child- and adolescent-level clinical outcomes, such as symptom reduction or improvement in functioning, that could be attributed to the system-level changes. Even though the studies have been done at very different settings, with Fort Bragg as a military post setting and Stark County as a civilian setting, the results have been remarkably comparable, suggesting that the findings are robust and not especially sensitive to widely different settings and service systems.

This lack of evidence for client-level benefit from the "system of care" initiatives is mirrored in the meta-analytic studies of John Weisz and colleagues. In a meta-analytic review of studies that compared children receiving treatment in a community setting with children receiving no treatment, Weisz, Donenberg, Han, and Weiss (1995) identified nine studies sufficiently well-designed for sound conclusions to be drawn. Across the nine studies reviewed, effect sizes for treatment relative to a no-treatment control had an overall mean effect size of .01, a result not significantly different from zero and one that clearly demonstrated that usual care in the community has no discernible clinical impact, as measured by the designs in these studies.

In striking contrast to the lack of beneficial outcomes in symptoms and functioning observed in community-based services, there is a large body of work showing that psychotherapeutic treatments delivered in highly controlled studies can produce improved clinical and functional outcomes for children receiving care. Extensive meta-analytic reviews of rigorous studies using randomized clinical trial designs (e.g., Kazdin & Weisz, 1998; Weisz, Weiss, & Donenberg, 1992) have examined the effects of psychotherapeutic as well as psychotropic interventions on symptomatology and functioning across a large number of published studies. Uniformly these reports have concluded that many of these interventions for children result in improved clinical outcomes.

The conclusions of these meta-analyses remain strong even when subjected to extensive reanalyses. For example, the positive effects of psychotherapy exist across years within the same meta-analyses and in meta-analyses spanning different years. Outcomes are more positive for domains related to the target of the intervention, but are not due to the use of outcome measures that are unnecessarily close to the actual treatment process. Effects of treatment are not limited to immediate posttreatment improvements, but remain relatively constant across follow-up periods of a year or more. Positive outcomes appear across different problem categories and across different kinds of potential outcome measures, including parental report and child self-report. The conclusions of meta-analytic studies are thus quite robust. Besides meta-analytic studies, alternative methods have been established to determine whether specific psychotherapeutic interventions result in improved outcomes for children. These methods involve establishing a set of criteria for deciding whether sufficient evidence exists to label a psychotherapeutic treatment as empirically supported (e.g., Chambless & Hollon, 1998). In a series of recent reviews, a number of different psychotherapies fulfilled the criteria to be judged either "probably efficacious or well-established" (e.g., American Academy of Child and Adolescent Psychiatry, 1998), including treatments for depression and conduct disorders, two of the most common problems presenting for care in public mental health service systems.

Therefore, from both the meta-analytic perspective and the criterion-based perspective, relatively clear evidence exists that psychotherapeutic interventions can result in moderate to large improvements in client outcomes both at the close of treatment and over follow-ups of one year or more. These types of beneficial findings have also come out of studies of psychotropic medication, especially the use of stimulants to treat problems of attention and hyperactivity. For example, treatment research shows that, for children who meet the criteria for Attention Deficit Hyperactivity Disorder (ADHD), stimulant medication, along or in concert with psychosocial interventions, is effective in over 70 percent of children (Jensen and Payne, 1998). Based on these divergent findings, a number of authors have argued that a relatively strong empirical and theoretical case can be made for focusing attention on the *quality of mental health treatment* that children receive (Bickman & Noser, 1999; Hoagwood, Hibbs, Brent, & Jensen, 1995; Noser & Bickman, 2000). These researchers make this argument on the following grounds, which have been generated by the research reviewed above. First, a large body of work shows that psychotherapeutic and psychotropic treatments delivered in highly controlled studies can produce improved clinical and functional outcomes for children receiving care. Second, the weight of evidence suggests that care provided in community treatment settings does not result in outcomes significantly better than normal improvements occurring over time. Third, large system-level interventions have failed to improve clinical and functional outcomes over the short or long-term. Taken together, these points suggest that attention to treatment process (quality of care) in community treatment settings could have substantial effects on the outcomes achieved by children receiving mental health care.

The next section will present and illustrate three different strategies that are currently being used to address the need to improve quality of mental health care and therefore result in greater benefit to children and families receiving services in community settings.[2]

CURRENT STRATEGIES TO IMPROVE QUALITY
OF MENTAL HEALTH CARE

Three general strategies have emerged over the past decade to improve the quality of services provided in systems of care for children and adolescents: (1) dissemination of efficacious treatments in community settings; (2) outcome assessment in community settings; and (3) use of quality of care indicators in tracer conditions within service systems. In this section, each of these strategies will be presented with examples from current projects under way at the CASRC. In addition, the discussion will reference chapters from this volume that provide excellent examples of one or more of these strategies being used in other cultural contexts.

Disseminating Efficacious Interventions
in Community Settings

The usual model for developing, testing, and disseminating efficacious treatments was developed by the National Cancer Institute (NCI) in the United States as a process for bringing drug therapies into widespread medical use. As described by Hoagwood et al. (1995), the NCI model is the prototypic approach to transferring treatment processes tested in efficacy studies to a broader range of community treatment settings and children within those settings. The model has five phases:

- hypothesis development;
- method validation;
- efficacy trial testing of hypotheses;

- intervention testing in defined populations; and
- demonstration and implementation trials.

This model is elegant and emphasizes high internal validity at all stages, with gradually expanding external validity in each successive phase.

Currently, the above approach is being used with a number of psychosocial interventions that have been shown to be beneficial to children and families in carefully controlled clinical trials in the United States. Wide-scale dissemination is being attempted with the "nurse home visitation model" developed by Olds et al. (1997) as an early preventive intervention targeting risk for child abuse and neglect and later development of aggression and conduct disorder in children. The model also being used in the dissemination phase is the "multisystemic treatment" developed by Henggeler (1999) to address delinquent behavior. In both of these examples, the intervention approach has been developed from a clearly specified theoretical model, includes a well-specified set of elements that are codified in a manualized protocol, and has been tested in a number of randomized clinical trials. This is the stage at which the intervention is ready to be disseminated in effectiveness studies, according to the NCI model.

A smaller scale approach is illustrated by a current project in which CASRC investigators are collaborating with the intervention developers from the Oregon Social Learning Center in Eugene, Oregon (OSLC). In a study from the above project, Chamberlain, Moreland, and Reid (1992) reported the results of a randomized clinical trial that examined the efficacy of providing foster parents with training and support through weekly groups and between-group telephone contacts in three counties. The study used a controlled design where foster families were randomly assigned to one of three groups: (1) enhanced services plus a monthly stipend (experimental condition); (2) a monthly stipend only; and (3) foster care as usual. Foster parents in the enhanced services group participated in weekly groups and between-group telephone contact that focused on the use of practical behavior management skills to address behavioral problems presenting in children who had been placed in their care. Compared to those in the two control conditions, foster families that received enhanced services reported a decrease in child symptoms, a decrease in rates of disruption from care due to the child's behavioral/emotional problems (i.e., changes in placement), and a decrease in the rate of foster parents who subsequently dropped out of providing foster care. Not only did the enhanced services lead to better child outcomes, but also retention rates of foster parents were higher for those who participated in enhanced services.

In several subsequent randomized clinical trials with diverse populations of youngsters from preschoolers to adolescents, Parent Management Training has been shown to produce positive outcomes. These subsequent trials all have demonstrated the continued positive effects with foster parents in three areas: (1) reduction of child symptoms, (2) lower rates of disruptions in foster care (changes in placement for negative reasons), and (3) fewer foster parents in the PMT condition dropped out of providing foster care. However, all of the clinical trials were tightly controlled with homogeneous subjects and carefully trained graduate students and staff, and they were implemented by the developer of the intervention, Dr. Patti Chamberlain. What is unknown is whether the efficacious treatment can be implemented within a much larger system of foster care and with more heterogeneous substitute parents, such as kinship foster parents, and still demonstrate the same benefits. Essentially, what is needed is an effectiveness study testing the outcomes for the intervention in the "real world" of services systems.

Using the same program model that is described above, through the collaborative project Cascading Dissemination of a Foster Parent Intervention, we are now testing the transferability of this intervention from Oregon to the foster care system in San Diego, California, which has six regions where the intervention will be successively implemented within two cohorts of three regions each. A cascading dissemination model is being used where, with each iteration of the implementation, the involvement of the original developers will lessen. During the first iteration, the Oregon staff has trained the San Diego staff and is monitoring the implementation from a distance. The second iteration will have the San Diego staff training a new set of staff members and monitoring the outcomes. In both iterations, randomized designs are being used. Outcomes are being evaluated at five levels (child symptoms, functional behavior, environments, consumer perspectives, and system) using a multimethod/multiagent strategy. If the outcomes from these two studies are comparable to those achieved in the Oregon-based randomized clinical trials, the intervention will be considered ready for dissemination to diverse child welfare service systems beyond San Diego County.

Outcome Assessment in Community Mental Health Service Settings

A second strategy for improving care is the implementation of outcome assessment in community treatment settings. One of the major shifts in the public mental health delivery system has been the relatively recent emphasis on outcome accountability. While this emphasis may have originated with the private sector, many government agencies are now requiring public system providers to submit outcome data to funders and policymakers (Koch, Lewis, & McCall, 1998). For example, the State of California has implemented a statewide performance outcome data collection system that has become an ideal naturalistic laboratory in which to study the process and outcome of implementing an outcome assessment protocol in community-based child and adolescent mental health service settings. In 1994, the California state assembly passed legislation mandating the collection of standardized outcome measures for all youths who remain in the publicly funded mental health system for at least sixty days (California Mental Health Planning Council, 1997). The California program is representative, in design and purpose, of similar initiatives in other states, and of other broad service system evaluations (Hodges & Hernandez, 1999; Rosenblatt, Wyman, Kingdon, & Ichinose, 1998).

The goals of outcome mandates include both the aggregate use of data to evaluate service system effectiveness and the collection of data for use by individual clinicians for diagnosis and treatment monitoring (California Mental Health Planning Council, 1997). The first goal is driven by increased emphasis on service accountability, and the second goal is driven by a history of research supporting the use of standardized clinical measurement in mental health practice (Meehl, 1954). Much of the literature in this area provides recommendations or guidelines for the implementation of outcome accountability protocols (Smith, Fischer, Nordquist, Mosley, & Ledbetter, 1997) and/or the use of specific measures in such protocols (Eisen, Leff, & Schaefer, 1999).

There have been few attempts to examine clinicians' utilization of outcome information. This raises serious concern, given the literature on the significant limitations of clinical judgment alone for decision-making (Bickman et al., 1995). Beginning with seminal work by Meehl (1954) and others (Dawes, Faust & Meehl, 1989), there has been strong empirical support for the use of standardized, clinical measurements in mental health practice, as opposed to reliance on clinical judgment alone. However, it seems that many clinicians do not incorporate such measurement into their assessment and intervention efforts. The reasons for this must be explored further, but may include barriers associated with feasibility (e.g., time constraints, high caseloads) and lack of perceived clinical utility of the measures. In addition, there may be education and training issues and/or attitudinal barriers whereby clinicians do not perceive any added value of systematic measurement beyond that of their own clinical judgment.

The acceptance or rejection of clinical practice guidelines in medicine offers a somewhat analogous paradigm for examining the implementation of outcome measurement in mental health. For example, Cabana et al. (1999) identified a number of barriers to acceptance of practice guidelines that may be related to outcome assessment: lack of familiarity with or awareness of the new procedures, disagreement with specific guidelines or mandates, general lack of agreement with guidelines, negative outcome expectations for the intervention ("it will not work"), lack of self-efficacy (belief in ability to perform the tasks), lack of motivation or readiness to change, external barriers (difficult to use), patient factors (e.g., unwilling to complete measures), and environmental factors (lack of time or resources or an increase in scrutiny of job performance).

In order to address the lack of evidence for the effectiveness of mental health services in community-based settings, we must increase our understanding of the process of integrating evidence-based practice into standard clinical practice, as also suggested by Whittaker and Maluccio (2002) and by Wright and Paget (Chapter 10 in this volume). In San Diego County, the Child and Adolescent Research Center (CASRC) is examining performance indicators on over seven thousand children and adolescents served at forty community clinics over the past three years. Annual reports are provided to the stakeholders of the service system to profile service provision.

In addition, the CASRC is involved in a number of studies that are examining this outcome performance assessment in both San Diego County and elsewhere in the State of California. In one study, fifty randomly selected clinicians from various service sites in San Diego, representing multiple mental health disciplines (e.g., psychology, social work, marriage and family therapy), have been interviewed individually or in focus groups. Preliminary analyses suggest that many clinicians hold strong negative attitudes about the validity and utility of standardized outcome assessment protocols. For example, when these clinicians were asked to rate the extent to which they used seven types of information to evaluate the effectiveness of their work with children and families, they rated "improvement in real life functioning" (e.g., school grades) and their "own intuition" as first and second most frequent, and standardized measures or scales as a distant seventh (last). Our experience with training clinicians to use outcome measures indicates that attitudinal barriers to use are not necessarily related to perceived competence, i.e., clinicians generally report adequate knowledge about the use of measures, but concurrently report minimal integration into practice (Garland, Culver, & Walton, 1998). We need to expand and deepen our understanding of clinicians' attitudes and practices regarding evaluating the effectiveness of their services (e.g., Cabana et al., 1999; see also Jergeby, 2002; Zeira, 2002).

In addition to qualitative data on the acceptance of standardized outcome protocols, we have quantitative preliminary data on collection compliance in the above-noted studies. Preliminary analyses of the performance outcome project implementation in San Diego County indicate that there is great variability in compliance across programs, ranging from approximately 40 to 95 percent of eligible clients per site. We have seen similar variability across counties within the state, with the range of 10 to 64 percent for the number of clients in the eligible target population on which baseline measures were completed. The follow-up rates have been much lower, in the range of 5 to 30 percent. Anecdotal reports suggest that the following variables may be associated with compliance: overall volume of clients in the program (inversely related to compliance), percentage of English-speaking clients (positively related to compliance), and attitudes about the value of outcome data. However, such anecdotal evidence requires empirical validation.

International interest in the use of outcome assessment and performance indicator strategies is seen in a number of chapters in this volume. In Chapter 4 Vecchiato addresses the difficulties of using science-based approaches to outcome measurement and the problems of moving beyond easily collected outcome data that are typically found in large-scale administrative databases to more sensitive measures of outcome and effectiveness that require data collection systems using more standardized measurement. Two chapters from researchers in the United Kingdom report on an innovative new program of outcome-based assessment and monitoring for children's services in England and Wales [Ward in Chapter 1 of this volume, and Rose (2002)]. Ward gives a detailed account of the Looking After Children Project, which represents a comprehensive approach to the use of outcome-based evaluation at the micro level. This project is similar to the development of performance outcome systems in the United States that have been described above; the major similarity resides in the efforts to use outcome measurement to influence practice at the level of client and practitioner interactions. Ward echoes the difficulties in implementing such a system that have been seen in the U.S. efforts, especially in the collection of complete and accurate information by practitioners. Those similar findings across national boundaries support the general need for more research on the barriers to implementation and the developing strategies for addressing these barriers.

Use of Quality of Care Indicators in Tracer Conditions

A third approach to improving mental health care has used a model called "quality of care." In the United States, the quality of care (QC) model for improving treatment processes has been developed and applied over the past several decades (Donabedian, 1980; Young, Sullivan, Burnam, & Brook, 1998), particularly to physical health problems and to mental health problems among adults, such as depression (Wells, Sturm, Sherbourne, & Meredith, 1996) and schizophrenia (Young et al., 1998). Quality of care research is more directly focused on identifying methods for improving care in community treatment settings and measuring the costs and benefits of interventions designed to improve quality of care. It is therefore in line with, but more detailed and flexible than, phases IV and V of the NCI model noted earlier.

The phases of QC research can generally be described as: (1) defining best practices (or what constitutes quality care), (2) evaluating the degree to which quality care practices are employed in community treatment settings, (3) evaluating how the use of quality care practices relates to treatment outcomes, (4) evaluating the costs and benefits of proposed quality improvement efforts, and (5) proposing quality improvement efforts to be tested in meaningful service systems (e.g., in a managed health care plan or public mental health service system).

From the perspective of QC research, it is recognized that quality care is an evolving concept that changes as the state of knowledge changes. In a QC framework a distinction is made between *technical* aspects of treatment process and *interpersonal* aspects of treatment process (Donabedian, 1980). The QC approach is exemplified by work within the CASRC in San Diego that is being done in collaboration with three other California research centers: the Center for Mental Health Services Research at the University of California at Berkeley and San Francisco, the National Research Center on Asian-American Mental Health at the University of California at Davis, and the Research Center on Managed Care at the University of California at Los Angeles. A current study being carried out by investigators from the four centers is using the QC framework to develop and examine specific process indicators for the three selected "tracer" conditions of ADHD, depression, and conduct disorder. Little is known about how to monitor the quality of care for child mental health problems or what "benchmarks" of quality could be used to assess this domain in a publicly funded mental health care setting. Fortunately, the development of treatment guidelines and national recommendations for quality of care indicators for child mental health services is under way. Data on the effectiveness of care for ADHD and major depression also are emerging. These advances make it possible to begin work on examining how quality of care indicators relate to child outcomes and the development of a quality evaluation method that is applicable to care delivered in a defined service delivery context.

In the current collaborative project, we are using an innovative approach to defining and assessing quality of care that was developed for an adult study of quality improvement for major depression (Wells et al., 2000). Specifically, data on both process and outcomes are used to define quality of care in the context of the clinical condition that applies over an episode of care. This permits one to distinguish between appropriate care for both a period or moment in time and a sustained period of appropriate care. This distinction is critical in evaluating the management of chronic conditions like ADHD, major depression, and severe disruptive behavior problems. The project has developed quality of care criteria for these three conditions in the following steps. A detailed literature review was performed over a period of three months. The review began with a MEDLINE search for all relevant articles about the efficacy of the clinical processes of the tracer conditions, categorized by identification, assessment, treatment, and follow-up. These classifications were chosen so that we could rate the variables that are measured in the technical domain of this study's quality of care indicators. Other evidence categories will include interpersonal skill, parent satisfaction, continuity of care, and child outcomes. The literature was categorized by study type, such as randomized controlled trial (RCT), prospective non-RCT cohort studies, prospective non-RCT registry studies, retrospective adjusted cohort and case-control studies, observational and unadjusted retrospective cohort studies, cross-sectional studies, surveys, editorials, and reviews. Individual case descriptions were excluded. Outcome evidence tables were produced to present the data. Insofar as possible, sociodemographic and treatment setting characteristics also were noted because we anticipated that many of the clinical samples in earlier studies will differ from this study's target population.

As the strength of the evidence was gathered, the project director and a panel of experts developed a proposed criteria list. When finalized, the expert panel of both researchers and clinical providers were sent a draft of the literature review and the proposed criteria structure. They were then contacted by conference call to assess their level of satisfaction with these materials. The research team then revised the literature review and proposed criteria, and send out these materials by express mail. The panelists were asked to read the final literature review and rate the proposed criteria (Round 1). These ratings were returned to UCLA Health Services Research Center for scoring. Finally, the panel convened for a fact-to-face meeting, where all criteria were discussed and rerated (Round 2). Panelists were asked to rate their level of agreement with the criteria, the criteria's level of importance to treatment outcomes for children with target conditions and key quality of care problems, and the level of difficulty to provide such care in a public-sector managed care treatment setting. A 1 to 9 scale was selected because this provided a range for categorizing the criteria as appropriate, equivocal, or inappropriate. A criterion was defined as appropriate if there was high agreement that it is important in determining treatment outcomes and that it would be easy to implement in this study's treatment setting. In sum, these steps illustrate the interplay of both published literature and the opinions of an expert panel that is drawn from both the research community and the clinical practice community.

Treatment and assessment quality of care criteria were developed from the operationalized practice parameters used in this study. Examples of proposed criteria are use of psychoeducation, use of rating scales for assessment and monitoring medication, use of psychotherapies that are supported by clinical consensus or have established efficacy, contact with school, referral for a medical evaluation, instruction in behavior interventions at home and at school, information on dietary interventions, information about medication and possible side effects, and regular monitoring of vital signs, height, and weight while on psychotropic medication. Based upon the quality of care indicators developed in this process, a medical record abstraction form was developed and is being implemented in a study of 1,100 medical records of those youths with a tracer condition who meet eligibility criteria and had an episode of care at a selected clinic within a randomly selected county. The quality of care ratings abstracted on medical records cases will then be linked to the performance outcomes data for these cases to determine whether there is a clear association between the quality of care as reflected in the medical record and the outcomes as measured by standardized instruments.

We believe the quality of care strategy represents a very promising formal approach to improvement of care efforts in large public systems. Several chapters in the companion volume might be related to this strategy, even though none of them report using the formal methods of quality of care improvement noted in our example. In Chapter 13 Zeira (2002) describes an attempt in Israel to develop outcome measures and integrate them into social workers' ongoing practices in a public social services system. The process includes a collaborative effort to define outcome indicators between a university and public agency representatives that appears similar to the collaborative processes described in the quality of care strategy above. In Chapter 3 Cinzia Canali and Paolo Rigon (2002) also describe similar collaborative processes in their discussion of evaluating services for children with multiple problems.

SUMMARY OF CHALLENGES AND LESSONS LEARNED

In this chapter we have discussed three major approaches that are being used in the United States to address the disappointing lack of beneficial child clinical outcomes observed in studies of community-based mental health services. These approaches are all currently seen as viable strategies to improve care and no approach has become dominant or shown the greatest promise. In fact, research testing of these three models is only now beginning in the child mental health care field. Nevertheless, a number of challenges and lessons can be offered about the current status of the field of outcomes measurement and the progress or lack of it over the past decade.

First, research over the past decade strongly supports the idea that system level changes do not necessarily result in micro level or individual clinical level changes. The Fort Bragg and Stark County studies (Bickman, Noser, & Summerfelt, 1999) have shown that system level changes such as greater integration of services can result in other system-level changes, such as less use of restrictive-level care. However, no evidence has emerged that supports the idea that greater integration of services will result in clearly beneficial clinical outcomes for the recipients of mental health care services.

Second, evidence-based interventions and treatments are difficult to transfer to the "real world" of service delivery. This is likely due to the many differences between studies that establish efficacy and the nature of community-based service delivery systems. Participants in efficacy clinical trials are likely to be considerably different from those in regular service systems. They are likely to have only one problem being addressed while public service system clients are likely to present with multiple conditions needing amelioration. Participants in clinical trials are likely to be volunteers, while public service system clients may have different reasons for seeking services, including mandated referrals. Service providers in clinical trials are likely to be highly motivated graduate students or experienced staff who undergo rigorous and specialized training in the methods of the interventions. In comparison, service system providers are seeing many more clients under less than optimal conditions, and often with widely divergent conditions requiring attention. These considerations suggest that the logic of studies establishing the evidence for interventions and treatments in clinical trials may not work well for the type of studies needed to address the effectiveness of these interventions in community-based settings. They also suggest the great need for studies of this kind so that we develop better methods for transferring efficacious treatments to community care systems.

Third, the implementation of standardized outcome assessment as part of accountability processes within ongoing service systems appears to engender several critical problems. The stakeholders in the service systems are not likely to agree on the actual domains to be measured. Service providers appear to have less tolerance than anticipated for the widespread use of these measures. There is growing evidence that the imposition of assessment outcome systems will not automatically translate into the use of these measures in the critical processes of clinical planning. Outcome assessment that is divorced from the clinical planning process would seem to have little promise for increasing the quality of clinical care provided. Finally, the very low rates of completion for outcome assessment measures, even at the baseline period, underscore the difficulties in implementing these systems on a wide scale.

In conclusion, the quality of mental health care in public service systems for children and adolescents is much lower than what is possible, given the research base that has developed for evidence-based treatments. However, much work needs to be done before *evidence-based treatment* is transformed into *evidence-based practice*.

NOTES

1. The Child and Adolescent Services Research Center in San Diego, California, is funded by the National Institute of Mental Health.

2. The importance of developing methods for improving treatment quality within community treatment contexts is highlighted by the recent federal reports published by the National institute of Mental Health, *Bridging Science and Service* (1999) and *Translating Behavioral Science into Action* (2000), both of which suggest specific directions for improving the translation of effective practices to broader treatment environments.

REFERENCES

American Academy of Child and Adolescent Psychiatry (1998). Practice parameters for the assessment and treatment of children and adolescents with depressive disorders. *Journal of the American Academy of Child & Adolescent Psychiatry* 37(Supplement): S63–S83.

Bickman, L. (1997). Resolving issues raised by the Fort Bragg evaluation: New directions for mental health services research. *American Psychologist* 52:562–65.

Bickman, L., Guthrie, P. R., Foster, E. M., Lambert, E. W., Summerfelt, W. T., Breda, C. S., & Heflinger, C. A. (1995). *Evaluating Managed Mental Health Services: The Fort Bragg Experiment*. New York: Plenum.

Bickman, L., & Noser, K. (1999). Meeting the challenges in the delivery of child and adolescent mental health services in the next millennium: The continuous quality improvement approach. *Applied & Preventive Psychology* 8:247–55.

Bickman, L, Noser, K., & Summerfelt, W. T. (1999). Long-term effects of a system of care on children and adolescents. *Journal of Behavioral Health Sciences Research* 26:185–202.

Cabana, M. D., Rand, C. S., Powe, N. R., Wu, A. W., Wilson, M. H., Abboud, P.-A. C., & Rubin, H. R. (1999). Why don't physicians follow clinical practice guidelines? A framework for improvement. *Journal of the American Medical Association* 282(15): 1458–65.

California Mental Health Planning Council (1997). *Adult Performance Outcome Study: Wave 1 to Wave 3*. Sacramento: California Mental Health Planning Council.

Canali, C. & Rigon, P. (2002). Evaluating outcomes for children with multiple problems. In T. Vecchiato, A.N. Maluccio, & C. Canali, (Eds.). *Evalution in Child and Family Services: Comparative Client and Program Perspectives*. Hawthorne, NY: Aldine de Gruyter.

Chamberlain, P., Moreland, S., & Reid, K. (1992). Enhanced services and stipends for foster parents: Effects on retention rates and outcomes for children. *Child Welfare* 71: 387–401.

Chambless, D. L., & Hollon, S. D. (1998). Defining empirically supported therapies. *Journal of Consulting and Clinical Psychology* 66:7–18.

Costello, E. J., Angold, A., Burns, B. J., Erkanli, A., Stangl, D. K., & Tweed, D. L. (1996). The Great Smoky Mountains Study of Youth: Functional impairment and severe emotional disturbance. *Archives of General Psychiatry* 53:1137–43.

Dawes, R. M., Faust, D., & Meehl, P. E. (1989). Clinical versus actuarial judgment. *Science* 243:1668–74.

Day, C. & Roberts, M.C. (1991). Activities of the child and adolescent service system for improving mental health services for children and families. *Journal of Clinical Child Psychology*, 20: 340-350.

Donabedian, A. (1980). *Explorations in Quality Assessment and Monitoring, Volume I: The Definition of Quality and Approaches to Its Assessment*. Ann Arbor, MI: Health Administration Press.

Eisen, S. V., Leff, H. S., & Schaefer E. (1999). Implementing outcome systems: Lessons from a test of the BASIS-32 and the SF-36. *Journal of Behavioral Health Services and Research* 26:18–27.

Garland, A. F., Culver, S., & Walton, R. (1998). Clinicians' response to mandatory training on outcomes measures. Paper presented at the 11th Annual Research Conference: A System of Care for Children's Mental Health: Expanding the Research Base, Tampa, FL.

Henggeler, S. W. (1999). Multisystemic therapy: An overview of clinical procedures, outcomes, and policy implications. *Child Psychology & Psychiatry Review* 4(1):2–10.

Hoagwood, K., Hibbs, E., Brent, D., & Jensen, P. (1995). Introduction to the special section: Efficacy and effectiveness in studies of child and adolescent psychotherapy. *Journal of Consulting and Clinical Psychology* 63:683–87.

Hodges, S. P., & Hernandez, M. (1999). How organizational culture influences outcome information utilization. *Evaluation and Program Planning* 22:183–97.

Jensen, P. S. & Payne, J. D. (1998). Behavioral and medication treatments for Attention Deficit Hyperactivity Disorder: Comparisons and combinations. Paper presented at NIH Consensus Conference on Diagnosis and Treatment of ADHD, Washington, D.C.

Jergeby, U. (2002). Outcome evaluation as performed by practitioners. In T. Vecchiato, A. N. Maluccio, & C. Canali (Eds.), *Evalution in Child and Family Services: Comparative Client and Program Perspectives*. Hawthorne, NY: Aldine de Gruyter.

Kazdin, A. E., & Weisz, J. R. (1998). Identifying and developing empirically supported child and adolescent treatments. *Journal of Consulting and Clinical Psychology* 66:19–36.

Knitzer, J. (1982). *Unclaimed Children: The Failure of Public Responsibility to Children and Adolescents in Need of Mental Health Services*. Washington, DC: Children's Defense Fund.

Koch, J. R., Lewis, A., & McCall, D. (1998). A multistakeholder-driven model for developing an outcome management system. *Journal of Behavioral Health Services & Research* 25:151–62.

Meehl, P. E. (1954). *Clinical versus Statistical Prediction: A Theoretical Analysis and a Review of the Evidence*. Northvale, NJ: Jason Aronson.

National Institute of Mental Health (1999). *Bridging Science and Service: A Report by the National Advisory Mental Health Council's Clinical Treatment and Services Research Workgroup*. Rockville, MD: Author.

National Institute of Mental Health (2000). *Translating Behavioral Science into Action: Report of the National Advisory Mental Health Council Behavioral Science Workgroup*. Rockville, MD: Author.

Noser, K., & Bickman, L. (2000). Quality indicators of children's mental health services: Do they predict client outcomes? *Journal of Emotional and Behavioral Disorders* 8:9–18.

Olds, D. L., Eckenrode, J., Henderson Jr., C. R., Kitzman, H., Powers, J., Cole, R., Sidora, K., Morris, P., Pettitt, L. M., & Luckey, D. W. (1997). Long-term effects of home visitation on maternal life course and child abuse and neglect: fifteen-year follow-up of a randomized trial. *Journal of the American Medical Association* 278(8):637–43.

Piening, S. & Warsh, R. (2002). Collaboration between evaluators and agency staff in outcome-based evaluation. In T. Vecchiato, A. N. Maluccio, and C. Canali (Eds.). *Evalution in Child and Family Services: Comparative Client and Program Perspectives.* Hawthorne, NY: Aldine de Gruyter.

Rose, W. (2002). Achieving better outcomes for children and families by improving assessment of need. In T. Vecchiato, A. N. Maluccio, and C. Canali (Eds.), *Evaluation in Child and Family Services: Comparative Client and Program Perspectives.* Hawthorne, NY: Aldine de Gruyter.

Rosenblatt, A., Wyman, N., Kingdon, D., & Ichinose, C. (1998). Managing what you measure: Creating outcome-driven systems of care for youth with serious emotional disturbances. *Journal of Behavioral Health Services & Research* 25:177–93.

Smith, G. R., Jr., Fischer, E. P., Nordquist, C. R., Mosley, C. L., & Ledbetter, N. S. (1997). Implementing outcomes management systems in mental health settings. *Psychiatric Services* 48:364–68.

Stroul, B. A., & Friedman, R. M. (1986). *A System of Care for Seriously Emotionally Disturbed Children and Youth.* Washington, DC: CASSP Technical Assistance Center, Georgetown University Child Development Center.

Weisz, J. R., Donenberg, G. R., Han, S. S., & Weiss, B. (1995). Bridging the gap between laboratory and clinic in child and adolescent psychotherapy. *Journal of Consulting and Clinical Psychology* 63:688–701.

Weisz, J. R., Weiss, B., & Donenberg, G. R. (1992). The lab versus the clinic: Effects of child and adolescent psychotherapy. *American Psychologist* 47:1578–85.

Wells, K. B., Sherbourne, C., Schoenbaum, M., Duan, N., Meredith, L., Unutzer, J., Miranda, J., Carney, M. F., & Rubenstein, L. V. (2000). Impact of disseminating quality improvement programs for depression in managed primary care. *Journal of the American Medical Association* 283:212–20.

Wells, K., Sturn, R., Sherbourne, C., & Meredith, L. (1996). *Caring for Depression.* Cambridge, MA: Harvard University Press.

Whittaker, J. K. and Maluccio, A. N. (2002). Issues for program design and outcome evaluation in residential group child care. In T. Vecchiato, A. N. Maluccio, and C. Canali (Eds.), *Evaluation in Child and Family Services: Comparative Client and Program Perspectives.* Hawthorne, NY: Aldine de Gruyter.

Young, A. S., Sullivan G., Burnam, M. A., & Brook, R. H. (1998). Measuring the quality of outpatient treatment for schizophrenia. *Archives of General Psychiatry* 55:611–16.

Zeira, A. (2002). Promoting self-evaluation of programs for children at risk and their families. In T. Vecchiato, A. N. Maluccio, and C. Canali (Eds.), *Evalution in Child and Family Services: Comparative Client and Program Perspectives.* Hawthorne, NY: Aldine de Gruyter.

8

Evaluating Social and Health Services for Children, Adults, and Elderly Persons

Alessandro Pompei

The general goal of social and health services is to promote health and the quality of life. Evaluation of the outcome of services should, therefore, concern their effectiveness, in addition to the current interest in assessing process, structures, and consumer satisfaction. One obstacle in evaluating outcomes is the difficulty in assessing case-by-case projects because of their lack of documentation. In this chapter we discuss an evaluative approach that encourages documentation, using pre-post comparisons for each case presented by a person or family. The purpose is to systematize record keeping so as to uncover methods considered necessary for an effective helping process that incorporates systematic understanding of the impact of professional paths for solving diverse problems.

EVALUATION APPROACH

The evaluation approach considered in this chapter proposes: (1) a series of stages in *providing a caregiving service* and (2) a range of phases of the *helping process*.

Stages in Providing a Caregiving Service

Any social or health service can be considered a caregiving experience that has a number of stages. As seen in Figure 8.1, these are:

- request for services;
- analysis of the request as defined by a person or family;
- definition of the problem in which to intervene for improving life conditions;
- choice of the best helping process for the problem;
- identification of the people and resources that can be brought to bear on the problem;
- definition of the expected results; and
- description of the person's or family's condition after the operational phase, permitting measurement of results.

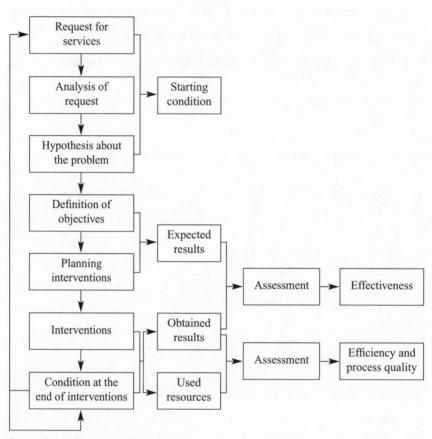

Source: Popei, Costanzi, and Risso (2000).

Figure 8.1.   Stages in provision of a care-giving service (Source: Pompei, Costanzi, &
        Risso, 2000).

After the end of the assessment, it should be possible to evaluate effectiveness
and efficiency of the helping process and, on the basis of that information, plan for
new services and end the caregiving process.

Phases of the Helping Process
As outlined in Table 8.1, the helping process reflected in the above stages includes the following phases, in particular:

Table 8.1. Phases of the Helping Process

Request *deals with the question that a person asks in accessing the service.*
Analysis of the request *requires gathering and recording necessary information about the person and her/his world.*
Definition of the problem *requires the professional to use all acquired information to form a* hypothesis about the problem. *Objectives and strategic operational lines are defined.*
Definition of goals of the service *deals with describing anticipated results in such a way that they can be measured and verified. The contract for caregiving is negotiated with the person.*
Planning and implementation of intervention *requires professionals to prepare the operational plan (who, what, what time, with what frequency). They then monitor interventions to verify their performance in relation to the plan.*
Evaluation conditions at the end of intervention. *This includes output evaluation and outcome evaluation.*

- statement of the request of service;
- analysis of the request;
- definition of the problem;
- formulation of goals of the service;
- planning and implementation of intervention; and
- evaluation of conditions upon termination of intervention.

The process presented above does not lend itself well to those standardized services that are based on legislated responses to particular conditions, for example, economic support or immunizations. Such interventions are characterized by administrative paths and minimize the importance of the practitioners' contribution. Evaluation on a case-by-case basis is therefore not so important. In other services, however, the helping process is born from the need to understand the roots of the request for services, to define goals and expected results, and to intervene with appropriate resources. The service delivery is oriented to each person's uniqueness and assumes that all the persons in each case will have responsibilities in the attainment of expected results. The focus is on competencies and abilities, not on insufficiencies and problems. The recognition of abilities, in fact, is the basis for turning the situation into a negotiated path that leads the person to the resolution of her or his need. Such an approach recognizes the necessity of personalized planning and implies a commitment between practitioner and consumer that is supported by organizational resources and by a network of professionals in which the consumer is included.

In the process of delivering the service, an information system can be designed to document each stage; for example:

- the requests;
- the synthesis of the social and health conditions before the intervention;

- the analysis of subjects and resources;
- the hypothesis about the problem in general and in its specific components;
- the general goals and the specific expected objectives;
- the contract between the person and the service;
- the intervention planning and its implementation;
- the condition of person/family after interventions; and
- the assessment and evaluation of the quality of the process and its outcome.

APPLICATION

We tested the helping process described above in three areas—children, adults, and elderly people—of the social and health service systems. The test included more than two hundred cases comprising

- territorial services (e.g., social work in the district, in urban, or in suburban areas; home care services for elderly people or for families with many problems; services for children);
- semiresidential services (e.g., daytime services for disabled people); and
- residential services for children or elderly people (e.g., residential communities, institutes).

The results and considerations described in this chapter refer to an experiment implemented in a town in northern Italy. The experiment involved both territory-based and residential services. The number of cases analyzed for the present study was thirty-seven. Professionals such as social workers, family doctors, and nurses were involved.

WHAT WE LEARNED[1]

A variety of issues were addressed in the course of planning the evaluation, as discussed in the following section.

Documenting the Helping Process

It is necessary to maintain an information system that correlates the health condition before, during, and after the intervention. The information system must measure the change that occurred after the provision of services, with regard to the expected results. A good information system allows the evaluation of obtained results, highlighting the different sources of information: practitioners, consumers, relatives, families, volunteers, and others. Designing and clarifying the information system helps in facilitating the access to services, the preliminary assessment rules, the economic assignments, and the evaluation (Diomede Canevini, 1993; Fasolo, 1993; Vecchiato, 1995).

Request for Service and Assignment of Responsibilities

The request for service made by the person must not be confused with the problems connected with it. If the planning is focused only on delivering services, the preliminary assessment of the need/problem will be inaccurate and it will merely

conform to the literal request made by the consumer, without verifying its reliability or exploring other relevant concerns.

The information gathered on the request must be recorded as formulated by the
person. Then the request can be used to compare it with information that emerges
through interviews or other forms of qualitative analysis. On the basis of available
information, we formulate the participation of consumers, relatives, services
providers, and others in the helping process. We should note that consumers and
resources are *real* when they assume their responsibilities and are involved in the
project; they are *potential* when they are not yet available to do something but
might eventually be involved.

Care-Giving Card

The analysis of the request reconstructs the determinants of the problem, on a
personal and family basis, and must be documented in the *care-giving card*. It
gathers all information—health, social, etc.—necessary for defining the problem.
In this way, it becomes a synthesis of the personalized project history.

The following information can be useful:

- who is requesting care;
- expressed needs or required interventions;
- problems and their characteristics;
- person's history, including in particular:
  —psychological and physical condition;
  —personal resources and abilities;
  —lack of independent activity;
  —economic abilities;
  —housing condition;
  —awareness about the problem; and
- people close to the person who is the focus of help (family, friends, etc.).

Defining the Problem

This is the stage in which the needs are interpreted with the aim of finding possible solutions. Discussing and sharing these possibilities means moving toward a
shared solution. Defining the problem becomes an *interpretation* of reality as re-
constructed by all involved parties.

If the work has been carefully documented, details may emerge that are contra-
dictory and it will be necessary to synthesize them. This can be done through a
data summary that highlights actions, capabilities, competencies, and limitations
of the person together with her or his interests and potentialities. In this stage,
the person's history needs to be understood in order to plan the personalized
intervention.

The Contract

The contract between the person and the service that is taking care of the case
is an important element of the process.[2] It can be an oral or a formal agreement.
In any case it must be considered a pact among the consumer, the family, and the

service. The negotiation process is not work *on* or *for* the person but *with* the person in order to address the difficulties. If there is no contract, a clear basis for achieving the expected results does not exist. The contract should specify objectives in relation to each problem. Each goal must be described in order to specify the result expected at the conclusion of a particular intervention (Maluccio, 2002).

Planning and Implementing Interventions

For each problem there is a specific service delivery or operational plan. The interventions need to specify a time frame, and all subjects and resources must be involved in the operational plan. The latter is an important part of the contract; it is its most tangible part because it can be shared with—and eventually undersigned—by the person and the family. For each intervention it is important to indicate who carries out the intervention, its frequency, and its length in time.

Evaluation of the Plan and the Case

The service delivery plan is monitored to determine if the interventions were implemented as planned. Moreover, it is checked not only at the end of the project, but also at critical points throughout the process of intervention. Indeed, the evaluation process in each case begins *before* the intervention when, on the basis of the preliminary analysis of the request, the problem is defined and services are planned. Evaluation continues as the intervention proceeds. It closes with the evaluation of effectiveness of the project (Blythe, Tripodi, Fasolo, & Ongaro, 1993).

The professional and/or colleagues define the measurable factors that describe the different dimensions of the problem. This will permit early measurements and subsequent evaluations. This depends on

- the nature of the problem;
- the professional, organizational, economic and technological resources; and
- the context in which service is provided.

If the goal is shared with the person and with service providers, it is possible to select result indicators that can document the implementation of the project. In selecting the indicators, attention must be devoted to strengths as well as weaknesses, with regard to the different responsibilities of the person, services, and others.

Termination of the Case

At the termination of the operational plan, the situation of the person is described. In doing so the project-group needs to answer the following questions:

- Have the interventions matched the goals?
- Did the interventions improve the person's quality of life?
- Did the interventions match the person's request?
- Was the contract respected?
- Was the helping process performed with regard for the person's rights?

- Is the project-group satisfied with the helping process and its results?
- Did the consumer share the evaluation process and is he/she satisfied with the obtained results?

Another important question to answer is whether the problem still exists. If so, it is necessary to define a new case.

Evaluating Effectiveness

Evaluating effectiveness means verifying whether the expected results, as defined at the beginning of the process, have been reached at the end of it. Effectiveness can be measured in case of positive outcomes; negative results should be highlighted before the termination of the project in order to redefine the process and its results (Liberati & Donati, 1996). Some negative outcomes can result from the following situations:

- *How the intervention is implemented.* It is possible to obtain results lower than expectations when the consumer/family does not consider the intervention valid. This may happen when the contract is not negotiated or when the information does not circulate among all subjects involved. Also it may happen when the relationships between consumer and practitioners is not positive: in this case it is important to understand motivations and ways of overcoming the difficulties.
- *If the conditions with the consumer change.* In that situation the planning needs to be revised, since maintaining the original contract would not be appropriate.
- Sometimes *objectives are too ambitious.* In this case the level of expectations is greater than the person's abilities and this will create tensions or contrary effects.
- In some cases the *objectives are lower* than the real capacities of the person and this can depress and discourage the person.
- The results can be different from the expected ones because the *hypothesis definition was incorrect.* The project-group could have underestimated some aspects related to physical conditions, psychological factors, or other issues. An incorrect hypothesis in the problem definition can also result from insufficient information.

CONCLUSION

The project considered in this chapter helped set up the conditions for evaluation of effectiveness in practice. In particular, it confirmed the importance of documenting the helping process in each stage rather than waiting until the end. Such documentation is a useful means of supporting practitioners' decisions through evidence-based guidelines (Sarpellon & Vecchiato, 1993; Vecchiato, 2000). Evaluation can help to focus the attention of practitioners on the person in need and promote the relevance and quality of interventions following a flexible planning process.

NOTES

1. For application of the consumer-practitioner contract in the human services, see Maluccio (2002).
2. For discussion of related evaluation approaches in family and children's services, see Chapter 3 by Chaskin and Chapter 10 by Wright & Paget in this volume.

REFERENCES

Blythe, B. J., Tripodi, T., Fasolo, E., & Ongaro, F. (1993). *Metodi di misurazione nelle attivitá di servizio sociale a diretto contatto con l'utenza*. Padova, Italy: Fondazione "E. Zancan."

Diomede Canevini, M. (Ed.) (1993). *Documentazione professionale e valutazione degli interventi*. Padova, Italy: Fondazione "E. Zancan."

Fasolo, E. (1993). Misurare gli interventi: Le ragioni e il come. In Diomede Canevini, M. (Ed.), *Documentazione professionale e valutazione degli interventi* (pp. 67–80). Padova, Italy: Fondazione "E. Zancan."

Liberati, A. & Donati, C. (Eds.) (1996). Raccomandazioni per la promozione, disseminazione ed implementazione di linee-guida di comportamento pratico. *QA* 7(2; June): 77–95.

Maluccio, A. N. (2002). Revisiting the "Case for the Contract." *Reflections: Narratives of Professional Helping,* 8:56–68.

Pompei, A., Costanzi, C., & Risso, A. (Eds.) (2000). *Il lavoro per progetti individualizzati. Linee guida per chi opera al servizio delle persone anziane*, Padova, Italy: Fondazione "E. Zancan."

Rose, W. (2002). Achieving better outcomes for children and families by improving assessment of need. In T. Vecchiato, A. N. Maluccio, & C. Canali (Eds.), *Evalution in Child and Family Services: Comparative Client and Program Perspectives*. Hawthorne, NY: Aldine de Gruyter.

Sarpellon, G. & Vecchiato, T. (Eds.) (1993). *Le frontiere del sociale. Primo rapporto*. Padova, Italy: Fondazione "E. Zancan."

Vecchiato, T. (Ed.) (1995). *La valutazione dei servizi socio-sanitari*. Padova, Italy: Fondazione "E. Zancan."

Vecchiato, T. (Ed.) (2000). *La valutazione della qualitá nei servizi. Metodi, tecniche, esperienze*. Padova, Italy: Fondazione "E. Zancan."

9

Outcomes Are Dependent on Inputs

Does Risk Assessment Inform Service Delivery?

Maryanne Berry and Scottye J. Cash

Public child welfare agencies are charged with the prevention and treatment of child abuse, with the priority of preserving families while keeping children safe (Barth & Berry, 1994). Achieving such a complex objective requires a sound knowledge base of risks associated with child abuse and neglect; the resources, services, and skills associated with adequate parenting and family well-being; and a strong practice base of the service techniques and programs that are effective in a variety of circumstances, cultures, and populations. Services to prevent child abuse and neglect have been criticized as a "one size fits all" model of service de-livery, in that all parents reported for abuse or neglect typically receive the same package of treatment services. Recent service models, however, are based on the premise that families differ in the risks they present and that services must be in-dividually tailored to these different risks to achieve positive outcomes. This prem-ise has not been sufficiently tested.

This chapter therefore describes a study in the United States through which we examined (1) whether risks differ across families served by a public sector child abuse program; (2) whether service provision differs across families served; and (3) whether family risks are indeed predictive of services provided.

BACKGROUND

Certainly, parents and families need to possess particular skills and resources in order to sustain and nurture their members. Child abuse and neglect are related to poor parenting skills, parental depression, family stress, economic hardship, and other characteristics and conditions (McDonald & Marks, 1991). Many studies have also identified social isolation as a key correlate of child maltreatment (Brunk, Henggeler & Whelan, 1987; Darmstadt, 1990; Leifer, Shapiro & Kassem, 1993; Strauss, 1980; Zuravin and Greif, 1989). Research is also identifying ob-servable outcomes of child abuse and neglect, including evidence that child neg-lect can result in a 20 percent reduction in brain size when children have been severely neglected in infancy (Perry, 1996).

The importance of effectively preventing or treating child abuse and neglect in families is established. Not all families, however, have the same combination or configuration of risks and service needs. Risk assessment is an important initial step in services to families, as agencies investigate the severity of the risk to the maltreated child and the presence or absence of specific resources and risks in the family and household. A detailed risk assessment instrument is completed for every family who is served by the child protective services agency under study. This risk assessment provides a means for prioritizing cases and is intended to lead naturally to the development of an individualized service plan for each family, based on its specific risks and needs.

Concurrent with the development and refinement of methods of assessing risk in families, treatment options for maltreating families have evolved as well. Service agencies charged with the prevention and treatment of child maltreatment (both child abuse and neglect) have developed a substantial repertoire of treatment strategies to ameliorate these risks over the past two decades, since the Child Abuse Prevention and Treatment Act of 1978 in the United States. These strategies have been categorized as clinical and concrete services (Feldman, 1991) and range from individual counseling of parents and children, family counseling, parent effectiveness training, and social support and psychoeducational group treatment to case management and brokering of concrete services, such as financial aid, housing, and legal assistance.

Intensive family preservation services are one form of service in the continuum of child protective and family welfare services. These services are labor-intensive and time-limited. The hallmarks of this program model include small caseloads, intensity of service time and effort, individualized service plans that are relevant to families' needs, a home-based approach, delivering as many services on-site as possible, and a dual focus on concrete services and clinical techniques (Kinney, Haapala, & Booth, 1991). Given the extreme intensity and individualization of services, such treatment is usually restricted to those families at greatest and most imminent risk of having their child(ren) placed into foster care. Individualization of the services provided is intended to ameliorate the specific risks that brought the family to this most dire and urgent state (Berry, 1992, 1997).

At the time of a family's introduction to the child welfare agency for services, usually at investigation of a report of child maltreatment, caseworkers conduct a risk assessment of the family and its situation. The process of risk assessment, at its most fundamental, is intended to determine the likelihood that a child will be maltreated in the future. In its more generic and popular form, however, it is an inventory of the risks and resources bringing the family to the attention of the agency so as to inform practice decisions (Doueck, Bronson, & Levine, 1992; Pecora, 1991).

So what is the pragmatic use of risk assessment? Is it performed as a simple screen in order to prioritize the cases to be opened and with the greatest urgency? Or is it an initial assessment of family conditions, characteristics, and complaints intended to inform case planning and service delivery? A logical progression model of practice (Alter & Egan, 1997) would indicate that an assessment of risks (and resources) would do both: it would inform case planning by identifying the most urgent families, and ultimately inform both service delivery and the identification of case outcomes [the most meaningful outcomes being those relevant to the specific risks that brought the family to treatment (Cole, 1995)].

Anecdotal and empirical evidence (Doueck et al., 1992; Lyons, Doueck, & Wodarski, 1996) indicates an abrupt and clear distinction between risk assessment (typically performed by telephone maltreatment report responders or by those who investigate reports of maltreatment) and family assessment (typically performed by the caseworker assigned to serve a newly opened or transferred case). This is a troubling distinction, suggesting that services can often "drift" from the original objectives of service: to prevent further child maltreatment.

Researchers in the field of risk assessment have found that the likelihood of future child maltreatment can be somewhat accurately predicted by a very small number of variables (Johnson, 1997; Pecora, 1991; Schuerman, 1994). Johnson (1997) has validated a list of seven parental risk factors predicting the risk of recurrence of child maltreatment. These include poor physical care of children, poor or moderate affect toward children, inability to use agency resources, female gender of primary caretaker, child not living with biological parents, prior abuse history, and four or more children in the home. These risk factors accurately predicted the recurrence of abuse at levels from 60 to 83 percent for different ethnic groups. If these are better-than-fair predictors of risk of maltreatment, then such a list should logically be embedded in practice decisions and case planning, particularly among programs targeted at families at imminent risk of child removal and, logically, child maltreatment.

PURPOSE

The study presented in this chapter provides important information on the match of services to family risk in the reduction of child maltreatment. While the two fields of risk assessment and child abuse treatment strategies have been in concurrent development over the past two decades, their congruence in the delivery of services to maltreating families has been overlooked. The services provided are intended to differ from family to family and be individualized to the strengths and needs of the family (based on a risk assessment). To date, however, only a few studies of services to prevent child abuse have delineated the specific services proffered in any detailed way (Staff & Fein, 1994).

Much of the basis of current risk assessment practice is the hypothesis that a thorough assessment of the strengths and risks present in a family will contribute to the more effective delivery of services, that is, services that are individualized to family need. This study will examine whether risks differ across families, whether service provision differs across families, and whether services are indeed matched to family risks. If the study finds that all families present the same risks at intake, risk assessment procedures in public sector agencies could be significantly streamlined. More importantly, if all families receive the same services, regardless of risk, then a fundamental premise of the purpose of assessment is being ignored.

METHOD

This study is a process and outcome evaluation in a large public child welfare agency. In that the overarching goal was to identify whether the risk assessment process played a meaningful role in the delivery of services, and ultimately case outcomes, the evaluator followed a utilization-focused model in its development (Patton, 1997). While most evaluation research in the field of family preservation has focused on family and problem characteristics improved by services, few have focused on specific service characteristics and fewer still have emphasized the utility of findings regarding best practice (Blythe, Salley, & Jayaratne, 1994; NASW News, 1998). The specific research question was, therefore, Do risk factors predict service delivery? In other words, Are the services delivered matched to the risks bringing the family to the agency?

Site

The agency that is the focus of this study is the Intensive Family Preservation Unit within a large metropolitan child protective services agency. This unit has the following objectives:

- to protect the child from an immediate or short-term danger of abuse or neglect;
- to help the parents build on family strengths and resources in order to reduce the risk of abuse or neglect; and
- to enable the family to ensure the child's safety without child protective service assistance after the case is closed.

Participation in the program can include working with the caseworker in the home as needed, going to individual therapy, participating in group therapy, and other activities as negotiated by the family and worker together.

Sample

The sample of the study is comprised of all families that were served by the Intensive Family Preservation Unit. The sampling frame was the following: the case must have been opened in the unit on or after May 1, 1996, and before March 1, 1997, resulting in a ten-month sampling frame for cases. All cases included in the sample were closed by August 31, 1997. This resulted in a final sample of fifty-three cases.

Eligibility for Services. The Intensive Family Preservation Unit receives referrals from the Child Protective Services Units, through (1) regular child protective services caseworkers, (2) intake/investigation child protective services caseworkers, (3) other child protective services regions in the state (in the event that the family has recently moved to this region), or (4) the court system. Families that are served by the Intensive Family Preservation Unit are believed to be at *imminent risk* of having the child removed from the home. *Imminent risk* is assessed by the intake/investigation worker or the regular child protective services worker, the intensive family preservation supervisor, and the assistant district attorney. The unit accepts the case based on the following criteria: at least one child is at risk of removal from the home; intensive services are likely to protect the family's children from abuse or neglect in the immediate or short-term future; the family is willing and able to participate in the services; the objectives in the referral are likely to be achieved in 60 to 120 days; and the public agency is not the possessory or managing conservator of any child in the family.

The family preservation caseworker and family preservation supervisor make the final decision regarding whether the complexity of a family's problems can be met through the services that the intensive family preservation program can offer. Exclusionary criteria can include parental substance abuse; the parent or primary caretaker is psychotic or mentally retarded; there is a history of sadistic abuse; or in the case of sexual abuse, the perpetrator is still in the home. In practice, these exclusions are seldom used.

Procedure and Design

This study was a one-group pretest-posttest design. A limitation of this design is the lack of a control or a comparison group. Once the study has established the utility of the instruments developed for this study, particularly the service tracking logs, it is expected that subsequent evaluations will compare the service delivery and outcomes of intensive units and conventional units serving less risky families.

The evaluation is descriptive as well as associational in design. The study described the strengths and stressors present within the family, provided information pertaining to the family's system and the risks that were present within the family identified at intake by the intake/investigation worker, described the services (concrete and clinical) provided, and documented the amount of time spent with each family. The study also examined the relationships between client characteristics and risks and subsequent service provision.

Given the nature of the research questions, a control group is not necessary; this study does not seek to establish treatment efficacy over other approaches. Ongoing research and analysis will examine the relationships of client characteristics and services to a range of case outcomes, but these are not discussed here.

Measures

A fundamental principle of this study of services was to utilize the large amount of information already gathered in the state management information system to the extent possible, so as to (1) avoid unnecessary burdening of caseworkers with additional paperwork and (2) identify for personnel the "marker" variables in a massive set of case data that are critical predictors of case outcomes.

Each case provided information on both client characteristics and service characteristics and case outcomes. Several of the data collection forms used to obtain

information related to client characteristics were already in place in the large number of Management Information Systems (MIS) case-tracking forms that are standard for public agency cases in this state. Other forms were introduced by the
researcher to obtain additional information on risks and service characteristics.

Client Characteristics.   Much of the information on clients was gathered from
that collected by caseworkers in the process of keeping case tracking forms on
standard state MIS forms. This information was categorized by the researchers
into the following classes of information:

- *demographic information* included household composition, geographic location of the household, and age and sex of each family member;
- *nature and severity of the presenting maltreatment* included type(s) of
  abuse, the abuser's sex and relationship to the victim(s), and severity of
  abuse;
- *family resources* included personal qualities and abilities of parents and
  children, knowledge and skill levels, social supports available, and income
  and material resources; and
- family stressors included history and chronicity of stressors (including child
  abuse), environmental stressors, and compounding problems such as drug
  use, etc. (see Table 9.1 in a later section). The information gathered on these
  preexisting forms is recorded by all child protective service units.[1]

Service Characteristics.   Information related to service characteristics was
gathered on three forms: the Client Contact Log, the Concrete Services Log, and
the Clinical Services Log, all developed for this study.[2] The Client Contact Log
tracks structural elements of the service: the amount of time the caseworker
spends in person with the family at a variety of locations (home, in the Intensive
Family Preservation Unit, in a support group, in another agency, and in the car).
The Client Contact Log also tracks the time spent on the phone, with the family,
with other agencies involved with the family, and with the school system. Finally,
this log assesses how much time the worker spends on paperwork, in staffings, and
in supervision. Each of the categories is measured in minutes per family, per day,
and then totaled at the end of the month, providing a total and an itemized accounting of time spent on each case, in minutes. This form also provides the date
the case was opened and closed to the Intensive Family Preservation Unit.

The remaining two service logs address the nature of services. The purchase of
the Concrete Services Log is to record nonclinical services or resources provided
to the family. The categories include parenting, financial, transportation, home,
bills, food, child care, moving, cleaning, medical, job, and recreation. Rather than
measuring the nature of services in increments of time (a structural detail), concrete services and resources were recorded in terms of incidents, with a checkmark
each time the worker utilized a specific approach. A complete listing of the oper-
ationalization of each of these categories was supplied to caseworkers in a set of
coding instructions with each form.

Table 9.1. Family Stressors[a,b]

	Total ($n = 53$)
History/Stress	
Abused or neglected as a child	60.4
Lack of education	47.2
Absence of burden sharing	34.6
Crisis lifestyle	25.0
Marital conflict	25.0
Health problems	17.0
Unable to form positive relationships	11.3
Diagnosed mentally ill	5.7
Environmental Stressors	
Single parent	57.7
Inadequate income	53.8
Housing problems	51.9
Recently moved	44.2
Young, immature parents	44.2
Several preschool children	36.5
Socially isolated	18.9
Unsupportive extended family	13.5
Compounding Problems	
Low self-esteem	47.2
Generalized anger	37.7
Victim of spouse abuse	32.1
Apathy or low energy	30.2
Codependent behavior	26.4
Drug or alcohol use	24.5
Criminal involvement	20.8
Irrational behavior	17.0
Perpetrator of spouse abuse	13.2
Parenting Issues	
Ignorance of child development	77.4
Inappropriate expectations	34.0
Inappropriate discipline	26.4
Unrealistic or rigid	26.4
Insensitive to child's needs	20.8
Failure to meet basic needs	18.9
Aversion to the demands of parenting	15.1
Lack of attachment	9.4

[a]Percentage of families for whom stressor is marked Yes.
[b]Multiple response.

The Clinical Services Log includes information on the types of clinical services that are provided by the intensive family preservation workers. The categories are broken into different theoretical frameworks of work with families; they include: client-centered, cognitive-behavioral, behavioral, problem-solving, psychodynamic, psychosocial, Adlerian, experiential, communicative, structural, and "other." The "other" category is used in case a worker utilizes a therapeutic modality that is not listed on the log. If the worker used a different therapy from those listed, he or she was asked to define the therapy and describe the technique used.

A limitation of this form is that many of the workers' activities borrow or combine techniques from a range of therapies. In order to increase the reliability of the form, during instrument development family preservation and family reunification workers were asked to describe the types of techniques that they use and these were then placed under the theoretical framework that was congruent with those techniques. Subsequent refinement and training resulted in a measurement instrument and training session for all caseworkers. In a codebook provided to each caseworker, each category was operationalized as to its theoretical background as well as techniques associated with the theoretical background. The development of these service-tracking instruments took several months of meetings with staff, followed by months for pilot testing and refinement. Program staff participated in all aspects of development and testing of the service logs.

DESCRIPTION OF FAMILIES AND SERVICES

Demographic Characteristics of Children and Families

The demographic characteristics of children and families that were served by the Intensive Family Preservation Unit were examined. The average age of mothers was twenty-four years old, and 40 percent of the sample consisted of single-mother-headed households (although a larger number of families were reported as single-mother-headed households elsewhere in the case records). Almost 40 percent of the mothers were married and 20 percent were cohabiting. For 18 percent of the sample, the mother's marital status was unspecified.

The presence of economic impoverishment is evident in this sample; two-thirds of the families reported an income below $9,000 a year. Another 18 percent of the families had an annual income between $9,000 and $17,999. Families with an income between $18,000 and $33,999 a year comprised 14 percent of the sample, and the remaining 2 percent of the families had an income between $34,000 and $64,000 a year. Information on the level of income achieved by families was obtained for forty-four of the fifty-three families in the sample.

The average number of children per family was two and the vast majority of the families in the sample (89 percent) had three or fewer children in the household. Fifty-seven percent of the children were female. The ethnicity of the oldest child was predominantly Anglo (68 percent), 16 percent were African-American, 9 percent Hispanic, and 2 percent Asian American. These proportions are comparable to those in the metropolitan area served. For the remaining 5 percent of the sample, the oldest child's ethnicity was unreported.

Nature of Maltreatment

There was some variation in the type of maltreatment for which the family was reported. A little over 40 percent of the families were reported for physical abuse

(43 percent). Over one-third of the families were reported for neglect (34 percent), including medical neglect, physical neglect, and neglectful supervision, and almost 10 percent for both physical abuse and neglect combined. Only 4 percent were reported for sexual abuse. For almost 10 percent, the type of abuse was unspecified. Caseworkers determined that the motivation for the maltreatment was often that the parent lost control (25 percent), that this was an act of omission (25 percent), a result of lack of knowledge (25 percent), or a failed attempt to discipline the child (23 percent).

There is also information on the relationship of the abuser in the household to the oldest victim; there could be more than one abuser in the household. In 92 percent of the cases served, the mother was an abuser; the father was an abuser in 45 percent of the cases; and the stepfather was an abuser in 6 percent of the cases. The parent's paramour (gender unknown) was an abuser in 8 percent of the cases and in approximately 3 percent of the cases an abuser was an unrelated household member. For the remaining 32 percent of the cases, the abuser's relationship to the oldest victim was unspecified.

Despite the designation of imminent risk of placement as a criterion for program participation, only 66 percent of the families were reported to be at imminent risk of having their child placed outside the home. Imminent risk was much more likely for neglect cases than for physical abuse cases.

At the end of treatment, and at a one-year follow-up assessment, most families that had experienced the placement of a child or children into foster care were those who were reported for child neglect, rather than child abuse. Child placement was not related to the designation of imminent risk of placement, nor was placement more likely for families with a single parent or of low family income.

Family Strengths and Supports

A family's strengths and supports include the personal qualities of parents and parent figures, knowledge and skills, social supports, income and material resources, and the child's characteristics. The caseworker, rather than the family, rated each of these attributes following an assessment interview in the home. Families were uniformly perceived by caseworkers to have multiple strengths. A little over 90 percent of the families were seen as cooperative. Over three-fourths of the families were perceived to be able to give and accept affection (79 percent), able to form healthy attachments (77 percent), wanting to make changes (77 percent), and open to new ideas (74 percent).

Approximately two-thirds of the families were aware of their problems (68 percent) and accepted responsibility for the child's maltreatment (66 percent). Workers reported that half of the families had a history of adequate functioning (51 percent) but only 36 percent had a positive image of themselves. Only 28 percent of the families were reported to have effective coping skills. Families were also assessed as to their knowledge and skills. Sixty percent of the families were reported to be able to solve problems. Specifically in relation to the children in the family,

43 percent were able to accept differences in their children while only 23 percent of families had knowledge of child development as a strength.

The caseworker also assessed a family's social support system in relation to the family's strengths and support. Sixty-six percent of families had a support system in place and almost 50 percent of families had positive relationships with people outside their family. External support systems were no more or less likely for single mothers.

Caseworkers reported that two-thirds of the families in the sample were able to meet basic material needs and approximately 60 percent of the families were able to manage income and resources. Reliability checks on the data showed that an assessment of the ability to meet basic needs was indeed related to a higher reported family income, and an assessment of housing problems was related to a lower income.

The caseworker also reported on the children's characteristics. For the purpose of this study, information on the oldest victim in the family is described. Children were not perceived to have as many strengths as were parents. Workers perceived that almost three-quarters of the children were able to form healthy attachments. Only one-third of the children, however, were able to accept limits and direction and/or were considered to be assertive. Twenty percent of the children had a positive self-image and almost 19 percent of the children had respect for self and others. Nine percent of the children were considered to be self-disciplined. However, it should be noted that a child's age was not taken into consideration when a worker determined if a child had a particular characteristic. For example, if an infant was the oldest victim, he or she, more than likely, would not be determined to be assertive.

Family Stressors and Risk Factors

The stressors that were present within a family were also assessed and rated by the caseworker. The family's stressors were organized around the following domains: history/personal stress, environmental stressors, compounding problems, and parenting issues (see Table 9.1).

A majority of the families had at least one adult family member who had been abused or neglected as a child (60 percent). Workers reported that almost half of the families lacked formal education and a little over a third experienced an absence of burden sharing in the home. A quarter of the families reported that they experienced marital conflict and/or had a crisis lifestyle. Crisis lifestyles were significantly more likely among families reported for child neglect. Eleven percent of the families were regarded as unable to form positive relationships. Only 6 percent of the families had a member who was diagnosed as mentally ill and no families had a member who was mentally retarded.

Families experienced a variety of environmental stressors as well. Over half of the families were single parent families (58 percent) and had an inadequate income (54 percent) or housing problems (52 percent). Forty-four percent of the families reported that they had recently moved and 44 percent of the families were considered to have young, immature parents; over a third of the families were stressed by several preschool children in the home. Social isolation was prevalent in 19 percent of the families. Thirteen percent of the families had nonsupportive extended family.

There was considerable variation in the type of compounding problems experienced by the families in the sample. Almost half of the families were assessed to have problems with low self-esteem; over a third experienced generalized anger; and just under a third were considered apathetic. Thirty-two percent of the families reported that they were a victim of spouse abuse and in 13 percent of the families, there was a perpetrator of spousal abuse in the home. Twenty-six percent of the families were assessed to exhibit codependent behaviors and 17 percent exhibited irrational behaviors. Twenty-one percent of the families had at least one member who participated in criminal activities, and almost a quarter of the families had some form of drug or alcohol use (despite drug use being an exclusionary criterion for service).

Parents were also assessed as to their parenting skills. Workers reported that 77 percent of families ignored or were not aware of child development issues. Other parenting challenges were not as common. Thirty-four percent of families had inappropriate expectations for their children; 26 percent of families used inappropriate discipline and/or were considered to be unrealistic or rigid in their parenting. Inappropriate discipline was significantly more likely when the family was reported for physical abuse. Eighteen percent of families failed to meet the basic needs of their children and 15 percent of families were characterized as having an aversion to the demands of parenting. Attachment difficulties were very rare; a little under 10 percent of families lacked attachment to one or more of their children.

Information on the oldest child victim was also reported by caseworkers. The characteristics of children thought to contribute to the stress experienced by the family included developmental delays (21 percent), health problems (15 percent), learning problems (8 percent), physical limitations (4 percent), drug-affected birth (2 percent), and mental retardation (2 percent). The behavioral problem of acting out was displayed by only 8 percent of the children.

Service Characteristics: Structure of Services

Information on what is considered the "black box" of services (Staff & Fein, 1994) was gathered. The structure of service delivery (i.e., days open, time spent per case, service intensity) was gathered on the 53 cases in the sample. The mean number of days cases were open was 124 days (17 weeks or 4 months), with an average total time expenditure of 60.28 hours per case (see Table 9.2). This is equivalent to an average of approximately 30 minutes of time spent per day on each case (which includes time spent in person with the family, on the phone with the family or with collaterals, or agency paperwork, staffing, and supervision).

Table 9.2.   Service Characteristics (Time)

	Total (n = 53)
Service Characteristic	
Mean number of days open (days)	124.0
Mean total time served (hours)	60.28
Service intensity-average time per day (minutes)	33
Mean time spent per month overall (hours)	15.41
Mean time (hours) spent in:	
Month 1 (n = 53)	14.13
Month 2 (n = 48)	16.41
Month 3 (n = 41)	15.96
Month 4 (n = 33)	15.14
Month 5 (n = 19)	14.69
Month 6 (n = 12)	13.57
Month 7 (n = 4)	10.42
Month 8 (n = 2)	8.3
Month 9 (n = 1)	4.0
Case closed within (%):	
1 month	11.4
2 months	7.5
3 months	7.5
4 months	24.5
5 months	24.5
6 months	11.4
7 months	7.5
8 months	3.8
9 months	1.9
Mean proportion (%) of time spent:	
In person	74.0
By phone	14.0
In agency	12.0
Mean proportion (%) of time spent in the home	35.0
Contact by phone (total hours)	
Family	4.14
Agency	2.50
School	0.22
Mean total contact (hours) by phone	6.87
Contact in person (hours)	
At client's home	19.82
In office	1.86
In support group	11.12
At another agency	7.83
In car	6.87
Mean total contact (hours) in person	47.52
Agency coordination (hours)	
Paperwork	5.89
Staffing	1.09
Supervision	0.27
Mean total agency time (hours)	7.26

Fifty percent of the cases were closed within four months, the recommended length of service in this family preservation program. Within five months of case opening, three-fourths of the cases were closed. The remaining fourth of the cases was closed by the ninth month. Table 9.2 also presents the average amount of time spent each month of a case. For the average length of time a case was open (approximately 4 months) the average time per month was 15.41 hours. This intensity remained fairly consistent during the first five months of treatment. Toward later months in a case, services became less intensive.

The method of contact as well as the amount of time per contact was also computed. For example, the mean total contact by phone was 6.87 hours. Workers averaged 4.14 hours of contact to the family by phone, 2.5 hours of phone contact to other agencies, and 0.22 hours of contact with the schools. The in-person contact was considerably higher, with an average of 47.52 hours of direct contact between worker and family. Approximately 19 hours of contact were in the client's home, while only 1.86 hours were in the office. Eleven hours of contact were while the client attended one of the psychoeducational groups offered by the agency. Workers had direct contact with families while visiting other agencies an average of 7.83 hours and in the car an average of 6.87 hours.

Finally, the average amount of time workers spent away from the family (doing paperwork, staffing a case, or in supervision) was 7.26 hours per case. The majority of this time was spent doing paperwork (5.89 hours), followed by time spent with other workers discussing a case (1.09 hours). The least amount of worker time was spent receiving case supervision (0.27 hours).

In addition to actual hours spent on each case, the proportion of time spent with the family in person and by telephone was also calculated. On average, workers spent almost three-fourths of their time in person with the family, with 35 percent of that in the family's home. Another 14 percent was spent on the phone either with the family or with collaterals, and the remaining 12 percent of the time spent was doing agency-based work.

Service Characteristics: Nature of Services

Congruent with the nature of intensive family preservation models, a variety of services was provided to families in the program. Services were characterized as clinical skills and concrete services. Clinical skills were categorized according to their theoretical perspective, and workers were expected to use multiple clinical skills and multiple concrete services per contact. Contacts were not measured in terms of time, but in terms of the number of contacts utilizing that service.

Clinical Skills. Client-centered skills were utilized by caseworkers with the greatest frequency, at an average of 22 contacts per family, and were provided to 96 percent of the families receiving services (see Table 9.3). Problem-solving skills were used with 100 percent of the families and averaged 16 such contacts per family. The other clinical skills were not used with the same frequency as client-centered or problem-solving skills; as is illustrated in Table 9.3, but a wide

Table 9.3. Service Characteristics (Type) (*n* = 53)

	Total contacts	Families Receiving (%)
Clinical Skills[a]		
Client-centered	21.75	96.2
Problem solving	15.67	100.0
Cognitive behavioral	7.89	88.7
Psychosocial	7.53	81.1
Behavioral	7.06	83.0
Psychodynamic	4.13	73.6
Communicative	2.62	67.9
Structural	1.94	43.4
Adlerian	1.52	43.4
Experiential	1.47	35.8
Concrete Services[a]		
Parenting	6.18	59.6
Transport	4.58	63.8
Child care	2.80	51.1
Food	1.58	46.8
Medical	1.42	29.8
Financial	1.24	42.6
Home	0.44	17.0
Bills	0.40	19.1
Move	0.24	8.5
Recreation	0.22	12.8
Clean	0.12	8.5
Job	0.10	10.6

[a] Multiple response.

variety of clinical skills was used with families. Cognitive-behavioral techniques were provided an average of 8 times, with 89 percent of the families experiencing this worker skill. Psychosocial and behavioral techniques were used an average of 8 and 7 times, respectively, and were provided to over 80 percent of the families. Structural, Adlerian, and experiential techniques had the lowest frequency of provision and were only used with 36 to 43 percent of the families served.

Concrete Resources.   A variety of concrete services were provided to the families as well. The number of concrete services provided, however, was considerably lower than the number of clinical skills used (see Table 9.3). As with the clinical approaches, multiple concrete services could be used during one visit, and concrete services were measured in number of contacts rather than the amount of time spent doing each service. Families received more concrete parenting services than other concrete services, and parenting services were provided to almost 60 percent of the families. Concrete services would include the provision of parenting help and other parenting supports, rather than teaching or discussing parenting. Of all

the concrete services offered, transportation services were provided to the majority of the families (64 percent), and families that received transportation services
received an average of 5 such services. Child care was the next most frequently
provided service, with 51 percent of the families receiving it; however, child care
was only provided an average of 3 times per family. Food and financial services
were provided to over 40 percent of the families and an average of 2 times and 1
time, respectively. Medical services were provided an average of 1 time per case,
and only 30 percent of the families received medical services. Home help, bills,
moving, recreation, cleaning, and job services were provided at very small levels
and were each offered to fewer than 20 percent of the families.

FINDINGS

Are Services Differentiated for Families
Presenting Different Risks?

There are few differences in services according to risks. Associational tests
(chi-square and t-tests) were performed to determine associations between risks
and services. Significance levels of tests had to be below .05 to be considered significant and reported here as an association.

The mean number of days a family was served did not differ between abuse
cases and neglect cases. The number of days served was also not related to whether
the family was cooperative, whether the family was socially isolated, or whether
the family had problems with housing, substance abuse, anger control, apathy, or
ignorance of child development.

The amount of time a caseworker spent with a family was not related to the level
of risk present. Nor did total contact time differ between physical abuse cases and
child neglect cases, between single-parent families and couple families, or between those families with or without an adequate income. The intensity of service
(the average amount of service time per day) also did not differ across selected
case characteristics, such as type of maltreatment, level of risk, marital status, income level, parenting skills, self esteem of parent, anger control, or education
level.

There was a significant difference between physical abuse cases and child neglect cases in the proportion of time a caseworker actually spent in the home, as opposed to other sites of service delivery. Physical abuse cases received an average
of 42 percent of case time in the home, while child neglect cases received an average of 27 percent of service time in the home. This may be due to the abundance
of time that neglectful families spend in the agency's support groups designed for
neglectful mothers. The proportion of time spent in the home did not differ by any
other family characteristics, including level of placement risk, level of parenting
skills, or level of income. Supervision (caseworkers' time with the unit supervisor)
and help acquiring food were the only areas where neglect cases received significantly more service time than physical abuse cases.

Clinical skills were provided in differing amounts and did vary with the abilities of the client served. For example, behavioral techniques were seldom used with clients who did not accept responsibility, were not aware of the problem, refused to make changes, or had attachment difficulties. Client-centered techniques were significantly more likely if the client displayed problems with attachment to his or her children.

Concrete services were provided with some relevance to the strengths and needs of the family. For example, parenting help was provided to older mothers and parents exhibiting irrational behavior, good cooperativeness, low self-image, and/or attachment difficulties. Financial services were most likely to be provided for parents who were victims of spousal abuse, mentally ill, in a crisis lifestyle, without the support of extended family, users of drugs or alcohol, single parents, had unstable housing, or were unable to meet the basic needs of their children. Transportation services were significantly more likely if the family had low income and/or experienced child neglect.

DISCUSSION

There are a number of limitations to the structure of this study. First, the sample consists of fifty-three families served in a ten-month period. These are the cases for which there are complete case data, and may therefore overrepresent cooperative/successful families. Because this study is neither intended to be representative of all family preservation programs nor an outcome evaluation, the skewed sample does not affect the validity of the specific research question at issue: do the risk factors present in this sample of families differentiate the services that they received?

Caseworker assessments and reports are the sole source of data for this evaluation. Such a single source for data collection was purposely chosen, in order to identify the key markers in the caseworkers' automated risk assessment system that are most useful to case planning and service delivery. Reliability checks on variables were performed when possible, and most data showed adequate reliability. Some variables, particularly parental marital status, were fairly unreliable, showing different frequencies at different points in data collection.

Intensive family preservation services have a number of key features that distinguish these models of service delivery from other models within child welfare services (and mental health and juvenile justice, for that matter). They are intended to be delivered to families at imminent risk of the placement of their child(ren) into out-of-home care due to such reasons as child abuse or neglect. These services are designed to be short-term and intensive, with caseworkers spending large amounts of time in direct contact with family members, and in the home when at all possible for the best transference of skills. Services are also intended to follow logically from a thorough assessment of the family's strengths and needs, and to be individually tailored to those strengths and needs. It is expected that different families will have different service needs, and service delivery is structured so that caseworkers have the ability to provide only those concrete services and apply only those clinical techniques that are relevant to the problems at hand.

This evaluation found that 66 percent of the families served by this unit were classified as being at imminent risk of child placement, indicating substantial variance from program policy or model parameters. There were few family characteristics at intake that predicted which families were categorized as being at imminent risk of child placement.

The way that services were structured in this unit was fairly faithful to intensive family preservation service models, in that cases were open an average of four months and each case received an average of sixty hours of service time by the caseworker. About three-fourths of service time was spent in direct contact with the family, with one-third of that time spent in the family's home. Services, therefore, do appear to meet the standards of being short-term, intensive, and home-based. Services did not span the usual range of home-based intensive family preservation services (Berry, 1997; Fraser, Pecora, & Haapala, 1991; Kinney et al., 1991), however, in that few families received help with home maintenance, bills and budgeting, moving, recreation, cleaning, and job services, which constitute traditional hallmarks of intensive family preservation services.

Another hallmark of intensive family preservation services is the individualization of services provided to family risks, making this program a prime source of data for a study on the utility of risk assessment. There were some differences in service delivery by risk factor. A home-based approach to services was significantly more common with physical abuse cases than with neglect cases. This may be due in part to the larger amounts of time that caseworkers spent in supervision when child neglect was an issue. While a home focus varied between physical abuse and neglect cases, the intensity of service did not vary. The intensity of service also did not vary with the level of placement risk present in the family. Caseworkers did utilize a variety of clinical techniques and concrete services with families, and this evaluation found that the techniques and services delivered were relevant and individualized to the strengths and needs of each family.

Finally, the findings suggest various implications for service delivery. First, the designation of imminent risk of placement continues to be an enigmatic condition. This study, like others (Fraser et al., 1991; Schuerman et al., 1997), did not find this categorization to be a reliable definition of risk nor a valid predictor of service delivery. While the exercise of determining the risk of placement is a sound one, and the limitation of intensive services to those at highest risk an efficient one, staff and referral sources need continuing support in their understanding of what constitutes an appropriate family for an intensive family preservation unit to serve.

More importantly, the only risk factor of any real utility in this study (in that it predicted the differential delivery of services) was the type of maltreatment present (abuse versus neglect). Families experiencing child neglect continue to require more time to serve, use more concrete and clinical services, and take more supervision time for the workers who serve them (and still experience less successful outcomes, on average).

Service delivery in this program does not appear to be driven by the assessment of risk at intake, but appears to evolve over the life of the case as more information is gathered. Risk assessment itself was not determinant of case planning decisions. Services did not vary significantly across cases, regardless of a number of substantial risk factors.

All of this brings into question the utility of risk assessment, both as a tool for determining overall level of risk (not established in this study) and as a case planning tool (also not established in this study). Clearly, further research is needed to replicate these findings, but the consistency of these findings with prior research (Berry, 1992; Fraser, Pecora, & Haapala, 1991) is disheartening. Child welfare service philosophies undergirding individualized assessment are little more than smoke and mirrors if families are simply provided whatever services are on hand, regardless of actual need. It is only when the services fit the need that families will truly be served.

CONCLUSION

Outcome evaluation research that focuses purely on outcomes relies on the assumption that the families entering the program are homogeneous, that the services provided are relevant and useful, and that the outcomes can be proximally connected to the program itself. Many evaluations of intensive family preservation programs in the United States have found these assumptions to be faulty (Fraser, Pecora & Haapala, 1991; Schuerman, Rzepnicki & Littell, 1998). The findings above were produced by an evaluation that focused on both process and outcomes in an intensive family preservation program. By going beyond the usual crude outcomes often identified (placements, recurrence of maltreatment) and measuring more proximal outcomes as well as service provision, this evaluation was able to more finely examine the interplay of *family risk factors* and *services provision* at intake, during services, and at case closure. The inclusion of measures of risk at intake and of service provision throughout the case will allow researchers to predict case and program outcomes with richer detail and greater accuracy, thus helping practitioners to predict what works best, for whom, and under what circumstances.

NOTES

1.   The agency under study implemented statewide computer automation of their recording system in September, 1996 (halfway through this study). Some of the case-tracking forms and their content changed in the process of automation, with much of the case information now collected in narrative, rather than categorical form. Categorical case information was retrieved and coded by the researchers from these narrative reports, beginning in September 1996.

2.   Available from the senior author.

REFERENCES

Alter, C., & Egan, M. (1997). Logic modelling: A tool for teaching critical thinking in social work practice. *Journal of Social Work Education* 33:85–102.

Barth, R. P., & Berry, M. (1994). Research on the welfare of children under permanency planning. In R. P. Barth, J. D. Berrick, & N. Gilbert (Eds.), *Child Welfare Research Review*. New York: Columbia University Press.

Berry, M. (1992). An evaluation of family preservation services: Fitting agency services to family needs. *Social Work* 37(4):314–21.

Berry, M. (1997). *The Family at Risk: Issues and Trends in Family Preservation Services*. Columbia: University of South Carolina Press.

Blythe, B. J., Salley, M. P., & Jayaratne, S. (1994). A review of intensive family preservation services research. *Social Work Research* 18(4):213–24.

Brunk, M., Henggeler, S. W., & Whelan, J. P. (1987). Comparison of multisystemic therapy and parent training in the brief treatment of child abuse and neglect. *Journal of Consulting and Clinical Psychology* 55:171–78.

Cole, E. S. (1995). Becoming family centered: Child welfare's challenge. *Families in Society* 76(3):163–72.

Darmstadt, G. (1990). Community-based child abuse prevention. *Social Work* 35:487–93.

Doueck, H. J., Bronson, D. E., & Levine, M. (1992). Evaluating risk assessment implementation in child protection: Issues for consideration. *Child Abuse and Neglect* 16:637–46.

Feldman, L. (1991). Evaluating the impact of intensive family preservation services in New Jersey. In K. Wells & D. E. Biegel (Eds.), *Family Preservation Services—Research and Evaluation* (pp. 47–71). Newbury Park, CA: Sage.

Fraser, M. W., Pecora, P. J., & Haapala, D. A. (1991). *Families in Crisis: The Impact of Intensive Family Preservation Services*. Hawthorne, NY: Aldine de Gruyter.

Johnson, W. (1997). Validation of a risk assessment inventory. Paper presented to the Children's Bureau National Child Welfare Fellows Institute, Berkeley, California, August 15.

Kinney, J., Haapala, D., & Booth, C. (1991). *Keeping Families Together. The Homebuilders Model*. Hawthorne, NY: Aldine de Gruyter.

Leifer, M., Shapiro, J. P., & Kassem, L. (1993). The impact of maternal history and behavior upon foster placement and adjustment in sexually abused girls. *Child Abuse and Neglect* 17:755–66.

Lyons, P., Doueck, H. J., & Wodarski, J. S. (1996). Risk assessment for child protective services: A review of the empirical literature on instrument performance. *Social Work Research* 20:143–55.

McDonald, T., & Marks, J. (1991). A review of risk factors assessed in child protective services. *Social Service Review* 65:122–32.

NASW News (1998). Researchers cite need for practice link. *NASW News* 43(9, October 1):7.

Patton, M. Q. (1997). *Utilization-Focused Evaluation: The New Century Text* (3d ed.). Thousand Oaks, CA: Sage.

Pecora, P. J. (1991). Investigating allegations of child maltreatment: The strengths and limitations of current risk assessment systems. *Child and Youth Services* 15:73–92.

Perry, B. D. (1996). *Maltreated Children: Experience, Brain Development and the Next Generation*. New York: W.W. Norton.

Schuerman, J. R. (1994). Will computer-based expert systems improve decisions made about children? In E. Gambrill and T. S. Stein (Eds.), *Controversial Issues in Child Welfare* (pp. 109–12). Boston, MA: Allyn and Bacon.

Schuerman, J. R., Rzepnicki, T., & Littell, J. (1998). *Putting Families First*. Hawthorne, NY: Aldine de Gruyter.

Staff, I., & Fein, E. (1994). Inside the black box: An exploration of service delivery in a family reunification program. *Child Welfare* 73(3):195–214.

Strauss, M. A. (1980). Social stress and marital violence in a national sample of American families. *Forensic Psychology and Psychiatry* 347:229–50.

Zuravin, S., and Greif, G. L. (1989). Normative and child-maltreating AFDC mothers. *Social Casework* 70:76–84.

10

A Learning-Organization
Approach to Evaluation

Lois Wright and Kathy Paget

The human services field, including child welfare, has a renewed interest in outcomes, defined as advantages for clients. In fact, in the United States, the federal Adoption and Safe Families Act of 1997 (ASFA) defines specific outcomes for children and families and addresses the need for adequate data systems to document outcomes. Measuring outcomes, however, does not necessarily result in improved services. There must be some connection between processes (what was done) and outcomes. ASFA addresses processes also through a call for innovation to discover better methods of achieving child welfare outcomes. This invites discussions about the relationships between processes and outcomes, and such discussions can be an important step toward integrating evaluation into agency culture.

This chapter draws upon the experience of the Center for Child and Family Studies, College of Social Work, University of South Carolina, to describe how it is using evaluation to broadly influence a public child welfare agency. It addresses current thinking regarding evaluation; the new interest in child welfare outcomes; the center's use of a learning-organization approach to evaluation; how this has redefined the evaluator roles and activities; the special skill of communicating results meaningfully; and challenges and unresolved issues.

EVALUATION AS AN EVOLVING FIELD

Evaluation is an evolving field that is just coming into its own. Though certainly evaluation of social programs has been around for a long time, the 1960s saw increasing interest in the United States. With large public expenditures aimed at reducing social problems during that decade came calls for accountability (Patton, 1997). Both the public and funding agents wanted to know what was working and how well the dollars were spent. But evaluation results largely failed to produce answers to the questions and did not result in improved programming decisions. Ambivalence toward and poor understanding of evaluation were exemplified by two extreme positions. On the one hand were calls for greater methodological rigor—stressing such aspects as experimental designs, quantitative results, validity and reliability, measurability, and generalizability—in reaction to what were viewed as compromised (unscientific) methods. On the other hand funders, though requiring an evaluation component to projects, undermined effective and useful evaluation by limiting the amount of money that could be spent on evaluation. Thus, evaluations were often perfunctory.

By the 1980s, however, social changes from the 1960s challenged our notions of valid research and evaluation. The push toward greater cultural relevance led to new notions of participatory research, in which the participants were involved in every step—from formulating pertinent questions through interpreting and applying findings. Considerable concern was expressed regarding the design and interpretation of research in a manner that captured cultural and individual variation (McCoy, 1983; Rogler, 1989). Jacobs (1988) emphasized the importance of accountability and the representation of multiple perspectives in a process of needs assessment, continual feedback, and clarification in order to ensure the appropriateness of research questions and the relevance of the results. Chavis, Stucky, and Wandersman (1983) referred to the interdependence between scientists and citizens. They suggested that scientists and research consumers need to examine and critique research assumptions and designs from a fresh perspective, consistent with what Wicker (1992:41) referred to as "getting out of conceptual ruts." Tyler, Pargament, and Gatz (1983) described an approach where expert-nonexpert interactions were viewed as a reciprocal process and the resources of all participants were shared. Thus, we began to rethink the relationship between the researcher and participants and to forge new notions of shared ventures generating meaningful information and leading to social change.

In the 1990s came calls for accountability as part of new notions of public management. This was embodied in the Government Performance and Results Act of 1993 (P.L. 103-62), which required all federal programs to develop goals and outcome measures to assess their performance. Within this context a Joint Committee on Standards for Educational Evaluation was tasked with rethinking the role of and standards for evaluation (Patton, 1997). Departing from the prior focus on traditional notions of methodological rigor, the group defined standards in terms "utility, feasibility, propriety, and accuracy" (ibid.:17). The group also formally addressed the issue of objectivity: "Unlike the traditionally aloof stance of basic researchers, evaluators are challenged to take responsibly for use" (ibid.).

As roles and standards continue to be redefined, we struggle with questions such as the following: Once we depart from the widely accepted notions of scientific rigor, what is left? Do we become ipso facto "unscientific"? Is that the right or most relevant question to be addressing? Is a better question whether evaluation accomplishes what it is intended to accomplish? How far can we depart from traditionally understood rigorous research methods and still produce valid results? What does objectivity mean within emerging notions of evaluation?

We at the Center for Child and Family Studies heartily embrace the new notions, which have helped us conceptualize how we support agencies' improving their programming decisions and moving toward better outcomes. However, we believe that caution and continuing self-examination are appropriate as we struggle with some of the tensions between traditional research and the emerging notions of evaluation.

NEW INTEREST IN CHILD WELFARE OUTCOMES

A particular (though not exclusive) focus of evaluation at the center is child welfare programs. Center involvement in evaluation with the state's public child welfare agency, the Department of Social Services (DSS), began as a result of federal legislation (the Family Preservation and Family Support program, part of the Omnibus Budget Reconciliation Act of 1993) directing states to develop five-year child welfare plans and to monitor plan implementation and outcomes. DSS contracted with the center to lead the statewide planning process, and we took a prominent role in evaluation of programs funded through the above act.

Several years later evaluation was reemphasized in the Adoption and Safe Families Act of 1997 (ASFA) (PL 105-89), which asked for a new level of accountability and for positive differences in the lives of children and families. This act unequivocally established that our national goals for children in the child welfare system were safety, permanency, and well-being; clarified that the child welfare system must focus on positive results and accountability, not just on procedural safeguards; required annual reports on state performance in relation to specified outcomes to be defined; and encouraged and provided flexibility to develop innovative strategies to find more effective ways of reaching goals. Thus, the law recognizes that we do not yet have all the solutions to achieve our goals, but it articulates a clear interest in generating solutions and using new knowledge for system improvements [Administration for Children and Families (ACF)—1/8/1998].

Administrative data are essential in helping agencies understand where they are strong or vulnerable and where their services are achieving or failing to achieve desired results, and also suggest areas for policy reconsideration and changes. However, administrative data alone are not apt to produce the kind of information the agency needs to make programmatic and service provision changes. The intent of ASFA was to document not only outcomes but also implementation of programs and services delivery to assist discovery of what works under what conditions and to support developing guidelines for replicability. This places evaluators in a critical position, as they form partnerships with agency staff to jointly embark upon an ongoing program improvement process. As the center has engaged in this process over the past six years, the relevance of a learning-organization approach to evaluation has become increasingly clear.

A LEARNING-ORGANIZATION APPROACH

A learning-organization approach to evaluation is based upon the notion of partnership between individuals who are implementing programs and individuals who are traditionally thought of as evaluators. The heart of the partnership is evaluative enquiry and the goal is to transform organizations into communities of enquirers (Preskill & Torres, 1999). The processes that facilitate evaluative enquiry are "dialogue, reflection, asking questions, and identifying values, beliefs, assumptions, and knowledge" (ibid.:xxiii). This sort of evaluative enquiry is not a substitute for the scientific process but rather a method for implementing it.

At the Center for Child and Family Studies we use the logic model to structure evaluations. It is a tool for thinking, for building relationships, and for guiding the evaluative enquiry. Logic models may take many forms. Figure 10.1 depicts the form used at the center.

The model is consistent with the scientific process and provides a visible focus on the logical connections among components, enabling us to engage others in that scientific process. Thus, it adds a structure to the evaluative enquiry that ensures its scientific integrity.

As we at the center have used the logic model with groups of practitioners and administrators, the processes discussed by Preskill and Torres (1999) have become alive for us and have added a deeper level of understanding to our work of promoting learning in organizations. Table 10.1 shows some of the evaluator roles, skills, and activities that have emerged from our work and depicts how they come into play at phases of the scientific process. The examples shown in the table cells only begin to suggest the complexity of the evaluation process. In reality evaluator activities will shift in unplanned ways during the evaluation, depending upon features of the situation and the individuals involved.

Evaluator Activities Revisited

Clearly, many of the activities listed in Table 10.1 are not those traditionally associated with evaluation. Though evaluators working outside a learning-organization approach may have used these activities, their importance would have been overshadowed by more technical activities (e.g., designing the evaluation and collecting data). A learning-organization approach to evaluation brings them into a place of prominence.

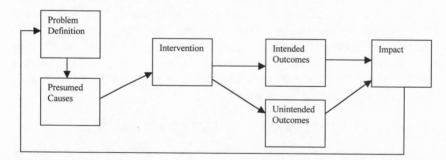

Figure 10.1. Logic model.

Asking Questions, Promoting Conversation.   Evaluation may be seen as ongoing conversation, and the evaluator must be skilled in knowing what questions to ask to sharpen and deepen participants' thinking. It is rare to be called upon to evaluate a program that has been well conceptualized, clearly thought through, and clearly defined. A long period of guided discussion is usually needed to help participants understand why they need greater clarity and to gain that clarity. For example, in a primary prevention program, center evaluators asked probing questions to help agency staff expand their thinking about risk factors in a target population and the implication of these factors for intervention. This was an insight-building process that was necessary for designing a program with integrity and also was effective in taking staff to a new level of thinking and self-awareness.

Forming and Managing Relationships (Conflict Resolution).   Evaluation involves an intense, continuous process of managing relationships with and among people directly involved with the program as well as people who are distant but significant stakeholders (administrators, politicians). Of those directly involved and who meet on a regular basis, differences of opinion and relationship clashes arise, and this impedes forward movement of both the intervention and the evaluation. The evaluator as an external party can help people gain perspective on their differences and see commonalities. For instance, when a local administrator had been told he had absolute authority over an initiative but was also told he had to work with a representative from the state office, the perceived inconsistency in the messages caused tension in the organization as roles and expectations were unclear. In a learning-organization approach, it is important for the evaluator to know how to communicate this problem to the appropriate administrators as well as to manage the conflict to which it gives rise.

Planning.   Most programs are not fully formed, conceptually or operationally, when evaluation begins, even if they have been in existence for some time. When evaluators are called in too late, resources may already have been squandered on poorly planned and fragmented activities. Thus, it is desirable that the evaluators become part of the team from the beginning. This, however, places them squarely amid program planning processes, where they contribute to program design as well as to evaluation. For example, a center evaluator called in to evaluate an existing pregnancy prevention program found that many program activities were unrelated to pregnancy prevention. Thus, much staff effort was being spent on activities that would not have achieved the desired results. The evaluator helped staff reshape the program to the extent possible, weeding out the extraneous activities and focusing the program better. If the evaluator had been called in earlier, he could have prevented many years of wasted effort.

Consulting.   As an agency comes to understand and value the knowledge and technical expertise of the evaluators as well as their unique view of the agency, staff begin to call upon them to consult in situations beyond the initial evaluation. This is something we welcome, as knowing when and how to ask for help is a hall-

Table 10.1. Evaluator Activities during Phases of the Logic Model

Evaluator Activities	Logic Model (Scientific Process)			
	Problem Impact Definition	Presumed Causes	Intervention	Outcomes
Asking questions, promoting conversation	Forcing specificity about why an intervention is needed, focus	Uncovering assumptions and assessing participant's understanding	Ensuring treatment integrity, fidelity, acceptability; Generating hypothesis and testing, promoting ownership of outcomes	Broadening perspective, system-level effects
Forming and managing relationships (conflict resolution)	Gaining consensus on initial problem definition	Gaining consensus on presumed causes	Facilitating discussion of connection between intervention and outcomes; Maintaining focus on connection between intervention and outcomes	Managing political agendas and stakeholders
Planning	Ensuring a sound problem definition as the basis of plan	Ensuring in-depth understanding of problem	Designing an evaluable program; Designing evaluation: measures, comparison groups	Maintaining focus on ultimate impact throughout planning process
Consulting	Providing new knowledge to promote insight	Promoting out-of-the-box thinking re: causes	Helping staff understand impact of program change on outcomes; Supporting staff in arriving at measurable outcome statements	Supporting staff to keep an eye on ultimate impact
Documenting	Providing history of thought process	Providing history of thought process	Providing detailed picture of intervention; Providing ongoing account of outcomes as basis for modifying intervention	Documenting events that occur throughout that affect ultimate impact

Bringing back information (summaries, reflections)	Conceptually organizing the group's understanding of the problem statement	Conceptually organizing the group's understanding of causes	Revealing lack of fidelity, difficulties in implementation	Maintaining interest in outcomes, revealing intervention problems, interpreting information	Interpreting political agendas to program staff and administrators
Bringing people together	Being aware of differences, and organizing people for negotiation of meaning	Being aware of differences, and organizing people for negotiation of meaning	Intervening when programs are floundering	Promoting discussion of procedural difficulties in data collection	Promoting intra-agency and inter-agency collaboration in data collection
Training	Helping separate problem definition from premature solution	Connecting to training resources about underlying causes	Ensuring staff competence to carry out intervention to achieve outcomes	Enhancing meaningful participation in evaluation	Ensuring infusion of outcome orientation throughout training
Designing the evaluation and collecting data	Helping the agency express problems using evaluation language	Helping the agency select the causes they can realistically address	Ensuring that the intervention addresses presumed causes	Designing & implementing collection methods acceptable to staff, unintrusive, ethical	Connecting the evaluation to large administrative data bases where appropriate
Formal reporting	Ensuring the report includes a problem definition that is meaningful to the agency	Ensuring the report reflects discussions about presumed causes	Ensuring the report contains a clear description of the intervention and possible variation across sites	Reporting findings often and in a user-friendly way	Adapting report format to the needs of various audiences

mark of positive organizational development. An administrator demonstrated this by asking for assistance in understanding his own emotional reaction to certain attitudes and behaviors of youth on a youth advisory council. The evaluator provided information on adolescent development and was able to help the administrator sort out what he was thinking and to share the legitimacy of what he was feeling.

Documenting.   Though agency staff complain about being swamped in paperwork and documentation, some very important things are never written down.

Evaluators document.   Documentation provides a history of the thought process throughout the stages of the logic model, facilitating the use of material from one stage as the basis for thinking in the next stage. Documentation signals that evolving understanding is important enough to be recorded. In addition, documentation is essential to replication. For instance, an extensive community-development project that had attracted visitors who wanted to know how to replicate it had never been documented adequately in writing. Though staff could talk about the program, they had never been forced, through the process of writing about themselves, to sharpen their thinking concerning what would be most helpful for others to know. Thus, the evaluator was called upon to provide documentation of the hundred-year history of the program, draft careful descriptions of current operations, and distill models and lessons. Through the questions the evaluator posed, staff understood their program at a much deeper level than previously.

Bringing Back Information.   The evaluator not only writes down activities and thought processes but also reflects upon these and discovers meaning. He/she then feeds this information back to staff in a more organized and useful way. Sometimes this process involves elaboration and sometimes reduction. For example, in an agency-driven primary prevention initiative, the process of determining guiding principles resulted in much redundant information. When we simplified the information to clear statements and key words, participants saw where their ideas were represented, came to consensus on the list of principles, and moved forward.

Bringing People Together.   The detailed process of following and promoting conversations around the logic model reveals any existing gaps in vertical and horizontal communication within the agency and with external organizations. Through the evaluation these gaps are recognized and communication is facilitated. For example, data collection needs around evaluation of a dual-track program required agency data that were not available from the existing databases. (In dual-track programs families are either sent through the usual legal track or diverted to an assessment and treatment track). The evaluator was instrumental in bringing together state- and county-level staff as well as groups within the state office that needed to be in communication. The result was statewide rethinking of and improvements in the automated data collection storage and retrieval system.

Training.   Integrity of the intervention to be evaluated depends upon the knowledge and skill of staff implementing the program. Because many initiatives require new knowledge and skills, training is a central issue. Process documentation can show where interventions are not being adequately implemented and thus point to the need for training. In addition, staff will most certainly need training in evaluation itself. Though they learn informally through their engagement in the evaluation, formal training may also be needed. The evaluator may have a role in suggesting that certain content be included in existing agency training or in conducting the training him/herself.

Designing the Evaluation and Collecting Data. This is the point at which traditional ideas of research and emerging notions of evaluation could clash. Strict adherence to "rigorous" scientific methods will not necessarily produce more valid and reliable results and in fact may produce no usable results. For instance, in an evaluation of a statewide teen pregnancy prevention program, the agency administrator insisted upon experimental groups and random assignment. However, on a local level the design could not be implemented. We were able to renegotiate the study using a strong quasi-experimental design that generated much better cooperation and more meaningful data. It is a paradox that the most rigorous evaluation design, when inappropriately applied, can fail to produce valid results.

Formal Reporting. Though frequent informal reporting throughout the evaluation processes ensures that participant input is evident in formal reports, we still discuss drafts of formal reports with participants to elicit their agreement or disagreement with our conclusions. We clarify and when appropriate negotiate meaning. Though our findings are not negotiable, the interpretations and implications may be. This process of producing reports increases ownership, dissemination of results, and subsequent learning throughout the agency.

Communicating Evaluation Results
to Promote Learning in Organizations

The communication of evaluation results is a process around which complaints are rampant (cf. Maluccio & Fein, 1994). Evaluators discover that their results are not used. Participants lament that evaluators do not know how to communicate with them. The result of communication difficulties is that important information may never be heard nor used by the agency. This is unfortunate, because information and how people use it play a critical role in determining the future of an organization.

As also considered by Piening and Warsh (2002), for information to be heard and used, it is critical that evaluators demystify the communication of results. This may include using appropriately nontechnical language, using a variety of presentation mechanisms, and creating opportunities for individuals to express attitudes, feelings, and opposing views. The evaluator must be attuned to the level of technical detail and words to which particular audiences resonate. Additionally, the evaluator must be creative in selecting reporting options that honor the variety of ways people take in and process information. If numbers are not meaningful to an agency administrator, the evaluator should convey information through words to the extent possible, even if this involves departing from a preferred mode of communication.

Regardless of how information is conveyed, until the recipients of information have had a chance to respond, communication remains incomplete. If their affective reactions and cognitive perceptions are not recognized and dealt with openly, distortions of information may result. Thus, the communication process must include opportunities for two-way interaction.

One consideration in encouraging two-way interaction relates to frequency of reporting. Indeed, the frequency may be as important as the mode of reporting. Though it is important not to overwhelm participants with information, evaluators can run the risk of underestimating the organization's desire for ongoing feedback. Participants do not like to receive information as a *fait accompli*. The prudent evaluator will report frequently enough to allow for cognitive and affective processing of information by participants, and for participant feedback and revision based on that feedback. Thus, any final reports would reflect these ongoing interactions.

Communicating negative findings warrants special consideration. Though always an issue for the evaluator, a learning-organization approach suggests constructive ways to do this. Having been involved in the evaluation's design, data collection, and data analysis, and having heard results frequently, stakeholders are positioned to be active problem solvers in discovering and responding to lessons learned from evaluation. Evaluators using a learning-organization approach avoid use of the terms "positive" and "negative" and use headings such as What We Have Learned, What Worked Well, or What Did Not Work As Well. Also, evaluators help participants understand results that may appear negative but have other explanations. For instance, sometimes it is helpful to provide a "big picture" as to the time necessary for change to take place. In an evaluation of character education program, center evaluators helped public education staff accept the time it takes for any educational reform to occur and produce measurable results.

A creative and flexible approach to reporting can be the deciding factor in whether evaluation results are used. Flexibility must include the possibility that the reporting process may need to change during the evaluation.[1]

CHALLENGES AND ISSUES

Emerging understanding of evaluation as an area of specialization related to but different from research combined with a learning-organization approach to evaluation has proven useful to the center in responding to the needs of our public child welfare agency. However, implementation challenges and unresolved issues are apparent. Those with which center evaluators are currently struggling fall into five categories, as described below.

Hiring and Managing a Research and Evaluation Team

To conduct evaluations using a learning-organization approach, the team of evaluators must consist of individuals representing many different skills. The team needs to be able to make methodological decisions to match the questions to be answered but also be skilled at communicating with staff. The members must feel comfortable spending hours interacting with data sets as well as interacting with people. Attitudes of evaluation staff are critical, as they accept and learn new roles, giving up any notion of being armchair scientists, learning to value a variety of evaluation designs, and learning to accept and manage ambiguity. This has implications not only for whom to hire but also for ongoing professional development and team management that involves judiciously combining evaluator skills and attitudes to fit particular evaluation initiatives.

Making Methodological Decisions

Making methodological decisions requires balancing feasibility and usefulness with scientific rigor as traditionally understood. This balancing process does not compromise quality, which continues to be supported through standards of practice (Joint Committee on Standards of Educational Evaluation, 1994). The range of methodological considerations include such things as overall design (e.g., types of comparison groups), testing of hypotheses versus generation of hypotheses, generating appropriate questions, determining appropriate dependent and independent variables, using qualitative versus quantitative designs, selecting sampling plans, choosing and/or creating instruments, and dealing with the question of statistical power.

Making decisions regarding these methodological considerations must include other factors besides scientific rigor. These factors include such aspects as resources available for the evaluation, kinds of problems addressed, information needs of decision-maker, ethics related to denial of services, and amount of structure that can be imposed upon a program. For instance, a center evaluation of a pregnancy prevention initiative began, at the request of a top manager, with a rigorous experimental design, including random assignment of participants to treatment and control groups. After two years of addressing extreme resistance from front-line staff, the evaluator reported to the agency that such a design was not feasible and needed to be changed. In the quasi-experimental design that currently guides the evaluation of this program, we are using an existing state data set on pregnancy rates for comparison purposes. The relaxing of traditional scientific rigor resulted in an evaluation that was feasible. In fact, insistence upon the most scientifically rigorous strategies can at times result in a false sense of security. What masquerades as rigor may be irrelevance. There is no safe and easy substitute for making methodological decisions program by program, accounting for the unique situation of each.

Using Good Judgment in Role Implementation

Once the role definition of the evaluator has expanded, boundaries relaxed, and objectivity reexamined, making decisions concerning the appropriateness of various roles becomes a challenge, and judgment is required in finding the right balance. Most difficult is the issue of objectivity: To what extent is the evaluator part of the agency versus separate from the agency as an impartial observer? The evaluator needs to understand the difference between becoming enmeshed in program planning with staff and maintaining his/her expertise as one who brings objective information to a process of program improvement. In addition, he/she must differentiate between inappropriately managing staff and appropriately facilitating resolution of differences among staff and administrators of a program.

Though the learning-organization approach does redefine objectivity, it is important that the evaluator safeguard the purity and accuracy of information. This aspect of objectivity must not be compromised. In addition, when the evaluator takes too much responsibility for program planning and implementation, he/she becomes vulnerable to taking ownership away from agency staff and being blamed by them for problems that may arise.

Owning and Sharing the Evaluation

Ownership of the evaluation, both a legal and an emotional/intellectual issue, is another area in which judgment and balance are required. Sometimes legal ownership of evaluation results becomes an issue between agencies, when the service agency and the evaluating agency (university) each claim ownership of the "intellectual property." Handling legal disputes over ownership can delay the contracting process. Yet this sends a confusing message. Regardless of legal ownership, from a practical point of view, the evaluation must be owned by both parties.

A challenge is to help the agency take ownership of information resulting from the evaluation and use it to benefit the agency. In fact, we evaluate according to a learning-organization approach specifically because the evaluation results need to be owned by the stakeholders. The previously noted Adoption and Safe Families Act has provided a mandate to the child welfare agency—not to us—to improve service provision and to achieve prescribed outcomes. As evaluators, we are assisting the agency in meeting its mandate.

On the other hand, the evaluators do maintain some ownership of the information, but our need is different. We have the responsibility to disseminate information to our colleagues in the field of evaluation. The challenge is to think of our need as secondary and the agency's need as primary. Agencies quickly discern when evaluators put publication needs above agency needs, and the resulting relationship problems can destroy the evaluation effort.

Redefining Expectations of Evaluation

Evaluation staff may feel discomfort as they struggle to recognize and appreciate the benefits of their work. A learning-organization approach to evaluation involves not only a reconsideration of evaluator roles and activities but also of expectations and benefits of evaluation. A value of the approach is that it allows evaluators to come to terms with shortfalls regarding some expected benefits within a context of larger benefits. For instance, information generated from evaluation may not result in immediate action in terms of modifying, continuing, or discontinuing an initiative. Yet there is cumulative knowledge building as the agency moves toward better understanding of clear program planning and decision-making. The benefit is greater potential for wise use of agency resources. The primary cultural change is an overall increasing openness to and respect for information and an intent to use information to lead organizations. Wheatley connects information to a new style of leadership in saying, "We need to have information coursing through our systems, disturbing the peace, imbuing everything it touches with new life" (1994:105). Thus, administrators who learn from and use evaluation information are not managing and controlling as much as they are generating an exciting, ongoing discovery process.

CONCLUSION

This chapter has addressed some of the current thinking in the field of evaluation and requirements for program evaluation in child welfare. It has focused on outcomes and the organizational learning that occurs through careful attention to processes leading to those outcomes. The Center for Child and Family Studies did not so much select a learning-organization approach to evaluation as that approach emerged as the most meaningful way to carry out its evaluations. The roles described in this chapter resulted from our experiences and were found to be consistent with that approach. Thus, the evaluation literature and our own experiences will continue to blend to enrich our understanding of evaluation and to produce increasingly useful results for the child welfare agency.

NOTE

1.   See Piening and Warsh (2002) for discussion of guidelines for collaboration between evaluators and agency staff.

REFERENCES

Administration for Children and Families, U.S. Department of Health and Human Services, Administration of Children, Youth and Families (1998). *Program Instruction,* Log. No: ACYF-PI-CB-98-02. Washington, DC: U.S. Department of Health and Human Services.

Chalofsky, N. (1996). A new paradigm for learning in organizations. *Human Resource Development Quarterly* 7(3):287–83.

Chavis, D. M., Stucky, P. E., & Wandersman, A. (1983). Returning basic research to the community. *American Psychologist* 38:424–34.

Jacobs, F. H. (1988). The five-tiered approach to evaluation: Context and implementation. In H. Weiss and F. H. Jacobs (Eds.), *Evaluating Family Programs* (pp. 37–48). Hawthorne, NY: Aldine de Gruyter.

Joint Committee on Standards of Educational Evaluation (1994). *The Program Evaluation Standards*. Thousand Oaks, CA: Sage.

Maluccio, A. N. & Fein, E. (1994). Tidiness in an untidy world: Research in child welfare. In E. Sherman and W. J. Reid (Eds.), *Qualitative Research in Social Work* (pp. 337–46). New York: Columbia University Press.

McCoy, M. M (1983). Personal construct theory and methodology in intercultural research.

In R. A. Neimeyer (Ed.), *Applications of Personal Construct Theory*. Toronto: Academic Free Press.

Patton, M. Q. (1997). *Utilization-Focused Evaluation: The New Century* (3d ed). Thousand Oaks, CA: Sage.

Piening, S. & Warsh, R. (2002). Collaboration between evaluators and agency staff in outcome-based evaluation. In T. Vecchiato, A. N. Maluccio, & C. Canali (Eds.), *Evaluation in Child and Family Services: Comparative Client and Program Perspectives*. Hawthorne, NY: Aldine de Gruyter.

Preskill, H. & Torres, R. (1999). *Evaluation Inquiry for Learning in Organizations*. Thousand Oaks, CA: Sage.

Rogler, L. H. (1989). The meaning of culturally sensitive research in mental health. *American Journal of Psychiatry* 146:296–303.

Tyler, F. B., Pargament, K. I., & Gatz, M. (1983). The resource collaborator role: A model for interactions involving psychologists. *American Psychologist* 58:388–98.

Wheatley, M. J. (1994). *Leadership and the New Science*. San Francisco: Berrett-Koehler.

Wicker, A. W. (1992). Getting out of our conceptual ruts: Strategies for expanding conceptual frameworks. In A. E. Kazin (Ed.), *Methodological Issues and Strategies in Clinical Research* (pp. 41–62). Washington, DC: American Psychological Association.

11

Outcome Studies in the Context of Organizational Inertia and Political Ideology

Frank Ainsworth

In this chapter I use examples from studies that I have carried out in diverse agency settings in Australia and South Africa, to explore how organizational inertia and political ideology affect the outcome research effort. In addition, I address the use of administrative data sets, study design and measurement, cross-national and cross-cultural differences, and funding in regard to outcome studies. The focus of the chapter is on the impact of process on outcome studies. I conclude with a plea for parallel research efforts to reduce the Australian dependence on culturally bound studies from the United States and Britain.

The four studies are (1) "Family conferences in a hospital setting: The caregivers' perspective," (2) an evaluation of a federal parental-child contact program that for reasons of confidentiality will be referred to as the "FDP program," (3) "Residential education for 'at risk' youth: Building knowledge," and (4) staff attitudes in a South African residential child care program.

THE STUDIES

The first study, "Family conferences in a hospital setting: The caregivers' perspective," was funded by the Australian Research Council (ARC) in 1999 and was completed by mid-2001. It is based in two hospitals, each in a different Australian state. This is a quasi-experimental, prospective cross-sectional study, using post-only measures. The aim is to examine the factors that influence family conference outcomes and objectives, and to measure the extent of family caregiver empowerment and the quality of the decision-making environment (Burford & Hudson, 2000). The study also compares the outcomes for caregivers involved in a family conference with a sample of caregivers who were not so involved.

The contract for the next study, of the federal "FDP program," was awarded in July 2000. The FDP program aims to assist in situations where there is parental conflict over child contact issues and resolve these matters without resort to time-consuming and expensive litigation. There are three programs, which commenced in early 1999, and each is delivered in a different state by a nongovernment community service agency. The evaluation is in two stages over eighteen months. First is a *qualitative* stage, involving focus groups with program staff, stakeholder interviews, and telephone interviews with service users. The second is a *quantitative* stage, involving statistical analysis of an administrative data set.

The third study is of "Residential education for 'at risk' youth." It aims to build knowledge about the benefits of residential living and alternative education programs for at-risk twelve- to sixteen-year old males. The study is of a five-day-per-week, twenty-four-hours-per-day program for youths with a history of truancy and disruptive behaviors, low self-esteem, poor peer relationships and chaotic family lives. It is framed as a quasi-experimental, prospective single group pre- and posttest design. It is the first Australian attempt to provide contemporary outcome data about this form of service. This study was unsuccessfully submitted for funding to the Australian Research Council (ARC) in 2000 and it has been submitted to an alternative funding source. It is included here since the initial unsuccessful bid for research funds illustrates, as explained later, a particular issue in relation to Australian outcome studies.

The final study is of a South African residential child care program, "What do children's homes staff let parents do? An international comparison." It uses data from an earlier study to compare staff attitudes toward parental contact in three U.S. programs and the South African program (Coughlan & Ainsworth, 2000). While technically not an outcome study, it is included as it highlights important cross-national and cross-cultural issues.

LESSONS FROM THE STUDIES

After briefly describing the circumstances surrounding the studies, in this section I indicate the particular lessons learned.

Organizational Inertia

Circumstance. In each of these studies organizational difficulties made the process of establishing the projects arduous. For example, the Australian Research Council's Strategic Partnership with Industry—Research and Training (SPIRT) grant for the above-noted hospital study was awarded in November 1998 and was scheduled to start early in 1999. In fact, receipt of the formal papers from the ARC by the university was delayed by three months and further delay was caused when the chief executive officer (CEO) of one of the hospitals initially refused to sign the research contract. There is an ARC requirement that under the SPIRT scheme the hospital Department of Social Work has to make a minimum cash contribution of $5,000 per annum toward the study costs. The hospital CEO thought this was unacceptable, as he was only familiar with grants for medical research bodies like the National Health and Medical Research Council, which do not run this type of scheme and do not impose that type of condition when funding medical research.

Eventually, the hospital CEO signed the contract but further delay was then experienced as the contract between the university and the hospital had to be signed by the university vice-chancellor, who was overseas for a period of weeks. Unfortunately, until the vice-chancellor signed the contract the ARC would not release the research funds to the university. The study commenced in November 1999, one year after the grant was awarded.

Since that time the federal government has introduced a Goods and Services Tax (GST). The federal tax office has ruled that the university is through this study providing research services to the hospitals involved. The result is that the university must now levy 10 percent GST on the $5,000 per annum cash contribution that the ARC requires from agencies. This applies to all the research projects noted in this chapter. In essence, this is an impost on research and knowledge development.

Comment. Initiating an outcome-based evaluation in a large, bureaucratic host medical setting like a teaching hospital is a hazardous enterprise. First, there is the issue of establishing the legitimacy of this type of outcome research in an environment where the traditional scientific paradigm is dominant. The fact that social work researchers are as yet unable to reach what is considered as the "gold standard" and instead have to use less rigorous methods is, in this context, viewed with suspicion rather than understanding. Furthermore, the high cost of medical research in comparison to the low cost of social work research tends to undermine this endeavor: "If it's that cheap it can't be serious research!" Second, the lack of legitimacy in Australia of this type of research in this type of organizational setting and the limited resources available for the activity can lead to political interventions from key organizational players that further endanger the outcome evaluation effort.

Ideological Impediments

Circumstance. The next issue concerns how personal and professional ideologies also act as impediments to outcome studies. For example, the hospital-based Family Conferences study had to be approved by three ethics committees, that is, two separate hospital groups and one university committee. The chairperson of one of the hospital committees, a professor of medicine, initially refused to place this study before the ethics committee as he described it as a "quality improvement" project and not a research study. This was in spite of the fact that the ARC, which does not fund quality improvement projects, was the source of the funds to support the study. This stance, although it was eventually abandoned, illustrates the way social work outcome research is viewed as lacking in rigor by some members of other professions.

Professional social work ideologies have also impeded this study. First, the hospital social workers remain reluctant to define or specify social work interventions, claiming that each case is different as is each intervention. This makes comparing the outcome of family conferences with cases where a family conference did not occur fraught with difficulty. In addition, when first collecting cases for this study, we became aware that some hospital social workers were only referring family conference cases in which in their opinion the outcome of the conference was positive. Although we have now been able, at least partially, to resolve this issue, for a while the integrity of the study sample was under threat.

Second, recruiting families to the study has proved difficult, especially for the comparison group, that is, cases in which a family conference did not occur. This appears to stem from social workers' low level of commitment to an examination of their practice and to building new models of practice. This possibly reflects the surprising fact that this is the first social work study using quantitative methodology ever to be mounted in the two teaching hospitals providing the sites for the research. In time a research culture that allows for both qualitative and quantitative studies may be established in these hospitals' social work departments but for now the going is tough.

More recently, the chance of success in the bid for an ARC grant for the "Residential education for 'at risk' adolescents" project was undermined when one assessor raised an "ethical issue" in relation to the proposal. According to this assessor, the ethical issue was as follows: "The Chief Investigator (CI) and Partner Investigator (PI) are intending to administer a number of standardized tests including the [acronym omitted] which I believe may be a restricted test. None of the investigators appears to be registered psychologists, which has the potential for adverse consequences" [unspecified]. This assessor also questioned the CI's statistical expertise. The two other assessors indicated that they were in support of funding for this project. The ARC—SPIRT scheme has no mechanism for questioning the comments of an assessor.

The claim that the test in question is restricted is untrue. The instrument measures problem behaviors, and is part of a battery of tests including measures of self-esteem, educational achievement, and the quality of peer relationships, all of which are sound outcome measures. Amazingly, one of the measures used in the study, and one that is frequently used by psychologists, was developed by a social work academic!

What is true is that we now have an absurd contradiction. In the same round of ARC grant applications as this unsuccessful application, the CI successfully submitted another project, which involved using the same test and an identical form of statistical analysis. In this instance no questions were raised by the three assessors about either the use of the tests or the appropriateness of the statistical analysis.

Comment.   The above shows how personal and professional ideologies can cut across attempts to develop outcome studies. The lack of status of social work research and social work researchers in the eyes of other professions is an issue that causes great concern. That it should be supported—if not promoted—by social workers themselves makes a depressing message for those who strive to create a more research-savvy, evidenced-based, and outcome-oriented profession.

The Use of Administrative Data Sets

Circumstance.   The federal FDP program evaluation contract involves both a qualitative and quantitative examination of program outcomes. As there was no clear service specification for the program, the three agencies involved have drawn with varying degrees of sophistication on different theoretical understandings of issue of parental conflict. The agencies have developed programs that have some commonality in terms of the services offered but are in fact very different. These differences relate to theoretical orientation and the type of services, individual or group, that they offer. Not surprisingly, the program funders are interested in the comparative outcomes of the three different models.

From the commencement of the program, the agencies contracted to provide the FDP services have been required to enter case and service activity data into an Internet federal database. The product is a typical administrative data set. The quantitative component of the evaluation calls for statistical analysis of data, with a view to establishing evidence that participation in the program leads to a reduction in parental conflict. The ultimate outcome measure is nonreappearance in the court that deals with family matters such as residency and child contact orders.

The final part of the evaluation is about statistical modeling and the building of a model that can predict which cases warrant referral to a FDP program. The hope is that a model of this kind will reduce the cost that the legal system incurs in these cases through the extensive use of court time. This will require the matching of information from the FDP and the legal systems Family Court database—a process that has yet to be adequately explored.

On examination of the administrative data a number of issues emerged. The first was in relation to the reliability of the data. In at least one agency neither the coordinator of the program nor the data entry person appreciated the need for comprehensive and accurate data collection. As a result there is a substantial amount of missing data, and items collected have for convenience of entry been changed by arbitrarily pushing items into inappropriate categories. Missing data is clearly a major issue when using administrative data sets and one that is not easily resolved (DiLeonardi & Yuan, 2000). In the other agencies data for some items have only been collected manually. There are also issues associated with downloading the data from the central database. All of the above means that data from different sources are arriving in different formats and time-consuming electronic and manual reconciliation is inevitable. Until this lengthy process is completed, the extent and type of statistical analysis that will be possible are unclear. The likelihood of the data being robust enough for various forms of statistical model building looks increasingly doubtful.

Finally, as this chapter was being written and as the interim report for the evaluation project was about to be prepared, the author was informed that the federal department was about to introduce a new database. This database will not collect all of the same items as the one that is being discontinued, and it is unclear as to whether the two databases will be compatible. Such a change in the midst of an evaluation project is not uncommon and illustrates the complexities of doing outcome-based research in government agencies.

Comment.   As this study shows, the increasing interest in the use of administrative databases for evaluation and research purposes is fraught with difficulties.

At the moment none of the parties, neither the funders nor the agencies involved, appear to monitor data inputs sufficiently to ensure that the accumulated data set has even a modest chance of being useful. This appears to stem from a lack of knowledge of the fundamental importance of quality data collection for evaluation and research purposes. Before the sound use of data from many of these sources is possible, these databases need to be redesigned to ensure measurement accuracy. This is not an issue that as far as can be seen has received any attention in the development of the shortly to be introduced new database.

Two things are now possible. First, the FDP outcome evaluation may be discounted because of the unreliability of the data on which it is based. But second, and possibly of longer-term consequence, administrators may be weary of spending large sums of money on outcome evaluations that cannot fulfill their expectations because of poor-quality data. The danger then is that this will set back attempts at building more empirically based outcome evaluations models. To avoid this outcome, a stronger link between academic evaluators and researchers and administrators at all level of government and agency management appears to be essential, as also suggested by Piening and Warsh (in the companion volume).

Study Design and Measurement Issues

Circumstance.   One further impediment that evaluators in Australia have to face is the apparent preference that community service practitioners and others have for evaluations based on qualitative methodologies. This is a position promoted by many, but not all, community service educators who hold university positions in key social science disciplines. Quantitative methods and the associated statistical data are classified as positivist and dismissed as politically and ideologically unsound because such methods, it is claimed, "fail to reflect the human story."

Unwittingly, a colleague and I may have recently added to the ability of those who dismiss quantitative methods to do so (Ainsworth & Hansen, 2000). In 1999 we attempted to replicate in Australia a U.S. study of social workers' beliefs about parents of emotionally disturbed children (Johnson, Renaud, Schmidt, & Stanek, 1998). We were unable to do so since the results from our efforts raised issues about the measurement validity of the instrument used in the original study to examine providers' beliefs about parents. The study has been seen by some practitioners as supporting the view that U.S. measurement instruments and quantitative type studies are of questionable value. This is not our position.

A further difficulty for researchers in Australia who are interested in quantitative outcome evaluations is obtaining study samples of sufficient size. For example, at any one time the number of children in all forms of out-of-home care in Western Australia is about 1,200. This is across the government and small nongovernment child welfare sectors. The government departments' limited interest in cooperating with university-based quantitative evaluators further reduces access to this population for research purposes. Fortunately, it has been possible to develop an innovative "lead agency" model in the nongovernment sector. This involves one nongovernment agency establishing an outcome project with a university-based evaluator but also negotiating with the other nongovernment agencies so that the project can draw cases for inclusion from other agencies. Only in this way has it been possible to draw study samples of sufficient size to permit analysis using advanced statistical techniques. This is an exciting development, as in a relatively short time the nongovernment agencies will hold outcome data superior to that held by government. In the contracting environment that now characterizes the Australian community services sector, this experience is likely to prove invaluable in negotiations for service contracts.

Comment. The struggle between those who favor qualitative evaluation methodologies and those who argue for at least some aspects of quantitative methodology is acute. Evaluation studies that combine both approaches are rare. While some changes, as illustrated above, are taking place, because of the funding environment there is emphasis in Australia on the notion that community services should only be evaluated against a set of established political and social values, not economic objectives. The preferred values are reflected in the term "community" and more recently "civic society." These ideologies impact on attempts to build a more robust quantitative approach to outcome evaluations, as these methods are seen as antithetical to these values.

Cross-National and Cross-Cultural Differences

Circumstance. At various points throughout this chapter, issues of cross-national and cross-cultural differences have surfaced. For example, the difference in results from the Provider Beliefs about Parents study may reflect differences between the cultural norms and values held by U.S. and Australian social workers that are embedded in their responses to the items in this instrument. Certainly, responses to individual items might be influenced by the way in which each country places a different emphasis on individual parental responsibility and the way professional services are made available to parents of emotionally disturbed children. Major differences in the social context such as how health and education services are funded and delivered in the U.S. and Australia may also influence practitioners' attitudes toward parents.

In addition, the way in which services in the U.S. that are similar or the same as services in Australia may have different titles. For example, the term "mental health" service is more common as a title in the United States due to the cultural ethos that emphasizes treatment and therapy interventions. (See Landsverk and Davis, Chapter 7 in this volume.) In Australia, the more generic "health care" or "family and children's service" terminology seems to be preferred, even when some of the services in these settings may address mental health issues.

In the South African study, the author and a colleague originally attempted to measure the extent to which a particular residential care program was family-centered. This program employed both English- and Xhosa-speaking staff. Accordingly, the Family Centered Group Care (FCGC) instrument that was validated in a U.S. study (Ainsworth, 1997) and that has a subscale about staff attitudes was translated independently into Xhosa. The staff then had a choice of language version when completing the instrument.

Discussions with the staff after they completed this task indicated that some items represented a cultural position that was unknown to South Africans. Even after translation items were not understood. An example is an item about family reunification, a term that is used extensively in the international child welfare literature. In South Africa the term "reconstruction" is preferred and the item that referred to reunification was unhelpful.

The researchers also found that the program staff lacked familiarity with the instrument format. For example, staff members were not familiar with Likert-type scales used in the instrument. By comparison, U.S. respondents who had earlier completed the FCGC instrument were comfortable with this approach to data collection. It is clear that the South African respondents found this format unusual, and this may have influenced the shape of the data that were collected.

Finally, in the South African context, it became clear that poverty limited the ability of parents, especially black parents, to remain involved with their children. This raised serious issues for the U.S. model of family-centered, residential group care practice. Unless parents are able to have regular contact with a residential care agency and their children, their involvement in the ongoing care process is limited. Yet, parental involvement is a core assumption on which this model of care practice and indeed one on which the contemporary family reunification movement is predicated. If parental involvement cannot be guaranteed, there is a question about the applicability of this model in the South African context.[1]

Comment.　　The results obtained in the PBAP study and the accompanying national preference toward qualitative methods in evaluation studies do mean that attempts in Australia to measure service outcomes using standardized instruments with sound psychometric properties are viewed with skepticism and given limited standing. This issue is further compounded from within the ranks of the few empirical evaluators when premature calls for "gold standard" studies are made. A recent example of this comes from a study of out-of-home care (Barber, Delfabbro & Cooper, 2000:8). These authors state, "In the absence of controlled experimental studies into this phenomenon, *i.e. parental visiting as an indicator of family reunification* [italics added], it is impossible to know whether parental visiting is causally related or merely associated with some other variable (such as a child's behaviour)." This comment does of course have validity. In a thriving, well-established outcome evaluation environment it would do no harm. When this is not the case, setting a standard that is not achievable in the foreseeable future only undermines the argument for the selective use of quantitative approaches to service evaluation.

The South African study also confirms the difficulty of using measurement instruments in a cultural setting different from that in which they were developed. But the issues raised by this study are even more fundamental. The study raises questions about the transferability of key concepts and model of practice from one cultural context to another. Translating instruments from one language to another is only part of the process of transfer. A rigorous checking of the key assumptions and cultural values embedded in instruments such as the BPAP or the FCGC is also needed. As part of this process, modification to an instrument may be needed and revalidation may be required. Only when these complex and arduous tasks are complete can an instrument be safely used to measure service outcomes in an alternative cultural setting.

Research and Evaluation Funding

Circumstance.   Of further concern, in the Australian context, is the arbitrary reduction of research grants. Of the three ARC—SPIRT research grants the author currently holds, the amount of funding requested for two of the projects was reduced without discussion or explanation—an experience that may also be common in other countries. Of course, the original funding requests may have been inflated and the reductions may be legitimate. The lack of feedback about the reasons for the reductions unfortunately undermines any sense of this legitimacy.

Of further concern is the lack of capacity in community service agencies to commit resources to rigorous research and evaluation efforts. All too often these agencies satisfy themselves with poorly drawn qualitative survey type evaluations that have limited value. While it is important to know about such items as client satisfaction that these studies address, they do not contribute to systematic building of knowledge about program effectiveness. Determining why a program benefits consumers and which components of a program are the most beneficial requires other types of evaluation studies. These other more quantitative approaches to outcome evaluations are also more powerful in the political arena when decisions about program continuity and funding are in question.

Comment.   When decisions to downgrade funding requests are made, the outcome researcher is placed in an invidious position. ARC research grants are allegedly given to support research that is internationally competitive; yet this type of arbitrary reduction inevitably undermines any such competitiveness. Options in this type of situation are few. Do you accept the lower level of funding or do you decline the grant in the full knowledge that to do so from this prestigious source will have a negative effect on your university research profile? Or do you reduce the complexity of the study and find a way to manage with the reduced level of funding? In Australia, this is a real dilemma since sources of funding are few.

The other source of funding for evaluation studies is the community services industry itself. So far the industry has shown considerable interest in developing outcome measures but limited interest in providing money to support such efforts. Federal government departments that have access to funds are the possible exception, although to date many of the evaluation and outcome efforts they have supported have been built around short-term qualitative studies. These studies have used a range of opinion-gathering survey type exercises that have included crude measures of client satisfaction as the primary source of data.

The university sector, with nongovernment agencies as the industry partner, has taken advantage of the ARC-SPIRT grant scheme as one source of money to support research and evaluation studies. Essentially, the SPIRT scheme seeks to promote academia—industry partnerships. It does this by allowing an industry partner to make an in-kind contribution, at least matching the ARC cash grant, to the cost of the research. The expectation is that once a research and evaluation culture has been established in a nongovernment agency, the agency itself will assume responsibility for the ongoing cost of such ventures. While this is an innovative way in which to promote research and evaluation studies of social programs, the assumption that an agency will eventually incorporate these costs into its operational budget may be fanciful thinking. As yet there is no evidence that when ARC—SPIRT type grants come to an end agencies will pick up the cost of these endeavors. Most of the large national nongovernment community service agencies do not have research staff, nor as they would say, the capacity to carry these costs.

THE WAY FORWARD

Nevertheless, one way forward is to build stronger agency—academia linkages.

Historically, for the service professions these linkages have primarily been for purposes of professional education. The emergence in all areas of the community services in Australia over the last decade of a service-contracting environment and demands for evidence of service effectiveness presents an opportunity for a new set of agency—academia relationships. Agencies increasingly have to undertake outcome evaluations, as part of service contracts, especially if funding for a contracted service is to be renewed. Internal agency personnel can rarely undertake these evaluations. In fact, Australian agencies, especially nongovernment agencies, simply do not have staff with the requisite knowledge and skill. This means that the door is open for agency-academic linkages of a different kind through which academia could offer agencies outcome research expertise, as also suggested by Wright and Paget (elsewhere in this volume). The building of these linkages is the positive aspect of the ARC-SPIRT funding model although what will happen to these relationships once they are no longer linked to money is an open issue.

The demand for outcome evaluations integrates well with the demand for evidence-based practice Macdonald & Sheldon, 1998; Vecchiato, Chapter 4 in this volume), and together they have the potential to put outcome research firmly on the Australian agenda. Interestingly, a completed study of trends in foster care in a nongovernment agency using a nine-year administrative data set is acting as a catalyst in this regard in this agency (Ainsworth, Ash & Summers, 2000). Building on that initial project it has been possible to mount with this agency as the industry partner two successful bids for ARC-SPIRT research grants.

Both of these grants examine foster care outcomes. In addition, as part of a deliberate attempt to establish a research culture among the workforce of this agency, a university research assistant for one of the grants has been located in the agency. The executive director views this as supporting the agency's long-term plans to convert an administrative position into that of a full-time research officer. This arises from the director's realization that in the future the agency will need to be able to access considerably more data about the value and effectiveness of its services than is currently the case. Hopefully, the executives of other community service organizations will embrace this position.

Finally, I would like to join other contributors to this volume in making a plea for cross-national, cross-cultural evaluation and research endeavors. From the onset the intention, not as yet realized, was for the "Family conferences in a hospital setting: The caregivers' perspective" study to have a parallel U.S.-funded site in a Boston teaching hospital. Tentative discussions are also under way with an Australian residential treatment program to parallel the U.S. "Coping and resiliency of boys following residential placement" study that is awaiting funding (Maluccio, 2000). Funding bodies in Australia value international research linkages of this type and positive funding responses are possible. Parallel studies would also help to address the issue of the overwhelming dependence of Australian social work on culturally bound studies from the United States and Britain and contribute to cross-cultural outcome evaluation in the area of family and children's services.

NOTE

1.   For discussion of evaluation of family reunification programs in the U.S., see Canali and Rigon (2002) and Pine, Healy, and Maluccio (2002).

REFERENCES

Ainsworth, F. (1997). *Family Centered Group Care: Model Building*. Aldershot: Ashgate.

Ainsworth, F. & Hansen, P. (2000). Social workers' views of parents of emotionally disturbed children: Replicating a U.S. study. *Australian Social Work* 53(3):37–44.

Ainsworth, F., Ash S., & Summers, A. (2000). Foster care trends in a Western Australian non-government family welfare agency 1991–1999. Submitted for publication.[[more information?]]

Barber, J. G., Delfabbro, P. H., & Cooper L. (2000). Aboriginal and non-Aboriginal children in out-of-home care. *Children Australia* 25(3):5–10.

Burford, G. & Hudson, J. (2000). *Family Group Conferences: New Directions in Community-Centered Child and Family Practice*. Hawthorne, NY: Aldine de Gruyter.

Canali, C. & Rigon, P. (2002). Evaluating outcomes for children with multiple problems. In T. Vecchiato, A. N. Maluccio, & C. Canali (Eds.), *Evaluation in Child and Family Ser-*

vices: Comparative Client and Program Perspectives. Hawthorne, NY: Aldine de Gruyter.

Coughlan, F. & Ainsworth, F. (2000). What do children's home staff let parents do? An international comparison. *Social Work/Maatshaplike Werk* 36(2):150–56.

DiLeonardi, J. W. & Yuan, Y. Y. T. (2000). Using administrative data. *Child Welfare* 79(5): 437–43.

Johnson, H. C., Renaud, E. F., Schmidt, D. T., & Stanek, E. J. (1998). Social workers' views of parents of children with mental and emotional disabilities. *Families in Society: The Journal of Contemporary Human Services* 79(2):173–87.

Maluccio, A. N. (2000). Coping and resiliency of boys following residential placement. Grant proposal. Chestnut Hill, MA: Boston College, Graduate School of Social Work.

Macdonald, G. & Sheldon, B. (1998). Changing one's mind: The final frontier? *Issues in Social Work Education* 18(1):3–25.

Pine, B. A., Healy, L., & Maluccio, A. N. (2002). Developing measurable program objectives: a key to evaluation of family reunification programs. In T. Vecchiato, A. N. Maluccio, & C. Canali (Eds.), *Evaluation in Child and Family Services: Comparative Client and Program Perspectives* . Hawthorne, NY: Aldine de Gruyter.

12

Family Service Centers

Lessons from National and Local Evaluations

Anita Lightburn

Major financial and professional investments are committed to outcome evaluations of new demonstration projects that are expected to produce useful information to inform policy, program, and practice for low-income families. The potential of evaluations to fulfill these expectations is often not realized because of the premature choice to do national studies with experimental designs. At the same time, limited investment in formative evaluations of local program demonstrations does not reflect their importance to program development and performance, which is essential as a foundation for large-scale experimental design studies. In the United States, too frequently, decisions about when and how to do outcome evaluations are based on politics rather than best practice in evaluation research. There is a rush to prove that the investment in new programs has worked with large-scale control group studies that are deemed the most reliable scientific method for evaluating the efficacy of new initiatives. A misconception about the right timing for such evaluations will be addressed in this chapter with suggestions for approaches based on current knowledge about program evaluation methodology and supported by lessons learned from experience in the field.

How decisions are made to support outcome evaluations, and how the research is accomplished, is a complex puzzle that, when examined through case studies, raises questions about their value. This value conundrum regarding outcome evaluation presents real challenges to government sponsors, program directors, practitioners, program consumers, and researchers. In the interest of further perspectives to solve this ongoing concern, this chapter reviews a case study of a national outcome evaluation and a local evaluation of a Head Start Family Service Center program demonstration.[1] Lessons learned are developed from this case study for those involved in evaluating programs that support low-income families. In particular, I will argue that the premature choice to do experimental design studies shortchanges the intent to demonstrate program efficacy. A rebalance to invest and support formative evaluations of local programs would reflect their importance as a foundation for experimental design studies.

THE VALUE CONUNDRUM

Outcome evaluations of family support programs that are both experimental design studies and formative evaluations have been substantially reviewed in the past decade. Experimental randomized studies of these programs have shown marginal results and do not provide relevant information, according to Weiss and Greene (1992), recognized experts in the evaluation of family programs. The deficits in these outcome studies include: (1) oversimplification of community-based family support programs, as the complexity of each program is not represented in the design of the study; (2) failure to describe or measure the real treatment provided; and (3) a "paucity of good measure to assess the effects of these programs on parents, families and communities" (ibid.:137). Describing program and practice processes has been regarded as the weakest part of family support services (Gershenson, 1995; Weiss & Halpern, 1990). From an ecological perspective, there is also little attention to the ways that context mediates parent outcomes (Bond & Halpern, 1988; Weiss & Jacobs, 1988; Weiss & Halpern, 1990).

Productive formative evaluations using action research methodologies emphasize participant involvement, evolve with the program, and contribute significantly to program development vital to family support programs. The quality and hence value of formative evaluation depend on adequate investment in both funding and support for developing the evaluator's capacity to implement action research methods so that there is adequate program and practice description. The value of the formative evaluation is in part determined by the time invested by the evaluator in working intensely with the program, providing program information and dissemination through reviews and retreats, and contributing to program effectiveness (Stroul et al., 1996; Bond & Halpern, 1988). Ongoing program development requires substantive evaluative information from a multiskilled evaluation team that can assist staff members, as suggested by Wright and Paget (Chapter 10 in this volume).

The Family Service Center (FSC) demonstrations were developed to provide a more comprehensive set of services to enhance Head Start's ability to respond to the needs of parents as well as their children through: (1) collaborative efforts with community organizations and (2) intensive case management that included a needs assessment and integrated services for families (Bernstein, Swartz, & Levin, 2000:1). For the FSC program, "community" included the Head Start leadership, staff, and the service providers, who were all essential to the responsiveness of the continuum of services required by the parents.

Comprehensive community programs such as the FSCs can benefit from including the whole community in the formative evaluation for longer-term program gains based on their investment in the outcomes. There were also considerable differences in local communities, such as geography, urban-rural settings, culture, socioeconomic status, state and town resource allocation, and quality and availability of the broad spectrum of health and human services. Therefore, specific attention to development of data that will enable comparison between sites should make it possible to increase understanding based on differences in context and program inputs. This is important background for a national perspective that is gained from studies across demonstration sites.

OVERVIEW OF THE FAMILY SERVICE CENTER DEMONSTRATION AND EVALUATION

The federal Office of Head Start funded Family Service Center demonstration projects in three waves from 1990 to 1993. FSCs were developed as part of Head Start's early childhood intervention programs in thirty-six states throughout the United States and also in Puerto Rico, to provide more comprehensive services for families. The demonstrations were funded for three years for an average of $250,000 each, with some of the early projects receiving funding for a fourth year. The FSC program goals were to develop innovative approaches to:

- identify problems of Head Start families[2] to train staff to understand and recognize families needs;
- motivate family members to seek necessary help and address their own problems;
- provide needed services directly or link families with appropriate services in the community; and
- support families as they work toward solving their problems.

Individual FSC program designs varied widely in their innovations, ranging from provision of increased case management to complex multisystem programs with co-located services provided by community agencies.

A major national evaluation and local project evaluations provided both formative and summative evaluation data for local Head Start programs and for the National Research Office of Head Start. I was both a local project evaluator and participant in the national evaluation. The demonstrations included a total of sixty-six projects in urban and rural areas, including programs associated with Migrant Head Start and Head Start on Indian Reservations. The demonstration sites were in greatly varied environments that stretched across the United States. For example, on the East Coast in Bridgeport, Connecticut, the FSC was in an impoverished neighborhood plagued by violence that was part of a well-known drug corridor. The main housing project was leveled at the end of the program (Lightburn, 1994). In contrast, on the West Coast in Coos Bay, Oregon, the FSC was part of a rural program where financial, social, and personal needs of families were major concerns because of changes in the fishing industry.

The national evaluation was a major undertaking that began in 1991 and concluded in March 2000. Abt Associates, Inc. conducted the national evaluation and was responsible for preparing a report to be presented by the Head Start Bureau to the United States Congress in the spring of 2000. Abt Associates included all local project evaluators as consultants to their work in developing and implementing the national evaluation at their sites.

As a social work educator, I highly valued the opportunity to do a case study of an innovation for poor, at-risk families. As the local project evaluator, being part of the national evaluation, I had the opportunity to learn from the other project evaluations across the United States in a host of contexts, different from my own, which was in Bridgeport, Connecticut. I was optimistic that the national evaluation would confirm the strong outcomes I was finding (Lightburn, 1994).

The Local Bridgeport Family Service Center Evaluation

The action-research approach to evaluation describes the formative part of my evaluation work with the administration, staff, larger community, and families (Bond & Halpern, 1988). Qualitative data included thick description in the ethnographic tradition that was gathered through intensive weekly work with the FSC program, a component of the Family Service Center at the Hall Neighborhood House in Bridgeport, Connecticut. The summative part of the local evaluation included pre-post tests with outcome measures of program participation, achievement of goals in education, employment, and substance abuse as well as use of standardized psychometric tests of family coping and individual mental health functioning. Baseline data were gathered when parents volunteered to participate in the FSC program. Follow-up data were collected eighteen months later, when the participants were no longer part of the intense five-day a week program.

The formative evaluation work that I carried out led to the redesigning of the FSC program that in the first half of the initial demonstration year did not meet families' needs. Subsequent designs were more effective, with exceptional results evidenced in the engagement of more families. Program structure mediated participation in unanticipated ways that were recognized after the first four months, when the approach failed to engage even 25 percent of parents who had volunteered to participate in the FSC program. Staff were discouraged and at a loss to understand the poor response. The initial program design, based on a family preservation model, focused on supporting parents with home-based services. However, few parents responded to this approach. Parents were rarely home when they said they would be. Reassessment with a focus group of parents revealed that for a number of reasons parents did not want case managers coming to their homes. First, there was real danger for parents and workers if strangers came to their homes, as drug deals were taking place all round them. Second, parents were also ashamed of their homes and hated being in them, so they often escaped for the day. Third, other mothers were put at risk for domestic violence from partners who did not want them involved with programs that could influence the women to leave them. Parents asked for a safe place, wanting to be taken care of and being able to go to "school again." They wanted to get away from their environments.

In the second phase of the FSC program, staff developed a five-days-a-week program at the community center, which became parents' "safe haven" (in their words). Participation varied between a high of 87 percent for one program year to 70 percent for the next program year (Lightburn, 1994:85). The provision of a safe haven that was responsive to parent need became one of the key factors that mediated participation. The redesign of the program, offering parents safety during the day and ready access to the services that they wanted, made an immediate and sustained difference in their level of participation. There was a definable difference in the quality of the program because of staff changes and reduced program supports for the next half of the program year, which contributed to the 17 percent drop in participation (Lightburn, 1994).

Program staff and administration were essential collaborators in the evaluation. They actively made program changes based on ongoing evaluative feedback. Weekly meetings with the evaluator built relationships that were pivotal to ownership of the program evaluation and subsequent program development. The focus for the evaluation included staff and parent concerns about what was working, taking into account program and parent goals. My ongoing observation of the program included weekly attendance at staff meetings and case reviews and meeting with the program director, supervisors, and agency administrator. These were all important in data gathering and working reflectively with those responsible for the program to understand what was observed. It was heartening to experience a research process that informed program and practice and helped to make them more responsive to the needs of low-income families.

An innovative continuum of services comprised the local Bridgeport FSC program, which coordinated and provided opportunities for parents who wanted to gain more control of their lives and increase their skills as parents, learners, workers, partners and friends (see Figure 12.1). The program model and practice in this community-based program succeeded in meeting the FSC program goals. Parent participation in the program over an eighteen-month period resulted in improved emotional well-being and expanded their connections to other parents, thus building important support networks. Families that were most at risk became actively engaged in the FSC programs, and many were able to make significant progress in meeting their goals (Lightburn 1994; Lightburn & Kemp, 1994a, 1994b).

The Bridgeport program was a well-defined case study that made it possible to track relationships between program inputs and parent outcomes. This action research or developmental research approach to formative evaluation, with a summative outcome evaluation, was deemed appropriate at that stage of the FSC's program development (Weiss & Halpern, 1990; Thomas, 1989). It can be viewed as a pilot study that provided case study information about whether the program was meeting the needs of participants; and including qualitative data allows the researcher to examine how outcomes may be linked with conditions and processes. Aldgate (2002) also demonstrates in her study of measuring outcomes in services to support children and families that the use of a variety of approaches combining qualitative and quantitative methods, with triangulation of data, provides a significant outcome evaluation report. Case studies such as these are important in their

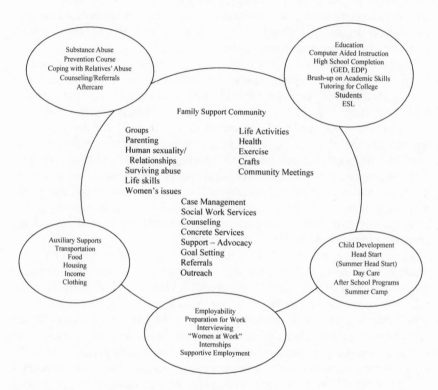

Figure 12.1. Family Support Program (1990–1993)

examination of relationships and outcome, and are therefore sensitive canaries (likened to the coal miners' canary) concerning what otherwise is not clearly heard from the frequently missing voice of all participants, parents, staff, and administration.

The National Family Service Center Evaluation

A national evaluation was planned within the first year of the initiation of the FSCs. An experimental design, with random assignment using control groups, was chosen, as there was confidence that this was the most suitable scientific approach to answer the research questions about the effectiveness of this type of program.

As Swartz, Bernstein, and Levin state in their final report: "The payoff for the evaluation is that randomized studies are seen as scientifically superior to non-randomized studies and, therefore, the results have more credibility and greater impact" (2000a:2.3). In support of this perspective, they report that the evaluation of an earlier project in another community provided convincing evidence to Congress about the effectiveness of early childhood programs precisely because it was randomized. Therefore, a randomized design was implemented that included treatment and control groups in twenty-four of the sixty-six project sites across the United States to examine short- and long-term outcomes. Participation in the FSC was considered as the short-term outcome, and milestones in literacy, employment, and substance abuse were the *longer-term outcomes*. Standardized literacy and substance use measures were used. FSC programs that provided services for participating parents were in their first program year when baseline data were gathered. Follow-up data were gathered from programs approximately nineteen months after random assignment. Only nineteen local site studies were chosen, based on their use of control groups, for comparison to the national study (Swartz, Bernstein, & Levin, 2000b:4.3–5). In general, these site evaluation reports supported the findings of minimal impact from program inputs on long-term outcomes as found in the national study.

Results of the national evaluation included: (1) an analysis that there were no discernible program effects on short- or long-term outcomes; (2) details describing the case management aspect of FSC programs; and (3) a positive evaluation of the transition of the FSC into Head Start, resulting in increased case management services. Extensive descriptive information about parents and programs provided a valuable picture of those Head Start parents who volunteered to be part of the FSC innovation. For example, low parent literacy skills were not a major problem as had been previously thought, while employment was a problem for many participants. FSC program response included increased case management with smaller caseloads than common in Head Start, with more face-to-face contact and as much time spent on families' basic needs and personal issues as literacy and employment needs (two of the primary program goals). There was an increased report of FSC parent use of external services, such as education programs or employment services, as compared to the Head Start parent control group. Of particular import was the reported positive integration of the FSC program into Head Start at the end of the demonstration, with reduction in case loads and increased visibility of Head Start (Swartz et al., 2000a). Indeed, the fact that FSC programs were developed, influencing the Head Start programs and their broader community, represented an exceptional effort in collaboration and outreach for a grassroots organization with professional service providers in their communities.

The national evaluation's finding of limited long-term impact for participants, even though FSC parents received more services than control group parents, was explained by the evaluators as: (1) possibly being mediated by quality of services that influenced participation rates; (2) showing variance in quality of community services; and (3) reflecting the recognized length of time that is required to make gains in education, employment, and self-sufficiency, particularly when the FSCs were not designed as specialized services, such as employment programs (Swartz et al., 2000a).

LESSONS LEARNED FROM THE NATIONAL EVALUATION

The findings from the national evaluation have ramifications for the future integration of family support into early childhood programs such as Head Start, as much as they do for the future of national experimental design outcome evaluations. Following are lessons learned to guide future evaluations that take on the challenge of demonstrating and explaining innovative program effects.

Timing of Study

Timing of a large-scale randomized study should follow an assessment of program maturity that includes evaluation of stability, integrity or fidelity, and potential for replication in order to ensure that there is meaningful explanation of outcomes from program inputs.

In the field of family and children services there is accumulated practice wisdom from the past two decades concerning the importance of the timing of randomized experimental design studies. Such studies should be done when they measure robust, well-established programs, and preferably those that have achieved positive results. Pressure to begin with an experimental design is seen as a political problem rooted in the need to demonstrate accountability and provide support for policy changes. A host of respected evaluators agree that in the best interest of good evaluation practice and science, such pressure should be resisted (Bond & Halpern, 1988; Ellwood, 1988; Weiss & Halpern, 1990; Weiss, 1998; Pecora et al., 1995; Weiss & Jacobs, 1988). This practice wisdom has particular significance for the FSC national evaluation. In many ways, the lack of results from the program input should be questioned because there was no evidence of the maturity of the FSC programs. The final evaluation report did not review the efficacy of the decision to do a randomized study of these new, widely varied FSC programs, other than noting that this approach was the valued scientific methodology for outcome evaluation (Swartz et al., 2000a).

Across the country FSC programs varied in their response to families' needs and hopes (Swartz et al., 2000b; Lightburn & Kemp, 1994a, 1994b). The Office of Head Start identified FSC program innovation as one of its goals to respond to parents' needs. With support for highly individualized programs, a more useful approach to evaluation would be to ensure that the first phase of the evaluation utilizes a model of action research with program development as part of the research design and realistic time line to move to program maturity. Focus on process evaluations to describe the difficulties in delivering these innovative services as planned should have been key to preparation for an experimental study (Pecora et al., 1995).

The first phase in experimental design program evaluation should require a description of program development and an examination of activities that define a program, including how much time is spent on the various aspects of service delivery that can inform policy, practice, and resource allocations. This defines what is inside the "black box," as Fein suggests (Chapter 2 in this volume). It also facilitates evaluating underlying program processes that are central in developing causal models (Weiss & Halpern, 1990). To make the investment in experimental design worthwhile, program maturity should also be determined as indicative of a level of program development that is deemed ready for evaluation. Process evaluation and action research in this first phase make it possible to advance program development through gathering of important program information. This should not be sacrificed with a premature move to outcome evaluation (Ellwood, 1988; Bond & Halpern, 1988). An alternative approach demonstrated by Henggeler et al. (1997) includes a pilot program that details and assesses program and service implementation using proposed outcome measures, for the randomized study, to enable refinements. This is an important example, as basic services that were central to the program intervention were not available and further development was necessary so that there was some degree of assurance that program implementation included the program services that were intended.

Zigler and Styfco (1993) have commented that one of the known facts about Head Start is that program quality varied widely, from outstanding programs to very poor ones. The quality of a program refers, among other things, to its maturity or stability and to program integrity or fidelity (providing what it has proposed). Head Start program quality influenced child outcomes. Head Start was the context and auspices for the FSC programs. It was obvious that there was considerable variance in the quality of the Head Start programs, which was also reflected in the FSC programs. The quality of programs has direct bearing on outcomes, whether it is the case of children or parents.[3]

In discussion at national meetings, FSC coordinators and program directors were for the most part positive about the help provided to parents. However, this represented their perspective rather than an assessment based on criteria that examined program maturity. Also, local project evaluators differed in their evaluation designs. Some evaluators were remote from the local programs, with little technical understanding of the service delivery, and without established feedback processes that provided programs with ongoing information (Swartz et al., 2000b).[4] Many program directors expressed concern at national meetings that their programs were not successful in engaging enough participants. They used the opportunity of national meetings to consult with other directors to find ways to develop further their approaches. In a review of lessons learned from comprehensive programs similar to many of the FSC programs, Stagner and Duran (1997) noted that experience in launching and sustaining these programs is very difficult work due to turf issues and differences in level of commitment between agencies. It was indeed very difficult work for the FSC programs, with their small staff and short time frame, to accomplish a well-developed program that usually takes years to build. There were a myriad of all too familiar concerns with constituency groups who were supposed to provide integral services for FSC parents, but were inconsistent in collaborative arrangements.

Assessing case managers' collaboration with service providers in education, employment, and substance abuse is one valuable means for also determining program quality, as collaboration was one of the primary objectives for the FSC programs. It is plausible that the variance in quality of these services, so central to the achievement of program goals, significantly contributed to the findings that program inputs made no difference in final outcomes. As the evaluators note in their explanation of outcomes, parents' participation and achievement in these areas would be mediated by the quality of service they received, because these are well-known factors that influence participation (Swartz et al., 2000a). It was evident from evaluators' meetings that many programs were struggling to keep staff, coordinate and gain services, and define program specifics that included engaging parents in effective ways. As Pecora et al. (2002) stress, lack of fidelity in program implementation compromises programs in real ways. There is ample reason to question fidelity in FSC program implementation across the various sites.

Program development was influenced by different challenges in each site. For many of the FSC programs it was a time of program development that included establishing integrity between program goals, objectives, and implementation. It was a challenging stage, with many barriers that program directors readily shared with each other. And, as Berry and Cash (Chapter 9 in this volume) discovered, there can be a lack of congruence between goals and practice that requires tracking and exploration. While responsive, creative, and innovative programs were developed, there was no review of program maturity across sites, or the evidence provided to support the view of FSC programs' readiness for randomized study, which was contrary to sound outcome evaluation practice (Devaney & Rossi, 1997). It was important to the local site leadership to meet the expectations of their Head Start project officers, so as not to jeopardize opportunities for future support for new programs. Neither local evaluators nor FSC leaders were prepared to suggest that their program should not participate in the national evaluation because it was not well enough developed. The fact is, no one asked about program maturity, whether or not programs were sufficiently developed to be evaluated. Instead, there was a sense of urgency, as staff scrambled to get their programs going to meet the expectations to participate in the national evaluation.

Attention given to the early formative evaluation work, where there is a fruitful collaboration between the evaluator and program, can result in support for the development of program objectives that are the foundation for both protocols and training to increase the likelihood that the intended service is delivered. Pine, Healy, and Maluccio (2002) in their work in family reunification detail the critical steps involved to improve the connection between goals and objectives that facilitate good practice and anticipated outcomes. This developmental process takes time, to ensure practice integrity through development of program and service protocols that are then supported through work with staff in training and supervision. It has been acknowledged that it takes at least three years for a program to mature in this way (Bond & Halpern, 1999; Weiss & Halpern, 1990; Weiss, 1998; Devaney & Rossi, 1997).

Assessment of Program Development

Assessment of program development that includes staff cohesiveness and staff development is an important indicator of program quality that is also a relevant mediating variable.

The maturity of the program depends in part on the knowledge and skill of the practitioners. When a program depends on paraprofessionals and undergraduate-trained workers, there is further need for staff development and support to enable them to fulfill program role and service expectations. Of the FSC case managers, only 12 percent had a master's degree, while 57 percent had a bachelor's degree and 27 percent either had an associate's degree or had attended a two-year program. With regard to staff development, over two-thirds of the programs had training sessions lasting no longer than a half-day, with many lasting only an hour or two, and just over a third of the programs held training sessions once a month. Building capacity in a new team unfolds with program development over the first program years, as demonstrated by Lindblad-Goldberg, Dore and Stern (1998) in a well-developed training program for home-based family services that made it possible to meet the mental health needs of children and adolescents. This is even more important when parents are part of a high-risk population that require intensive case management so instrumental in helping them with serious life struggles (Weiss & Jacobs, 1988; Stroul et al. 1996). Preparation and supervision of case managers is reflected in the quality of staff relationships with participants. In an example drawn from a local FSC program it was clear that it took time for relationships to develop to build a foundation for parents' subsequent achievements in education, employment, and ability to deal with substance abuse. A necessary phase of the work with families included building community and family for those who had not had these experiences. A dimension of program maturity was evident in the process of building community for parents that was intertwined with staff skill in group and family work supported through training and supervision. Again from the Bridgeport example there is this observation:

> Parents who were isolated, withdrawn, angry, and distrustful took time to respond to the nurturing of staff and other parents. From the evaluator's observations many of the women in the program lacked a "voice," believing that they had nothing to contribute to the FSC community. They would sit silent, rocking in a locked depressed position for as long as three months before they began to speak. For these parents lacking social and personal skills and afraid to trust others, the development of a sense of connection is a fundamental building block for other program goals. Fostering mutual aid

requires staff skilled in group work, which patiently helps parents discover their ability to help and receive help from each other. (Lightburn & Kemp, 1994b:84)

The maturity of a program can make a significant difference in the outcome for
participants. In the interest of all that is invested in innovations to support low-
income families, it is important that evaluations measure the services that were
intended.

The FSC program itself may also be in a developmental phase. For example, as
program staff become more cohesive, they build alliances that strengthen their
ability to reach outside the program to work in their community. This can involve
work with local police for a safer environment, which only became possible when
they engaged in collective action. Environmental realities in a high-risk environment, as those in Bridgeport, mediate outcome in ways that need to be understood
to assess program quality, such as staff cohesiveness and work in community that
can moderate a high-risk environment. If outcome data are collected from FSC
programs at an early phase in program development, when staff are not as cohesive and as effective in working on behalf of parents in the community, basic issues such as those that concern parent safety can influence participation in the
program. Staff cohesiveness is one measure of program development that defines
the capacity of the program to influence context. It is probable that staff capacity
to respond to parent need was related to their own professional development. Sites
that participated in the experimental design had less than two years to develop
their program and considerable variability in staff development was reported in the
final evaluation that would also potentially influence effective work with parents.
Since participation in family support programs has been well documented as dependent on the responsiveness of the program (Weiss & Halpern, 1990; Powell,
1988), there is reason to consider program development as staff cohesiveness and
staff development as they relate to program quality.

These examples suggest that further attention needs to be given to (1) qualifying program inputs (the availability and stability) of essential services in key areas
that were the focus of the innovation; (2) obtaining the knowledge of program development and processes that promotes access and sustains service utilization; and
(3) defining the synergy between program quality (relevance) and engagement of
parents to understand how it impacts both short- and long-term outcome. How did
all this work for parents who wanted help? The quality of services in a multitude
of ways influenced parents' desire, motivation, and capacity to participate in the
program. Participation in turn mediated achievement in all three long-term goals.
The investment in quality programs should be the priority of demonstrations such
as the FSCs, before they are evaluated with large-scale experimental studies.

Influence of Local Context

*The influence of the local context on programs can be addressed through map-
ping risk, opportunities, and the assessment of resources or assets in the ecosystem to explain outcomes.*

FSC programs were embedded in other systems, such as community centers, Head Start programs, and broader communities, that were potent influences on both the programs and families. Contextual realities mediated outcome in ways that were not accounted for in the development and interpretation of outcomes in the national study. For example, with respect to participation (a short-term outcome), consider the influence of context in the Bridgeport FSC, where violence in the community was a daily experience. For these parents, participation was influenced by their estimation of the risk involved in attending the program. Richters and Martinez (1993) document the traumatic effects of witnessing street violence, which can be debilitating. Some of the FSC program mothers were targeted when gang warfare erupted, and parents would not return to the program for a considerable length of time after one of the FSC mothers was shot dead. These highly motivated parents were making significant strides toward their goals. Nonetheless, to avoid danger for themselves and their children, they sacrificed progress in their education and employment programs (Lightburn, 1994). In such high-risk environments, FSC participation patterns can look different than in other programs. Evaluating the impact of such mediating contextual realities is important in understanding the effects on parents' achievement of both short- and long-term outcomes.

Reciprocity and Cohesiveness

Description of reciprocity and cohesiveness in the ecosystem should be developed as both an outcome and mediating variable.

From an ecological perspective, Garbarino and Kostelny (1992) raise critical issues and compelling concern about the expectations of programs and participants in impoverished communities where in essence there is little community, with diminished resources and higher-risk factors than in other neighborhoods. What is it that the program and participants are expected to be able to do in such circumstances? For low-income families the quality of resources and support is critical to their success in meeting their program goals. Therefore, gathering such information should be a priority, describing the capacity within the community as this influences programs and participants. There exists an inordinate challenge to contextualize program and represent the synergy between the program and its community as both an important outcome as well as a means of mediating other client-focused outcomes.

It is useful to think of ecology, as Chaskin (Chapter 3 in this volume) suggests, by addressing the need to understand capacity building within communities. This includes measuring the dynamic interaction between a program and the community, as well as assessing community assets and social cohesion to provide a more realistic evaluation of program inputs as contextual factors that influence outcome. An example from the Bridgeport evaluation describes how FSC parents were unsuccessful in completing high school, in an adult education program provided by the city of Bridgeport. In contrast to these discouraging experiences, parents discovered that they were very successful in the adult education program provided on-site by the FSC. This program included individualized computer instruction and was supported by their case manager, who frequently spoke with their instructor, interpreting parents' learning blocks and personal needs that made significant differences to instructors' responsiveness. The relationship between the FSC case managers and the educational instructors was vital to parents' success. The synergy among the FSC program, parents, and its providers from the community influenced parent short- and long-term outcomes (Lightburn, 1994).

Developmentally Sensitive Outcomes

Developmentally sensitive outcomes based on an understanding of the ecosystem, culture, gender, risk factors, and social norms of response that have been developed and tested in pilot studies with the demonstration population will increase value of outcome measures.

Obviously parents function very differently, and there is evidence that within the group of FSC parents there are those who would be considered high-risk mothers. Serious depression is recognized as a factor for high-risk families, and the profile gained from the national study data identifies 39 percent of mothers as seriously depressed (Swartz et al., 2000a). Examples already noted from the Bridgeport FSC program describe parents who were in high-risk environments, with many parents frozen in their ability to respond to staff and other parents in the program. This example points to the importance of considering outcomes that are realistic, capturing what is really happening as parents move toward self-sufficiency. If parents function differently, then those who take more time to take advantage of opportunities should be recognized for the impact that they have on the program, the resources they require, and the impact all of these factors have on outcomes. It is also necessary to choose outcome measures that will measure parents' progress.

Outcome measures should also be sensitive to cultural norms as well those that take into account social norms of response, as discussed by Ortega and Richey (1998) with respect to depressed women of color, and Sayfer et al. (1998) with respect to socially determined responses to substance abuse questions. Indeed, some of the parents who were seriously depressed and those who were substance abusers indicated that they were providing socially acceptable responses to evaluation questions. They said that their answers were given to make sure that they continued to receive welfare benefits and FSC program support. As one poly-substance-abusing parent reported, "Our family knows how to work with substance abuse, why should I bring shame on us?" [by reporting the degree of use]. In fact, the national evaluation findings on substance use, based on implementing the Addiction Severity Index,[5] reported FSC parents' profile as below the national norm in amount of substance use (Swartz et al., 2000a). This finding was of concern in light of other information that indicated many of the FSC families did have serious problems with substance abuse. This was certainly the case for the Bridgeport site, where parents similarly underreported their substance use. At the same time they had widely discussed the seriousness of their own and their family's abuse, to the point where they worked with the FSC staff to establish an Alcoholics Anonymous and support group for family members. The majority of the Bridgeport FSC parents disclosed in genograms that substance abuse had been a problem for their families over the last three to five generations. Pilot tests and use of multiple measures, such as genograms to gather qualitative data, would further understanding of how to develop sensitive outcome measures that have meaning for all involved and thereby increase their value, working constructively with the reality of linguistic differences and socially determined responses to sensitive issues.

The Bridgeport FSC learned during the first years of the program how to adapt the program to respond to high-risk parents' special needs, providing services that engaged them, to allow for their inconsistent participation. The evaluator also had to find developmental measures that would track their progress, such as standardized family coping measures (Lightburn, 1994). It was an added challenge working with those parents and families who were most in need. It was a choice that many FSC programs openly discussed deciding against, as they expressed the belief that they would produce better outcomes with those parents who were more able to engage in productive learning and work. There is a distinct advantage to giving serious consideration to risk factors so that more accurate developmental measures are used to chart progress for parents and for the program. Sensitive measurement would then provide information that could be used to advocate for the supports that these families need, instead of excluding them from programs because they are more likely to be harder to engage, and slower to meet program goals. Expected outcomes should be refined based on theoretical understanding, with review and participation in their construction by consumers as well as program staff, as has been suggested from extensive field experience (Berry, 1998; Bond & Halpern, 1988; Devaney & Rossi, 1997; Fink & McCloskey, 1990; Friedman, 1994; Weiss & Green, 1992; Zigler, 1998).

LESSONS LEARNED FROM EVALUATIONS OF LOCAL PROJECTS

The Head Start Bureau emphasized the importance of both the local and national evaluations, even though there was a considerable difference in the amount and type of investment made in each of these. Major investments of time, support, and funding were made in the national evaluation, which required large resources to develop the experimental design, the outcome measures and instruments, the protocols and training of data collectors, management and analysis of data, and site visits to develop case studies. The local evaluations were much more circumscribed by limited resources, even though substantive formative and outcome data were expected. Evaluators were given minimal direction and no additional training to support their work. The following lessons learned from the local project evaluations are drawn from observations made by the national evaluators who collected all available local evaluations, and the perspective drawn from the Bridgeport local evaluation case study.

Increase Value of Local Evaluation

Increase the value of the local evaluations by investing in the support and development of capacity in the local evaluator through development of knowledge and skill in action research.

Local Head Start programs contracted with local evaluators, who were paid out of the grant award. The national evaluators observed that there were limited "thick" program descriptions that described program development and service delivery for these local evaluations (Swartz et al., 2000b:2.1, 2.5, 6). Local evaluators provided outcome studies and/or prepared and collected data for the national evaluation. In many instances the data gathered from the local site for the national evaluation were used as the basis for the required local summative evaluation. There is much that the local evaluations could have revealed had there been greater attention to fulfilling mandates for evaluative information.[6] It was disappointing that fifty-eight local evaluation reports of innovative FSC programs for Head Start parents were so diverse in methodology, data collection, analysis, and reporting that it was not possible to compare the different approaches. In the summary of the local evaluations many useful observations about the FSC programs were presented as collective lessons learned, but it was not possible to compare or aggregate local evaluation findings.

Swartz et al. observed that "it was not apparent that all local evaluators took advantage of the opportunity . . . to observe first-hand the workings of the program on a day to day basis" (2000b:5, 6). Local evaluators had a wide range of backgrounds; some were full-time evaluators and others were academics in disciplines that were far from or near to the experiences of programs and practitioners in family support services. As Bond and Halpern (1988) have noted, creation of effective action research teams is demanding, requiring someone who can understand program and practice, as well as having the general skills of evaluation (Friesen & Koroloff, 1990; Nauta & Hewitt, 1988; Pecora et al., 1995; Powell, 1988). Understanding program and practice makes an enormous difference to whether or not the evaluator successfully joins with program staff, and to the process of describing and analyzing practice. Local evaluators made expedient choices that sacrificed thick description and involvement in service delivery processes. Simplistic tabulations of service inputs were chosen, thereby reducing the complexity of service provision to a unit of time rather than capturing the ongoing development and work in program relationships.

Academics and practitioners alike need to become involved in evaluations. It could have well been the case that local evaluators had neither the skill nor knowledge to produce the expected formative evaluation. It is also possible that evaluators did not have the time to invest in the intense on-site collaborative work required to provide thick program descriptions. Increased financial support and investment in research training for local evaluators, such as that provided for the national evaluation, could have increased the value of these local evaluations. This would have assisted evaluators in developing skill in action research methods, particularly in ethnographic methods for analyzing relationships among all aspects of the program, context, and outcomes.

Guidelines for Developing Local Evaluations

Guidelines for developing local evaluations, with accountability for implementation across sites, is essential so comparison and synthesis is possible, thereby increasing means for utilizing local evaluations in guiding program development and policy.

The lessons learned from the disappointments in the local evaluations emphasize the need to increase collaboration among the funders, consumers, and evaluator to develop more productive formative evaluations. There are basics for which there needs to be accountability, such as requiring an evaluation plan with a list of research questions, description of proposed sample and research methodology, and data collection plan and analysis, as well as expectations for structured reports. In general, the need to build capacity to strengthen local evaluations could begin with consultation to review the advantages and disadvantages of employing and implementing alternative designs, and specifically attend to how the local evaluation can prepare for cross-site experimental studies (Weiss & Halpern, 1990). And when there are multiple sites, as in the FSC programs, special attention should be given to promoting collaborations for comparative studies where there are different contexts and populations—studies that can advance knowledge about program development and impact. Evaluation activities varied greatly among sites, as did the final reports.

The national evaluators summarized the contents of the evaluation, covering the following areas: planning and development, community context, program operations, description of services, participant characteristics and needs assessment, participant participation patterns, staff and participant perceptions, and participant goal attainment and outcomes. In doing so, the evaluators found that synthesis of data across sites was difficult. More rigorous requirements for local evaluators would have increased the quality of observations that could have been made. The possibility of cluster analysis could then be explored with real potential to increase understanding and application of statistical tests because of the increase in the sample numbers (Sanders, 1997). Such support would take advantage of the opportunities for culling important lessons from each site that should be shared in final reports useful for the program site as well as other local programs.

CONCLUSION

This Family Service Center evaluation case study has brought to light a range of concerns about the value gained from both the national experimental design study and local project outcome evaluations. The key question is: How much has been learned from the FSC evaluations that furthers development of program and practice and informs policy for Head Start in their efforts to develop support for low-income families? The complexities of outcome evaluation in family support programs have been considered in this chapter within the larger context of field experience over the past two decades, to help explain the limited findings from the FSC national evaluation. In this review many issues were raised that identify areas for further attention. What happened in these programs? Was there a mismatch in the assessment of parent need and program offerings? Were the FSC program and services "good enough" to result in the hoped for outcomes? If they were not, was there a problem in program integrity or quality? And if the programs were good enough, would more sensitive or different outcome measures be required to tell the story of what this type of support meant to families? Could such outcome measures reflect developmental steps toward the outcome goals? Or, from another perspective, were the inputs inconsistent and services of such varied quality that evaluating the sum of these program services meant that they were not potent enough to make a difference? There is also the possibility that both program quality and insensitive outcome measurement contributed to the findings. These questions will be important to explore and to answer in future studies with some of the different approaches to evaluation that have been suggested in this case study.

It is reasonably clear that a great deal more would have been achieved with a rebalance of investment to support formative evaluations as the important first phase of outcome evaluation and then preparation for a national experimental outcome evaluation. Experimental design studies, while important, require development of more sensitive outcome measures and attention to measuring mediating ecosystemic variables that also should be considered as program outcomes. Demonstration programs should also be assessed for program maturity and replicability to determine when they are ready for an experimental design study. Considerable advantage would be gained from providing detailed description of process that includes all essential service activities and their support, as a basis for determining program quality and an assessment of program development. An assessment of the congruence between goals and practice based on specified goals, objectives, and guides for implementation with a sober assessment of barriers to program implementation is also equally important in determining program stability and readiness for evaluation.

Assessment of readiness would make it more likely that demonstrations would develop into programs that are viable, stable, mature, and worthy of testing in a large-scale experimental design study. It is possible that this type of progression would create more effective studies, instead of the marginal results that are part of outcome evaluation history. Decades of evaluation research can guide our work and aid us in our advocacy for best evaluation practice that will undoubtedly triumph over politics and prove that the value conundrum of outcome evaluation can be solved, based on all that we have learned.

NOTES

1.   The demonstration was supported by the United States Department of Health and Human Services, Administration for Children, Youth and Families, Office of Head Start, Washington, D.C.

2.   As reported from the national evaluation, Head Start families include low-income parents, with about 34 percent white, 38 percent African American, 21 percent Hispanic, 4 percent Native American, and 3 percent Asian. The families are comprised of 44 percent single-parent households. Ages of parents participating in the FSC program were as follows: 6 percent twenty years and younger; 61 percent between twenty-one and thirty years; 28 percent between thirty-one and forty; and 5 percent forty-one years and older.

3.   The quality of the program does not refer to "standardization across sites" required in random assignment to increase the interpretability of study results, as defined by Weiss (1998) in her guide to evaluation practice.

4.   Referring to the most passive level of functioning, from the developmental perspective of Belenksy, Clincy, Goldberger, and Tarule (1986).

5.   The Addiction Severity Index was developed by the National Institute of Drug Addiction and is believed to be suitable for this study based on norms from other national samples (Swartz et al., 2000a).

6.   Representing 89 percent of all local evaluations that were provided to Abt Associates for their final summary (Swartz et al., 2000b).

REFERENCES

Aldgate, J. (2002). Measuring Outcomes in Short-Term Fostering Services. In T. Vecchiato, A. N. Maluccio, & C. Canali (Eds.), *Evaluation in Child and Family Services: Comparative Client and Program Perspectives.* Hawthorne, NY: Aldine de Gruyter.

Belensky, M., Clincy, B., Goldberger, N., & Tarule, J. (1986). *Women's Ways of Knowing.* New York: Basic Books.

Bernstein, L, Swartz, J., & Levin, M. (2000). *Evaluation of the Head Start Family Service Center Demonstration Projects: Executive Summary.* Washington, D.C.: U. S. Department of Health and Human Services.

Berry, M. (1998). *Families at Risk: Issues and Trends in Family Preservation Services.* Columbia: University of South Carolina Press.

Bond, J. T. & Halpern, R. (1988). The cross-project evaluation of the Child Survival/Fair Start Initiative: A case study of action research. In H. Weiss and F. Jacobs (Eds.), *Evaluating Family Programs* (pp. 347–70). Hawthorne, NY: Aldine de Gruyter.

Devaney, B. & Rossi, P. (1997). Thinking through evaluation design options. *Children and Youth Services Review* 19:587–606.

Ellwood, A. (1988). Prove to me that meld makes a difference. In H. Weiss and F. Jacobs (Eds.), *Evaluating Family Programs* (pp. 303–14). Hawthorne, NY: Aldine de Gruyter.

Fink, A. & McCloskey, L. (1990). Moving child abuse prevention programs forward: improving program evaluation. *Child Abuse and Neglect* 14:187–206.

Friedman, R. M. (1994). Restructuring of systems to emphasize prevention and family support. *Journal of Clinical Child Psychology* 23(Supplement):40–47.

Friesen, B. & Koroloff, N. (1990). Family centered services: Implications for mental health administration and research. *Mental Health Administration* 17:13–25.

Garbarino, J. & Kostelny, K. (1992). Child maltreatment as a community problem. *Child Abuse and Neglect* 16(4):455–64.

Gershenson, C. (1995). Social policy and evaluation: An evolving symbiosis, in P. Pecora,

M. Fraser, K. Nelson, J. McCroskey, & W. Meezan (Eds.), *Evaluating Family-Based Services* (pp. 261–76). Hawthorne, NY: Aldine de Gruyter.

Henggeler, S. W., Rowland, M., Pickrel, S. G., Miller, S. L., Cunningham, P. B., Santos, A. B., Schoenwald, S. K., Randall, J., & Edwards, J. E. (1997). Investigating family-based alternatives to institution-based mental health services for youth: Lessons learned from the pilot study of a randomized field trial. *Journal of Clinical Psychology* 26:226–33.

Lightburn, A. (1994). Hall Neighborhood House Family Support Program Demonstration, 1990–1993. Final evaluation for the Office of Head Start, Administration for Children, Youth and Families, Health and Human Services, New York: Author.

Lightburn, A. & Kemp, S. (1994a). Family support programs: Opportunities for community-based practice. *Families in Society: Journal of Contemporary Human Services* 75:16–26.

Lightburn, A. & Kemp, S. (1994b). Urban family support: empowering high-risk minority families. In R. Fong, P. Sandau-Beckler, & D. Haapala (Eds.), *Empowering Families* (pp. 77–86). Riverdale, IL: National Association of Family Based Services.

Lindblad-Goldberg, M., Dore, M. M., & Stern, L. (1998). *Creating Competence from Chaos.* New York: W. W. Norton.

Nauta, M. J. and Hewett, K. (1988). Studying complexity: The case of the child and family resource program. In H. Weiss & F. Jacobs (Eds.), *Evaluating Family Programs* (pp. 389–404). Hawthorne, NY: Aldine de Gruyter.

Ortega, D. & Richey, C. (1998). Methodological issues in social work research with depressed women of color. In M. Potocky & A. Y. Rodgers-Farmer (Eds.), *Social Work Research with Minority and Oppressed Populations* (pp. 47–70). Binghamton, NY: Haworth.

Pecora, P., Fraser, M., Nelson, K., McCroskey, J. & Meezan, W. (1995). *Evaluating Family-Based Services.* Hawthorne, NY: Aldine de Gruyter.

Pecora P. J., Williams, J., Downs, A. C., White, J., Schockner, L., Judd, B. M., & Stenslie, M. (2002). Assessing Key Results in Family Foster Care Using Multiple Approaches. In T. Vecchiato, A. N. Maluccio, & C. Canali (Eds.), *Evaluation in Child and Family Services: Comparative Client and Program Perspectives.* Hawthorne, NY: Aldine de Gruyter.

Pine, B. A., Healy, L. M., Maluccio, A. N. (2002). Developing Measurable Program Objectives: A Key to Evaluation of Family Reunification Programs. In T. Vecchiato, A. N. Maluccio, & C. Canali (Eds.), *Evaluation in Child and Family Services: Comparative Client and Program Perspectives.* Hawthorne, NY: Aldine de Gruyter.

Powell, D. (1988). Toward understanding of the program variable in comprehensive parent support programs. In H. Weiss & F. Jacobs (Eds.), *Evaluating Family Programs* (pp. 267–86). Hawthorne, NY: Aldine de Gruyter.

Richters, J. & Martinez, P. (1993). The NIMH Community Violence Project: I, children as victims of and witnesses to violence. *Psychiatry* 56:7–21.

Sanders, J. R. (1997). Cluster evaluation. In E. Chelimsky & W. R. Shadish (Eds.), *Evaluation for the 21st Century: A Handbook* (pp. 396–404). Thousand Oaks, CA: Sage.

Sayfer, A. W., Griffin, M. L., Colan, N. B., Alexander-Brydie, E. & Rome, J. Z. (1998). Methodological issues when developing prevention programs for low income, urban adolescents. *Journal of Social Service Research* 23(3–4):23–46.

Stagner, M. & Duran, A. (1997). Comprehensive community initiatives: principles, practice and lessons learned. *Children and Poverty* 7(2):132–40.

Stroul, B. A., Friedman, R. M., Hernandez, M. Roebuck, L. Lourie, I. S., & Koyanagi, C. (1996). Systems of care in the future. In B. A. Stroul (Ed.), *Children's Mental Health: Creating Systems of Care in a Changing Society* (pp. 591–612). Baltimore, MD: Paul H. Brookes

Swartz, J., Bernstein, L., & Levin, M. March (2000a). *Head Start Research: Evaluation of the Head Start Family Service Center Demonstration Projects,* Vol. 1: *Final Report from the National Evaluation.* Washington, DC: U.S. Department of Health and Human Services, Administration for Children and Families, Commissioner's Office of Research and Evaluation, and the Head Start Bureau.

Swartz, J., Bernstein, L., & Levin, M. (2000b). *Head Start Research: Evaluation of the Head Start Family Service Center Demonstration Projects,* Vol. 2: *Summary of Local Evaluation Reports.* Washington, DC: U. S. Department of Health and Human Services, Administration for Children and Families, Commissioner's Office of Research and Evaluation, and the Head Start Bureau.

Thomas, E. (1989). Advances in developmental research. *Social Service Review* 63: 589–97.

Weiss, C. H. (1998). *Evaluation.* Englewood Cliffs, NJ: Prentice Hall.

Weiss, H. & Halpern, R. (1990). *Community-Based Family Support and Education Programs: Something Old or Something New.* New York: National Center for Children in Poverty.

Weiss, H. & Jacobs, F. (Eds.) (1988). *Evaluating Family Programs.* Hawthorne, NY: Aldine de Gruyter.

Weiss, H. B. & Green, J. C. (1992). An empowerment partnership for family support and education programs and evaluations. *Family Science Review* 5:131–48.

Zigler, E. (1998). By what goals should head start be assessed? *Children's Services: Social Policy, Research, and Practice.* 1:5–17.

Zigler, E. & Styfco, S. J. (1993). *Head Start and Beyond.* New Haven, CT: Yale University Press.

Author Index

Academy for Educational Development, 35
Acheson, D., 7
Ainsworth, F., 4, 42, 142, 146, 148, 151
Aldgate, J., 6–8, 156
Alter, C., 108
American Academy of Child and Adolescent Psychiatry, 86
Anderson, E., 38
Ash, S., 151

Barber, J. G., 148
Bardo, J. W., 36
Barrera, M., 37
Barth, R. P., 107
Berkowitz, S. D., 37
Bernstein, L., 154, 159
Berry, M., 3, 20, 40, 107–108, 123–124, 162, 167
Bickman, L., 85, 87, 90, 95
Blythe, B. J., 104, 110
Bond, J. T., 154, 156, 160–161, 163, 167–168
Booth, C., 108
Brekke, M. L., 71
Brent, D., 87
Briggs, X., 36–39, 41
Bronson, D. E., 108
Brook, R. H., 92
Brown, P., 30–31
Brunk, M., 107
Burford, G., 141
Burnam, M. A., 92
Burt, R. S., 38
Burtless, G., 62
Butler, B., 31

Cabana, M. D., 90–91
California Mental Health Planning Council, 89–90
Cash, Scottye J., 3, 40, 162
Chamberlain, P., 88–89
Chambless, D. L., 86

Chaskin, R. J., 3, 29–31, 41–42, 165
Chavis, D. M., 36–37, 39, 128
Cheetham, J., 19–20
Children Act 1989, 6
Chipenda-Dansokho, S., 31
Cleaver, H., 15
Cole, E. S., 109
Coleman, J. S., 38
Colwel, L., 71–72
Connell, J. P., 30–32
Cooper, L., 148
Costanzi, C., 100
Costello, E. J., 84
Coughlin, F., 142
Coulton, C., 32
Coulton, C. J., 33
Culver, S., 91

Darmstadt, G., 107
Davis, I., 3, 19, 147
Dawes, R. M., 90
Day, C., 85
Delfabbro, P. H., 148
Department for Education and Employment, 6–7
Department of Health, 6–7, 11–13, 15
Devaney, B., 162–163, 167
DiLeonardi, J. W., 145
Diomede Canevini, M., 102
Donabedian, A., 92
Donati, C., 105
Donenberg, G. R., 85–86
Dore, M. M., 163
Doueck, H. J., 108–109
Drisko, J. W., 19
Duncan, G. J., 39
Duran, A., 161

Earls, F., 39
Edwards, B., 39
Egan, M., 108
Eisen, S. V., 90

Ellwood, A., 160–161
European Health Indicators, 54

Fasolo, E., 102, 104
Faust, D., 90
Fein, E., 2–3, 19–21, 23, 109, 117, 170
Feldman, L., 108
Fetterman, D. M., 31
Fink, A., 167
Fischer, C., 38
Fischer, E. P., 90
Florin, P., 36
Flynn, P., 33
Focarile, F., 70, 78
Foley, M., 39
Fraser, M., 19
Fraser, M. W., 123–124
Friedman, R. M., 167
Frieman, R. M., 85
Friesen, B., 168
Fullbright-Anderson, K., 30

Gabor, P. A., 50
Garbarino, J., 165
Garland, A. F., 90
Garrett, P. M., 10
Gatehouse, M., 14
Gatz, M., 128
George, C. C., 62
Gershenson, C., 154
Goerge, R., 3, 33
Goerge, R. M., 65–66
Goodman, R. M., 36–37
Granger, R. C., 42
Granovetter, M., 38
Green, J. C., 154, 167
Greif, G. L., 107
Grinnell, R. M., 50
Gueron, J. M., 42
Guest, A. M., 36

Haapala, D., 108
Haapala, D. A., 123–124

Halpern, R., 154, 156, 160–161,
    163–164, 167–169
Hamilton, R., 31
Han, S. S., 85
Hansen, P., 146
Healy, L. M., 19, 162–163
Heckman, J., 63–64
Henggeler, S. W., 88, 107
Hernandez, M., 89
Hewett, K., 168
Hibbs, E., 87
Hoagwood, K., 87
Hodges, S. P., 89
Hollister, R., 33
Hollon, S. D., 86
Holmes, S., 49
Home Office, 6
Hotz, J., 63–64
Hudson, J., 141
Hughes, J. R., 71
Hughey, J., 36
Hughey, J. B., 36

Ichinose, C., 89

Jackson, S., 6–8
Jacobs, F., 154, 163
Jacobs, F. H., 128
Jaro, M. A., 66
Jayaratne, S., 110
Jensen, P., 87
Jensen, P. S., 86
Johnson, H. C., 146
Johnson, W., 109
Joint Committee on Standards
    of Educational Evaluation,
    137

Kaftarian, S. J., 31
Kassem, L., 107
Kazdin, A. E., 86
Kemp, S., 156, 160
Kingdon, D., 89
Kinney, J., 108, 123
Knitzer, J., 84–85
Koch, J. R., 89
Koroloff, N., 168
Kostelny, K., 165
Kottke, T. E., 71
Kretzmann, J. P., 35–36
Kubisch, A. C., 29–32

Landsman, M. J., 19
Landsverk, J., 3, 19, 147
Ledbetter, N. S., 90
Lee, B. A., 36
Lee, B. J., 33, 65–66

Leff, H. S., 90
Leifer, M., 107
Lerner, S., 19
Levin, M., 154, 159
Levine, M., 108
Lewis, A., 89
Lewis, D. A., 62
Liberati, A., 105
Lightburn, A., 4, 156, 160,
    165–167
Lindblad-Goldberg, M., 163
Littell, J., 26, 124
Littell, J. H., 41
Lyons, P., 109

McCall, D., 89
McCloskey, L., 167
McCoy, M. M., 128
McCroskey, J., 19
MacDonald, I., 16
McDonald, T., 107
McKnight, J. L., 35–36
Maluccio, A. N., 19, 151, 162–
    163
Mamon, J., 74–75
Marks, J., 107
Martinez, P., 165
Meehl, P. E., 90
Meezan, W., 19
Meredith, L., 92–93
Merriman, R., 70, 78
Milligan, S., 32
Mitchell, J. C., 38
Moreland, S., 88
Mosley, C. L., 90
Moyers, S., 9
Mueller, E., 36–37, 39, 41

NASW News, 110
Nauta, M. J., 168
Nelson, K. E., 19
Newcombe, H. B., 66
Nicholson, D., 10
Nordquist, C. R., 90
Noser, K., 85, 87, 95

Olds, D. L., 88
Ongaro, F., 104
Ortega, D., 166

Paget, K., 4, 32, 90, 150, 154
Pargament, K. I., 128
Parker, R., 6–8
Patton, M. Q., 110, 127–128
Payne, J. D., 86
Pecora, P., 160, 162, 168
Pecora, P. J., 108–109, 123–124

Peel, M., 9
Perkins, D. D., 36
Perry, B. D., 107
Peterson, N. A., 36
Piening, S., 26, 32, 135
Pilati, G., 3, 74–75
Pine, B. A., 19, 162–163
Pinnock, M., 16
Pompei, A., 3, 100
Ponti, A., 71, 80
Powell, D., 164, 168
Preskill, H., 130
Puntenney, D., 62
Putnam, R. D., 38

Ramsay, T., 37
Raudenbush, S., 39
Raudenbush, S. W., 39
Register, R., 32
Reid, K., 88
Renaud, E. F., 146
Rich, R. C., 36
Richey, C., 166
Richters, J., 165
Risso, A., 100
Robbins, D., 12
Roberts, M. C., 85
Rogler, L. H., 128
Rohe, W., 38
Rose, G., 71–72
Rosenblatt, A., 89
Rossi, P., 162–163, 167
Rossi, P. H., 19, 30–31
Rosso, S., 71, 80
Russell, M. A. H., 70, 78
Rzepnicki, T. L., 26, 124

Salley, M. P., 110
Sampson, R. J., 39
Sanders, J. R., 169
Sandler, I., 37
Sarpellon, G., 105
Sawicki, D. S., 33
Sayfer, A. W., 166
Schaefer, E., 90
Schmidt, D. T., 146
Schuerman, J. R., 26, 109,
    123–124
Schwartz, J., 70–71, 80
Scott, J., 9
Segnan, N., 71, 80
Senore, C., 71, 80
Shapiro, J. P., 107
Skuse, T., 13, 16
Smith, G. R., Jr., 90
Smoot, P., 41
Social Exclusion Unit, 13

Solberg, L. I., 71
Speer, P. W., 36
Staff, I., 19–21, 23, 109, 117
Stagner, M., 161
Stanek, E. J., 146
Stapleton, J., 70, 78
Stern, L., 163
Stetzer, P. S., 31
Strauss, M. A., 107
Stroul, B. A., 85, 154, 163
Stucky, P. E., 128
Sturn, R., 92–93
Styfco, S. J., 161
Sullivan, G., 92
Summerfelt, W. T., 85, 95
Summers, A., 151
Sunstein, C. R., 49
Swartz, J., 154, 159–162, 166, 168

Tamang, E., 75
Taylor, W., 70, 78
Temkin, K., 38
Thomas, E., 156
Toler, A. K., 31

Torres, R., 130
Tripodi, T., 104
Tyler, F. B., 128

ULSS 21, 75
University Associates, 20
Unrau, Y. A., 50

Van Voorhis, J., 65–66
Vecchiato, T., 3, 48–49, 102, 105
Venkatesh, S., 30
Vidal, A., 30
Voorhis, J. V., 33

Walton, R., 91
Wandersman, A., 31, 36–37, 39, 128
Ward, H., 2, 6–11, 13, 16, 92
Warsh, R., 19, 26, 32, 135
Wedge, P., 6–8
Weiss, B., 85–86
Weiss, C. H., 31, 160, 163
Weiss, H., 154, 156, 160–161, 163–164, 169

Weiss, H. B., 154, 167
Weisz, J. R., 85–86
Wellman, B., 37
Wells, K., 92–93
Whelan, J. P., 107
WHO, 52–53, 74
Wicker, A. W., 128
Wodarski, J. S., 109
Woolcock, M., 38–39
World Health Organization, 52–53, 74
Wright, L., 4, 32, 90, 150, 154
Wyman, N., 89

York, P., 32
Young, A. S., 92
Yuan, Y. Y. T., 145

Zannoni, F., 74
Zeira, A., 91
Zigler, E., 161, 167
Zuravin, S., 107

Subject Index

Abt Associates, Inc., 155–156
ACF, 129
Activity categories, 21
ADHD, 86
Administration for Children and
    Families (ACF), 129
Administrative data, use of, 32,
    144–146
Adoption and Safe Families Act of
    1997 (ASFA) (P.L.
    105–89), 127, 129
Aid to Families with Dependent
    Children (AFDC), 64
Alcoholics Anonymous, 167
Antitobacco counseling (see
    Smoking habit interven-
    tion)
ARC, 141–142, 144, 149–151
ASFA, 127, 129
Assessment and Action Records,
    8–9, 12, 14
Associational tests, 121
Attention Deficit Hyperactivity
    Disorder (ADHD), 86
Australian Research Council
    (ARC), 141–142, 144,
    149–151
Automated Intake System (AIS),
    67

"Black box" of service delivery, 3,
    19, 117, 161
Body Mass Index (BMI), 56
Bridgeport Family Service Center,
    156–158, 167

Cascading Dissemination of a Fos-
    ter Parent Intervention, 89
CASRC, 84, 90–91
CASSP, 85
CCIs, 29–30
    evaluation of, 30–32
CDCs, 29, 39
Center for Child and Family Stud-
    ies, 127, 130, 139

Centre for Health Education in
    Padova, Italy, 70, 72, 81
Chicago Public Schools (CPS), 62,
    67
Child Abuse Prevention and Treat-
    ment Act of 1978, 108
Child and Adolescent Service Sys-
    tem Program (CASSP),
    85
Child and Adolescent Services Re-
    search Center (CASRC),
    84, 90–91
Child Protective Services Units,
    110–111
Child welfare outcomes, new inter-
    est in, 129
Children Act of 1989, 6
Children's services (see England's
    children's services; Family
    service centers; Mental
    health care for children and
    adolescents)
Client Contact Log, 112
Clinical Services Log, 112–113
Collaborative strategies for cross-
    cultural outcome-based
    evaluation, 4–5
Collective efficacy, 39
College of Social Work (University
    of South Carolina), 127,
    130, 139
Communication of evaluation re-
    sults, 135–136
Community Action program, 29
Community assets, 34–36
Community attitudes and perspec-
    tives, 36–37
Community building
    administrative data for studying,
        32–34
    comprehensive community ini-
        tiatives and, 29–30
    evaluation of, 30–32
    context and, 28
    focus on, 28–29

organizing principle and, 28
outcome-based evaluation of
    community assets, 34–36
    community attitudes and per-
        ceptions, 36–37
    social effects of, 42–43
    social structure and behavior,
        37–39
    theories of change and, 3,
        31–32, 34, 40
Community Development Corpo-
    ration movement, 29, 39
Comprehensive community initia-
    tives (CCIs), 29–30
    evaluation of, 30–32
Concrete Services Log, 112
Conflict resolution, 131
Cost of Rights, The (Holmes and
    Sunstein), 49–50
CPS, 62, 67
Cross-cultural outcome-based
    evaluation
    collaborative strategies, 4–5
    future and, 4
    issues in, 1–2
    themes of, 2–4
    Volterra seminar and, 1, 5

DALE, 53
DALY, 53
Design for a Set of European Com-
    munity Health Indicators
    (2000), 54
Disability-adjusted life expectancy
    (DALE), 53
Disability-adjusted life years
    (DALY), 53

England's children's services
    historical perspective, 6–7
    integrated, 7, 14–16
    Looking After Children project,
        2, 7–11, 14–15, 91
    outcome-based evaluation of
        effective services and, 13–14

England's children's services (*continued*)
outcome-based evaluation of
(*continued*)
outcome indicators and,
13–14
Performance Assessment
Framework and, 7, 11–12
performance indicators and,
12–13
overview, 2, 6–7
vision for, 15–16
Evaluator activities
asking questions, 131
bringing back information,
134
bringing people together, 134
collecting data, 135
conflict resolution, 131
consulting, 131, 134
designing evaluation, 135
documenting, 134
forming and managing relationships, 131
logic model and, 130–133
planning, 131
promoting conversation, 131
reporting, formal, 135
training, 134–135
Evidence-based treatment and
practice, reaching goal of,
95–96

Family Centered Group Care
(FCGC), 148
Family Court database, 145
Family reunification program
(U.S.)
background information, 19–20
described, 20–21
outcome-based evaluation of
findings, 21–24
implications, 25–26
methodology, 21
significance, 26–27
practice implications and, 25
program outcomes and, 2–3, 19,
26–27
program planning and, 25–26
services provided, 23–24
intensity of different stages of
intervention, 23
intensity of, 23
nature of, 21–22
site differences, 22
in intensity of service, 23
workers' role differences, 22
at two sites, 22–23

Family risk factors, 3–4, 124
Family Service Center (FSC)
demonstrations
lessons learned from local projects
guidelines for developing
local evaluation, 169
increase value of local evaluation, 168–169
lessons learned from national
projects
assessment of program development, 163–164
developmentally sensitive
outcomes, 166–167
influence of local context,
165–165
reciprocity and cohesiveness,
165–166
timing of study, 160–163
overview, 153
projects
local, 156–158
national, 158–160
overview, 155–156
questions raised by studying,
169–170
value conundrum and, 154–
155
FCGC, 148
FDP program, 144–145
Framework for Assessment of
Need, 14–15
FSC demonstrations (*see* Family
Service Center demonstrations)

General practitioner (GP) counseling (*see* Smoking habit intervention)
Geographic information system
(GIS) technology, 33
Goods and Services Tax (GST),
143
Government Performance and Results Act of 1993 (P.L.
103–62), 128
GP counseling (*see* Smoking habit
intervention)
Gray Areas Projects, 29
Great Britain (*see* England's children's services)
GSCE examinations, 12
GST, 143

Hall Neighborhood House
(Bridgeport, Connecticut),
156–158, 167

Head Start Family Services Center
program, 4, 154–155,
158–160
Health World Report, 52
Helping process with children,
adults, and elderly persons
assignment of responsibilities
and, 102–103
care-giving card and, 103
caregiving service stages and,
99–100
contract and, 103–104
defining problem and, 103
documenting helping process
and, 102
effectiveness of, evaluating, 105
evaluating plan and case and,
104
helping process stages, 100–
102
interventions and, planning and
implementing, 104
outcome-based evaluation of
application of, 102
approach to, 99–102
implications of, 105
lessons from, 102–105
overview, 3, 99
request for service and, 102–
103
terminating case and, 104–105
HIV, 56

IDB, 65–67
Illinois client database records,
66–67
Illinois Department of Employment Security, 67
Illinois Department of Human Services, 66–67
Integrated Children's System, 7,
14–16
Integrated Database on Children
and Family Services (IDB),
65–67
Intensive Family Preservation
Units, 110–112
Issues in cross-cultural evaluation,
1–2
Italy, 1, 5 (*see also* National health
and social programs;
Smoking habit intervention)

"Lead agency" model, 147
Learning-organization approach to
evaluation
challenges and issues

hiring and managing research
and evaluation team,
136–137
making methodological decisions, 137
owning and sharing evaluation, 135
redefining expectations of
evaluation, 138–139
using good judgment in role
implementation, 137–138
data in studying, 127
described
communicating evaluation results, 135–136
evaluator activities, 130–135
overview, 129–130
evaluation as evolving field and,
127–129
future and, 139
implications of, 139
interest in child welfare outcomes and, 129
measuring outcomes and, 127
Local Health Unit 21, 75
Looking After Children project, 2,
7–11, 14–15, 91

Management Information Systems
(MIS), 112
MEDLINE search, 93
Mental health care for children and
adolescents
challenges of, 94–96
history of, early, 84–87
improvement strategies
disseminating efficacious interventions in community
settings, 87–89
outcome assessment in community mental health ser-
vice settings, 89–92
using quality of care indicators in tracer conditions,
92–94
lessons learned from past,
94–96
overview, 3
in past decades, 84
MIS, 112
Model cities program, 29

National Cancer Institute (NCI),
87
National Health Plan (1998–2000),
49, 52
National Health Plan (2001–2003),
52, 56

National health and social programs (Italy)
improved planning for, 50–52
issues of, 48
limits of, 48–50
outcome-based evaluation of, 3,
52–57
guidelines for, 57–59
solidaristic nature of, 49
utilitarian nature of, 49
National Priorities Guidance targets, 12
National Research Office of Head
Start, 155
NCI, 87
Nonexperimental methods of evaluating social programs
approach to analyzing, 62–65,
67
selection of comparison
group, 63–64
statistical methodology,
64–65
data in analyzing, 65–67
overview, 3, 61–62
study example, 62
variables, 67–68

Oregon Social Learning Center
(OSLC), 88
Organizational inertia, 142–143
Organizational inertia and political
ideology on outcome re-
search
future and, 150–151
lessons learned from
administrative data sets,
144–146
cross-cultural differences,
147–149
ideological impediments,
143–144
organizational inertia,
142–143
research and evaluation findings, 149–150
study design and measure-
ment, 146–147
overview, 4, 141
studies, 141–142
OSLC, 88
Outcome indicators, 13–14
Outcome-based evaluation (see
also Cross-cultural out-
come-based evaluation;
Learning-organization ap-
proach to evaluation)
at aggregate level, 14

of community building
community assets, 34–36
community attitudes and perceptions, 36–37
social effects of, 42–43
social structure and behavior,
37–39
of community mental health service settings, 89–92
of England's children's services
effective services and, 13–14
outcome indicators and,
13–14
Performance Assessment
Framework and, 7, 11–12
performance indicators,
12–13
as evolving field, 127–129
of family reunification program
findings, 21–24
implications, 25–26
methodology, 21
significance, 26–27
of helping process with children,
adults, and elderly persons
application of, 102
approach to, 99–102
implications of, 105
lessons from, 102–105
interest in, 1
of national health and social
programs (Italy), 3, 52–57
guidelines for, 57–59
organizational inertia and political ideology on
future and, 150–151
lessons learned from,
142–150
overview, 4, 141
studies, 141–142
of risk assessment methods
data, 122
findings, 121–122
implications of, 123–124
limitations of, 122
methodology, 110–114
seminar on, 1, 5
of smoking habit intervention,
78–81
implications of, 81–82

Parent Management Training,
88–89
Performance Assessment Framework, 7, 11–12
Performance indicators, use of,
12–13

Performance management program, 11–12
Personal Responsibility and Work Reconciliation Act of 1996 (PRWORA), 64
P.L. 103–62, 128
P.L. 105–89, 127, 129
Political ideology, 143–144 (see also Organizational inertia and political ideology on outcome research)
Poor Law, repeal of, 12
Post Qualifying Award in Child Care, 11
Program outcomes, 2–3, 19, 26–27 (see also Outcome-based evaluation)
Provider Beliefs about Parents study, 147
PRWORA, 64
Purpose categories, 21

Qualitative stage in research on parent-child visiting, 141–142
Quantitative stage in research on parent-child visiting, 142
Quality of care indicators, use of, 92–94
Quantitative stage, 142

Risk assessment methods
background information, 107–109
client characteristics and, 112
clinical skills and, 119–120
concrete resources and, 120–121
description of families and services and

demographic characteristics of families and children, 114
family strengths and supports, 115–116
family stressors and risk factors, 116–117
nature of maltreatment, 114–115
nature of services, 119–121
structure of services, 117–119
family risk factors and, 3–4, 124
outcome-based evaluation of
data, 122
findings, 121–122
implications of, 123–124
limitations of, 122
methodology, 110–114
overview, 3–4, 107
purpose, 109–110
service characteristics and, 112–114
services provisions and, 3–4, 124

Service provision and risk factors, 3–4, 124
Smoking habit intervention (Italy)
design of study, 74
effectiveness of general practitioner counseling, 70–72
materials and methods of study, 74–75
objectives of, 72–74
outcome-based evaluation of, 78–81
implications of, 81–82
overview, 3, 70
results of study, 75–78
Social capital, 38

Social Security number (SSN), 67
Social solidarity, 49
Social structure and behavior, 37–39
South African residential child care program, 142
SPIRT, 142, 144, 149–151
SSN, 67
Strategic Partnership with Industry-Research and Training (SPIRT), 142, 144, 149–151

TANF, 64–65
Templates for conducting evaluation research, need for, 4
Temporary Assistance for Needy Families (TANF), 64–65
Theories of change approach, 3, 31–32, 34, 40

UCLA Health Services Research Center, 93
UI wage report data, 67
Unclaimed Children (Knitzer), 84–85
Unemployment insurance (UI) wage report data, 67
Utilitarian approach, 49

Value conundrum, 154–155
Volterra (Italy) seminar (March 2001), 1, 5

Wales (see England's children's services)
WHO, 53–54, 74
"Work Pays," 64
World Health Organization (WHO), 53–54, 74